ILLNESS AS A WORK OF THOUGHT

The term 'psychosomatic' has gained an increasingly wide currency during the twentieth century, and yet its meaning remains difficult to define. Some may use it to imply that an illness is 'all in the mind', and therefore not quite real. Others may use it to advocate a more sympathetic medical outlook, one that is willing to address the psychological and personal dimensions of disease. Contradictory in its many associations and implications, the term 'psychosomatic' stands at the centre of dilemmas concerning the ethics and the politics of health, as exemplified recently by the controversial cases of ME or AIDS.

Illness as a Work of Thought responds to a rising interest in the study of the 'psychosocial' aspects of disease for the purposes of prevention or, more generally, towards a 'care of the self'. The book adopts a historically reflexive approach to the study of illness and modernity, in a practical application of Foucault's archaeological and genealogical methods. The author argues that a distinctly modern field of 'psychosomatic' research has existed since the early decades of the twentieth century, involving widely different types of discourse into complex mutual relationships. From medicine and psychiatry to psychoanalysis and the social sciences, she explores how the history of these different disciplines and of their encounters has shaped the meanings of the term 'psychosomatic' for modern individuals. She analyses how the discourse of psychosomatics may unsettle and transform the way we think of illness, subjectivity, and sociability, and hence the terms in which we discuss the ethical and political dimensions of health.

Monica Greco is lecturer in sociology at Goldsmiths College, London.

INTERNATIONAL LIBRARY OF SOCIOLOGY
Founded by Karl Mannheim

Editor: John Urry
University of Lancaster

ILLNESS AS A WORK OF THOUGHT

A Foucauldian perspective on psychosomatics

Monica Greco

London and New York

First published 1998
by Routledge
11 New Fetter Lane, London EC4P 4EE

Simultaneously published in the USA and Canada
by Routledge
29 West 35th Street, New York, NY 10001

Typeset in Garamond by Routledge
Printed and bound in Great Britain by Biddles Ltd, Guildford and King's Lynn

British Library Cataloguing in Publication Data
A catalogue record for this book is available from the British Library

Library of Congress Cataloging in Publication Data
Greco, Monica.
Illness as a work of thought: a Foucauldian perspective on psychosomatics/Monica Greco.
Includes bibliographical references and index
1. Medicine, Psychosomatic. 2. Foucault, Michel.
I. Title.
RC49.G635 1998
97–32080
616.08–dc21
CIP

ISBN 0–415–17849–5 (hbk)

CONTENTS

ACKNOWLEDGEMENTS

The research I publish here was carried out at the European University Institute in Florence, in a setting where different academic styles and languages constantly mix together to produce a very particular and rich local culture. This book is in many ways a product of this setting. The material I discuss includes work from Anglo-Saxon, French, German, and Italian authors, consulted in the original whenever possible or in the translations available – translations that were not necessarily English. For the purposes of quotation I have translated some texts into English myself, and the reader should assume this is the case whenever a text appears in another language in the bibliography.

My research for this book was generously sponsored by the European University Institute and by the Italian Ministry for Foreign Affairs. While I gratefully acknowledge this material support, my debts of gratitude certainly do not end here. I was fortunate to benefit from the countless opportunities for discussion and exchange provided by an international environment of renowned scholars and young researchers. Among these I wish to thank especially Professors Arpád Szakolczai, Alessandro Pizzorno and Steven Lukes, for their inspiration, their unflinching support and curiosity, and their guidance. To Arpád in particular I owe, among other things, the opportunity of visiting the Foucault archives at the Bibliothèque du Saulchoir in Paris while working as his research assistant, which proved to be a turning-point in what seemed like an impossible task. I also wish to thank Professors Hubert Dreyfus and Alberto Melucci, who examined an earlier version of this text and provided useful comments which helped me to define its limits more clearly. Among my fellow researchers at the Institute I would like to thank Roberta Sassatelli, Emilio Santoro, Sebastian Rinken, Stefan Rossbach and Luca Guzzetti, for both their seriousness and their ability to laugh. I owe a special debt to Davide Sparti and to Paul Stenner, who read and commented on the manuscript several times in the very different cultural and academic contexts of Italy and England, respectively. I owe thanks to the Centro Studi Storici di Psicoanalisi e Psichiatria, for inviting me to present this research to a mixed audience of historians, philosophers, psychotherapists, physicians, and authors in psychosomatics, whose feedback is invaluable and often difficult to seek. In that context my gratitude goes especially to Patrizia Guarnieri, who offered many useful pointers at the initial stages of my work.

Outside Italy, my thanks are due to Professor Stephen Mennell who introduced me to the Norbert Elias research network and gave me the opportunity to present my work at Leicester and in Dublin; on both occasions, I received useful comments and discussion. I thank Cas Wouters for responding with interest to my queries about Elias and psychosomatics, and for alerting me to unpublished material that confirmed me in my intuitions; I gratefully acknowledge the Elias Foundation in Amsterdam, for allowing me to quote from the unpublished transcript 'Civilization and Psychosomatics'. My gratitude goes also to Professor Nikolas Rose and to the History of the Present network, for organizing the 1992 conference on neo-liberalism where I first presented a provisional outline of the ideas of this book.

During the long, slow Florentine years in which this book was written, a number of groups and individuals significantly contributed to the forming and testing of my ideas outside a strictly academic setting. My gratitude in particular goes to: Marilena Carrino, who introduced me to the 'psychosomatology' workshops of Michel Marteau, organized in Florence under his supervision by APERTURA, which I attended between 1993 and 1997; Ilaria Capasso, Pino Pini, and the Istituto Andrea Devoto, who introduced me to the work of the Italian Mental Health Association and self-help movement; Professor Giovanni Guerra who invited me to join a research group on epilepsy at the Careggi teaching hospital in Florence in 1995, whom I acknowledge for this as much as for the many private conversations that enabled me to come closer to the everyday practice of medicine; and the working group on bioethics at the Florence Gramsci Institute, where I had the opportunity to discuss with biologists and physicians alongside political philosophers and sociologists, around questions of ethical practice and new legal norms.

Last, I wish to acknowledge what is most difficult to acknowledge adequately: the support of friends and family who gave me a home, symbolic and actual, in the course of many wanderings. I dedicate this book to their strength, to their generosity, to their faith. To Annalisa Fedelino, to Helga Dittmar, to Marilena Carrino; and to my parents, Augusto and Marina.

INTRODUCTION

> Remember what you know of human beings, and the first virtue of doctors, humility, will be yours automatically; for you know how little you know. Of course you might say here is somebody who is neither chair nor carpet, neither animal nor flower, neither stone nor wood. Yet is what you are saying true? No. This person is in reality animal and flower, stone, wood, carpet, and chair too. Beware, if you attempt to pry him away now from his connection with the universe, do not forget how many mistakes this attempt at isolation brings about and must bring about, mistakes which, perpetrated thousands of times, have heaped up so much debris around you that it requires all your strength and all your greatness to lift up your eyes over the pile. If you isolate man and deny that he is animal and flower, stone, and wood, then you are like a person who does nothing else during his whole life but look through a microscope: he is in danger of denying heaven, earth, the stars, since he cannot look at them through a microscope. Remember that the human being in front of you is an arbitrary figment of your lack of imagination . . . .
>
> The mistakes of the expert – and our kind of diagnosing constitutes an expert's mistake – continue long after they have been recognised as such by experts; they are tough, inert masses and difficult to get rid off [sic]. This is why the doctor who takes his profession seriously and enjoys it will have to repeat to himself again and again: to diagnose an illness of little use, can often be dispensed with and is often very, very damaging.
>
> (Groddeck 1977c [1927]: 241–2, 243)

In commonsense usage, the word 'psychosomatic' is full of disparate associations. It is a mysterious word, and in an everyday conversation between non-specialist, but informed participants, few would claim to know exactly what it means. And yet the word will be used, as if its meaning were obvious and understood by all. Some of its connotations are negative: to say that an illness is 'psychosomatic' may be a way of saying that it is 'all in the mind', and therefore not quite real. Hence the word conveys associations of deception and self-deception; or it conveys that one has failed to 'get oneself together' in managing the situations of one's life. There is the suggestion that we are responsible for having a 'psychosomatic' illness, in a way that we are not if we suffer from a broken leg, an infection, or an inherited metabolic dysfunction. Other connotations are more positive: here the word points to a more comprehensive medical outlook, capable of addressing the psychological and personal dimension of disease. But significantly, the words that most often describe this connotation are 'holistic' and 'alternative' medicine, not 'psychosomatic'. A 'holistic' approach to cancer suggests a special attention paid to the patient as a whole. An 'alternative' approach suggests non-invasive diagnostic and therapeutic procedures, gentle techniques of management and cure. It is not clear what a 'psychosomatic' approach to cancer immediately suggests to the layperson, apart from an initial surprise that can be easily explained by the negative associations of the word. 'Psychosomatic' in this case may literally appear to add insult to injury.

If we move to one domain of expertise, and specifically to the sociology of health and illness, we find a similar ambivalence. The terms 'psychosomatic', 'sociosomatic' and 'psychosocial' are often employed positively. But they are employed, for the most part, to define a position that is antagonistic and critical of the work of mainstream medicine (Gerhardt 1989). Thus, the term 'alternative' might well describe what psychosomatic also refers to in this context; the implication is that Western medical rationality is unable or unwilling to address the subjective and social aspects of disease. What is the nature of the sociological alternative? More immediately, sociology proposes to investigate the 'psychosocial' aspects of the aetiology of disease. These remain invisible to a biomedical perspective, because they stem from the social context of interaction before becoming concrete and recognizable as illness in the body of the patient. For example, the burgeoning field of a sociology of emotions shows that the experience of 'stress' is rooted in emotional responses that are not simply individual, but rather regulated and structured by social norms (Freund 1988; 1990). This type of research enables the scope of health and illness, and therefore the medical outlook, to be broadened beyond the individual body. On this basis, sociology may then take a further turn to fulfil its value-commitment towards a *critical* function. It may invite us to recognize that the disease of the patient is not only his or her own problem, but rather the symptomatic manifestation of underlying relations of power and inequality. At this level of analysis, sociology addresses medicine as one of the elements of social conflict, and particularly as an agent of forms of social control and domination legitimated through knowledge. This allegedly explains the reluctance of medical discourse to adopt perspectives that would radically undermine this role, despite any palliative claims to the contrary. David Armstrong (1987), for example, has warned the social sciences against being seduced into a relationship of cooperation whose terms remain dictated by medicine itself. Rather, to the extent that alternative viewpoints are selectively incorporated into medical work, they must be regarded as a dangerous extension of power and surveillance further and further into the lives of individuals and the community (Arney and Bergen 1984; Armstrong 1983). In this discursive context, the stigmatizing connotations of terms like 'psychosomatic' do not appear accidental but require explanation, rectification, and reappropriation (Figlio 1987). The sociological alternative is a challenge to what is perceived as a form of epistemological 'imperialism' in the definition of health and disease (Strong 1979; Waitzkin 1979; Conrad and Schneider 1980a). Thus sociology honours its task of 'siding with the underdog' by juxtaposing 'psychosomatic' or 'sociosomatic' understandings of disease to the biological definitions that are operant in medical institutions.

If we move to the opposite end of the spectrum of expertise, to the discourses of medicine, psychiatry and health psychology, we gain yet another perspective on the term 'psychosomatic'. It is not a diagnostic label, nor a diagnostic criterion. There are no clear definitions of what a 'psychosomatic' illness might be (Lask 1996). On the other hand, there is a *Journal of Psychosomatic Research*, a journal called *Psychosomatic Medicine*, and one called *Psychotherapy and Psychosomatics*. To quote the *Oxford Textbook of Medicine*, 'current theories are multicausal and make no attempt to separate a special group of psychosomatic illnesses. Rather, psychological factors are seen as having some part in the onset and course of all medical conditions' (Mayou 1983, in Lask 1996: 457–8; also in Wetherall (1983)). The term 'psychosomatics' as a collective noun expresses a theoretical and therapeutic ambition to account for the psychosocial dimension of any disease. This ambition was made explicit in the call for a 'biopsychosocial' alliance that would integrate the work of researchers in medicine, psychology, and sociology to produce a 'new medical model' (Engel 1977; see Kimball 1983). Predictably, we find here different explanations of why medicine fails to employ psychosomatic approaches clinically to the extent that the ambition would suggest, that is, for the entirety of medical conditions. The reason, we are told, is scientific and epistemological. Psychosomatic research is rapidly growing and has challenged many naive assumptions of biomedical knowledge, but so far it has not crossed the threshold of a 'scientific revolution' (Von Uexküll and Pauli 1986; Levin and Solomon 1990). What is needed is a meta-language capable of integrating the work of extremely diverse fields of research (Von Bertalanffy 1964). Psychosomatic hypotheses remain unviable as mainstream approaches as long as there is no consensual, 'truthful' paradigm to guide diagnostic and therapeutic practice in this new direction (Todarello and Porcelli 1992). Thus medical discourse appears to corroborate the impression of the sociologist and of the layman that 'psychosomatics' is a marginal element in the everyday practice of current medicine, even if the reasons that are given for this marginality are very different.

This book was born from an attempt to give due credit to each of these positions. Or, put differently, it was born from a refusal to endorse any one coherent version of what the word 'psychosomatic' signifies, either as a perspective in the present or as an ambition for the future. The term is a contentious one, so much is clear. What is also clear is that it is referred to a marginal position and to the role of offering an 'alternative' to existing practices, whether by medicine itself or against medicine. What accounts for this marginal position, and what the nature of that alternative might be, is not equally clear. The reasons, I propose, are more complex than those suggested by the opposite perspectives of medicine and sociology. The 'epistemological' reasons offered by authors in the clinical disciplines will appear naive to any sociological observer. They seem oblivious to the relevance of power relations not only to the production of knowledge, but also to the implementation of existing psychosomatic approaches, regardless of how 'scientific' they are. On the other hand, the sociological perspective based on a 'conflict-theory paradigm' (Gerhardt 1989) appears naive in the opposite sense. Its arguments are structured in terms of a logic of power and resistance, where medicine is identified as inherently dominant and sociology as inherently liberating. Medical knowledge is described as a 'construction' to challenge its monopoly over the definition of disease. But the faithfulness of sociological understandings to another 'authenticity' of disease is not equally doubted – or at least this is the implication of supposing that sociology *can* offer a workable diagnostic and therapeutic alternative. The terrain of psychosomatics is a slippery one for the discipline of sociology. It is a terrain where the customary ways of constructing a 'critical' position in relation to medicine easily fall into contradiction. In Uta Gerhardt's words,

> It is ironic that medical sociology investigates far-reaching causes of illness because, at the same time, it accuses the medical profession of extending its realm further and further into non-medical fields of social behaviour. Thus it appears to denounce conceptions of treatment derived from its own analysis of illness.
>
> (1989: 257)

Can a critical value-commitment be compatible with the aim of producing a diagnostic and therapeutic alternative? Is it a case, for sociologists and clinical disciplines alike, of having to choose between one role or the other? Are there different ways of conceiving the relationship between producing 'critique' and producing 'health'? These are some of the questions that arise when we are prepared to acknowledge the multiple versions and uses of the term 'psychosomatic' as genuine and valid, each in their own terms.

This attitude amounts to approaching 'psychosomatics' as a form of *problematization* (Foucault 1984a; 1988a; 1988b; 1990). From this perspective, the word 'psychosomatic' does not refer to a specific content nor to a specific method, all of which can be and are indeed the object of polemics. Rather, 'psychosomatics' is approached as what defines a space, a multiple and contradictory space, where something new is introduced as an object for thought. It is a space that includes the discursive and non-discursive practices that emerge when a domain of action or behaviour, illness in this case, has lost its customary familiarity and has become uncertain, as a result of social, economic, or political processes. Here the primary connotation of the word 'psychosomatic' is its contentiousness, its ambivalence, its availability for a definite variety of constructions and appropriations, which amount to its *problematic* character. This problematic character does not disappear once we have listened to the reasons of the different encampments that argue to define how the word should be used. On the contrary, the reasons offered by the medical establishment lead us, through their limits, to recognize the reasons of critical sociologists; and the alternatives offered by sociologists lead us to acknowledge the reasons of the medical establishment. As Foucault writes, 'what has to be understood [as a problematization] is what makes them simultaneously possible: . . . it is the soil that can nourish them all in their diversity and sometimes in spite of their contradictions' (1984a: 389).

The type of critical analysis based on the notion of problematization does not yield answers that are any more just or definitive to the questions involved, but it allows for a sense of perspective to be developed in relation to ongoing debates. Incommensurable alternatives may appear less radical when envisaged as stemming from the same conditions of possibility. Opposite viewpoints may result to have more in common than either would be comfortable to admit, which opens for discussion what other shared values their disagreement may safeguard. The analysis of problematizations does not propose new solutions, but attempts to clarify what is at stake in the different solutions that are proposed. Hence the agnostic title of this book: *Illness as a Work of Thought*. The expression points at once in two directions. One is the direction of the forms of knowledge, medical, psychological and sociological, that have come to investigate the 'work of thought' as a pathogenic variable. The other is the direction of social constructionism, where these forms of knowledge appear contingent and embedded in a field of power relations: concepts of illness are always, in this sense, the work of thought. To acknowledge one meaning of the expression does not imply, in my view, to deny the other meaning. On the contrary, the two meanings imply *each other* in a rather uncanny way. What can social constructionism make of a medical thought that acknowledges the role of thought itself, in all its historical contingency, in producing disease? What can medical thought make of a social constructionism that regards this too as a manifestation of power enforced through knowledge? What must each side relinquish to be able to acknowledge itself in the other? The two meanings of 'illness as a work of thought', in their mutual implication, point to the specifically modern quality of 'psychosomatics' as a form of problematization, and this modern quality is the object of this book. What I propose is to step back from the definitions of what is right or wrong, or what is true and what false, to examine how discursive relations that are specific to modernity frame the problem of psychosomatics and hence the forms that solutions can take. What is at stake in psychosomatics, I argue, is neither simply an epistemological problem nor a single politics either for or against the value of emancipation. Rather, what is at stake is this entire and historically specific set of relations, institutional and discursive, that allow for the management not only of illness, but of illness as opposed to, and distinct from, other social categories of evaluation. To redescribe illness in psychosomatic terms implies redefining these relationships too. While not adding any new items to the debate, this analysis frees a space or a time for reflection: it makes it more difficult to regard psychosomatics immediately as either a 'good' or a 'bad' development.

The structure of the book is circular: I begin with the social construction of subjectivity in chapter one, and I end with the social construction of subjectivity in chapter eight. In between I offer an analysis of the discourse of psychosomatics as drawn from research in medicine, psychology, psychoanalysis and sociology. Chapter one examines a historically specific set of assumptions concerning the self, to suggest that these assumptions make room for a certain way of posing 'psychosomatic' questions. I argue that this historical background constitutes a set of 'conditions of possibility' for the specificity of the modern problem of psychosomatics. In chapter eight I discuss the 'alexithymia construct' to illustrate how those initial assumptions are followed to their logical conclusions, to produce new effects of truth with which knowledge confronts individuals and collectivities.

From chapter two to chapter seven I reconstruct the discourse of psychosomatics as a space of problematization. This reconstruction adopts various strategies at different stages, and the reader should expect that at times the subject-matter will appear elusive and full of displacements: this is the inevitable price of rejecting any single, positive definition of 'psychosomatics' as a starting-point for inquiry. Chapters two and three focus on the construct of 'somatization' as a historical byproduct of the rationality of biomedicine. The example of 'somatization' is used to illustrate the normative power and pragmatic values that are implicit in the operative distinction between the 'body' and the 'mind'. In these chapters I acknowledge, in agreement with specialists in the field, that the distinction between 'mind' and 'body' contributes towards creating certain management problems in the work of medical institutions; but I then go on to suggest that these problems are relatively limited, if compared to the situations that an absence of the distinction invites us to imagine. In later chapters I illustrate that the spectre of these possibilities applies more widely and more radically in psychosomatics as a space of problematization, to the extent that it may be regarded as an organizing principle in the field of discursive relations. Chapter four introduces in some detail the methods of archaeology and genealogy as ways of approaching the propositions of psychosomatics. In particular, I examine the descriptive strategies that refer to 'tradition' and to 'biomedicine' as ways of establishing psychosomatics as a 'new' scientific endeavour. These strategies, I argue, obscure rather than clarify relevant continuities and discontinuities between the discourses of psychosomatics and of biomedicine; I then offer a different account based on Foucault's genealogies of madness, punishment, and the clinic. On this basis, chapter five offers an interpretive grid, a key to read and sort the variety of psychosomatic positions according to their mutual relationships and conditions of coexistence. Finally, chapters six and seven fill this interpretive grid with a narrative description of various theoretical positions, whose different implications as modes of questioning become intelligible under a more comprehensive light.

In the course of the book a tension between the two meanings of 'illness as a work of thought' is always apparent. This reflects the attitude I have adopted here in relation to the question of 'truth'. This attitude always regards 'truth' as a construction rather than a representation, but that as such does not lend itself to easy dismissals or arbitrary replacements for two reasons: first, that 'truth' is rooted in definite historical conditions of possibility, and second that what we know as 'true' effectively structures reality into the concrete forms of experience. This epistemological position is shared explicitly by some of the authors I discuss, such as Michel Foucault or Georg Groddeck; it remains implicit in the work of other authors who speak from a medical perspective, like Viktor Von Weizsäcker or Georges Canguilhem; and it is not shared by others, like Norbert Elias, Edward Shorter, and much of the literature on psychosomatic illness. The contrast between different authors in this respect can be subtle but all-important: very often they write about similar things but in a way that makes the implications of their work very heterogeneous indeed. In the course of the narrative I exploit these contrasts in various ways. In chapter one, for example, I use the work of Elias and Foucault to discuss the conditions of possibility of psychosomatics in terms of the historical construction of subjectivity, which both authors address. Their accounts, while being similar and complementary in some respects, enable this task in very different ways. Thinking through Elias, the problematic refers to the historical processes whereby modern individuals have come to develop certain forms of pathology; thinking through Foucault, it refers to the historical processes whereby these forms of pathology became an object for thought. For the purposes of this book, chapter one serves to highlight both these historical processes *and* two different understandings of the expression 'conditions of possibility'. The chapter thus introduces the relation to be established with the forms of knowledge discussed in the rest of the book. Subsequent chapters build on this initial contrast, and develop new ones; in each case it is not a question of denying the relative validity of each position, but rather of moving toward those that enable the space of problematization to be opened and unfolded, rather than settled and closed.

1

THE SYMPTOMS OF TRUTH

A historical search

> Nothing in man – not even his body – is sufficiently stable to serve as the basis for self-recognition or for understanding other men.
>
> (Foucault 1977: 153)

In what sense is the problematic of psychosomatics a specifically modern one? This question can be approached and answered at a variety of levels. First, we may consider 'psychosomatics' as a configuration of knowledge(s) that is specific to modernity in terms of what questions may be pertinently asked, and how. Second, we may regard this configuration of knowledge as addressing a problem, or the perception of a problem, that is itself historically specific. But what does 'historically specific' mean in this case? It could mean, in a realist vein, that the actual ways of falling ill changed historically, giving rise to different, new complaints and/or new pathologies. Or finally it could mean that a different way of thinking about illness – both on the part of laypersons and of experts – became pertinent to and for modern individuals, as a result of certain historically specific ways of envisaging the 'mind', the 'self', the 'body', and the relations between these and other concepts. Or it could mean both – indeed, if we were to accept the psychosomatic hypotheses that thematize the role of thought (and therefore culture) in the pathogenetic process, this is what we would have to conclude.

In this chapter I explore the historical conditions of possibility of psychosomatics from the perspective of 'subjective relations to the self'. I will lay the ground to show that psychosomatic illness emerges, as a problem for knowledge, in the context of a historically constituted experience of the 'self'. In order to map this historical context, I propose that we distinguish analytically between the process whereby modern individuals have come to *think* of themselves as bearers of psychosomatic illness and the process whereby they actually fall ill. The historical account I provide of the changing organization of subjective experience will thus avoid any reference to the biological substratum of human beings or to notions of psychophysiological functioning. I shall not be asking whether modern individuals 'function' in such a way as to be subject to specific forms of pathology; I shall only ask how it is that they have come to envisage themselves that way. This is necessary in order to devise a critical vantage-point to later examine the production of modern psychosomatic questions. Without such a vantage-point we would inevitably reproduce, in our historical account, the forms of knowledge whose genealogy we are trying to chart.

The work of Norbert Elias and of Michel Foucault provides the backbone of this chapter. Their approaches respectively to the 'genesis' and 'genealogy' of modern subjectivity are complementary at a descriptive level, and yet contrast in fundamental ways. I will attempt to show that this contrast is productive when it comes to approaching the historical dimensions of psychosomatics. Elias offers a framework within which it is possible to move without breaks of continuity from the psychological dimension to the political one. The central problem addressed in his work is the relationship between changes in social structures and changes in personality structures. These changes he empirically investigated and described in *The Civilizing Process* (1978b), with reference to the transition from the warrior society of the Middle Ages to the court society of the Renaissance. The themes developed in that empirical investigation recur throughout Elias' later work, including his sociology of knowledge, some aspects of which are relevant to this discussion.

Elias' historical arguments provide a diagnosis of modern forms of self-perception, and hence a critique of dominant categories of explanation in the social sciences. In particular, Elias challenges the notion that various opposite concepts, such as 'individual' and 'society', 'nature' and 'nurture', 'fantasy' and 'reality', can be assumed to refer to an unchanging essence of things. Instead, he proposes, they should be regarded as historically specific ways of perceiving the world and the relationship of human beings to the world; to understand how they have historically emerged implies also understanding that they cannot be treated as universally applicable categories of explanation. At all times, Elias presents this critique as a 'destruction of myths' (Elias 1978a), in the sense of facilitating the advent of a more adequate, detached, and objective knowledge of reality (Elias 1994). It is thus possible to distinguish between two overlapping aspects of Elias' work: one descriptive and diagnostic, the other indirectly prescriptive. Diagnosis and prescription overlap, for example, in the claim that:

> at this stage [scientists] are not yet able to detach themselves sufficiently from themselves to make their own self-detachment, their own affect-restraint – in short, the conditions of their own role as the subject of the scientific understanding of nature – the object of knowledge and scientific inquiry.
>
> (Elias 1978b: 256)

Some concepts in Elias' historical analyses are invested with this double, descriptive and prescriptive function. One such concept is that of 'psychologization'. This concept, which I discuss in more detail below, describes a historical process that accounts for how modern subjects perceive their 'selves', and their 'minds' in relation to their 'bodies'. These perceptions are shown by Elias to be not universal and pre-given, but rather historically generated and often deceptive (when they are assumed to be ahistorical givens). But 'psychologization' also prescribes the route towards a second-order distancing on the part of the subject of future (more detached, more reality-congruent) knowledge. Thanks to this ongoing process, Elias hoped that,

> We [would] one day succeed in making accessible to more conscious control these processes which today take place in and around us not very differently from natural events, and which we confront as medieval man confronted the forces of nature.
>
> (Elias 1978b: xvii; see also Mennell 1989: 99)

There is thus a fundamental continuity for Elias between the subject of action whose characteristics he describes, and the subject of scientific knowledge whose characteristics he embodies. Both partake in the process of 'psychologization' and are shaped by this process. 'Psychologization' is a source of illusion; but further 'psychologization' enables illusions to be revealed for what they are. All branches of knowledge move in this direction, although detachment is more easily achieved at present in some fields than in others.

This makes Elias' work problematic as a means for approaching the historical dimension of psychosomatic illness as a question for thought. For Elias, 'psychosomatic illness' is a feature of modern reality before being a construct of modern knowledge; knowledge comes to address psychosomatic illness because historical processes produce it as a phenomenon in its own right. It is one of those phenomena 'which today take place . . . not very differently from natural events', whose understanding and whose control are one and the same task. The theory of the civilizing process can indeed be read as a socio-patho-genetic theory of psychosomatic illness, that is, as an account of why modern subjects actually tend to fall ill in a specific way. Norbert Elias himself presented such a reading at a medical congress on psychosomatics held in Marburg in the 1980s, in a lecture entitled 'Civilization and Psychosomatics' (1982b). Elias' approach constitutes a valid sociological complement to medical theories of psychosomatic illness. For this very reason, however, it cannot provide a critical vantage-point on psychosomatics as a form of problematization. Rather, it is an element within the horizon of that problematization.

This point can be maintained quite independently of the fact that Elias' original theory was produced at a very significant time in the history of modern psychosomatics. Yet readers may find it useful to have a minimal reference to that context at this stage. The year 1939, during which the two volumes of *The Civilizing Process* first appeared in their original German form, is also the founding year of the journal *Psychosomatic Medicine*. This US journal still exists, and was created as a forum for a rapidly expanding field of research that had developed in the wake of work by Smith Ely Jelliffe, Flanders Dunbar, Franz Alexander, and others during the previous two decades. In Germany itself, during the interwar years and later, important debates were taking place as to the prospects of a medical reform in the direction of psychosomatics, exemplified by the writings of Viktor Von Weizsäcker and Karl Jaspers among others.

Returning to Elias, for our purposes his approach usefully describes the self-experience of modern individuals in terms of the figure of *Homo Clausus* ('enclosed man'). As a description, *Homo Clausus* is crucial in answering the question: for what kind of subject is the problem addressed in psychosomatic discourse a relevant problem? As an analytical concept, *Homo Clausus* designates a historically contingent form of self-perception, but also a concrete mode of organization of practices relating to the self. As such, the concept appears *prima facie* compatible with what Foucault named a 'critical ontology of ourselves' (Foucault 1984b). A critical ontology of ourselves involves an epistemological attitude that treats reality as a series of contingent, historical constructs; and yet that treats these constructs as, for all purposes, real in their effects (see Hacking 1986). It is an attitude that persistently refuses to search for general or fundamental truths behind the contingency of appearances. And it is an attitude that refuses to adopt extra-historical postulates as explanatory tools.

In what follows, I shall argue that Elias offers a valid, dynamic description of the passages that culminated in *Homo Clausus* as a modern form of self-perception. I shall also argue, however, that Elias grounds this description in general postulates concerning the nature of human beings as 'social animals'. Precisely this kind of postulate must be foregone in order to free the historical account from any epistemological co-dependence on forms of knowledge (such as psychology, psychoanalysis, or biology) that will later become the object of this book. Thus, I propose to use Elias' description by rethinking it, recasting it, through the work of Foucault. In particular, I shall draw on Foucault's proposal to give up the search for a theory of the subject that might form the basis of a 'history of subjectivity', in favour of the study of 'forms of experience' as these are made accessible by the history of thought. 'Singular forms of experience', Foucault writes,

> may perfectly well harbor universal structures; they may well not be independent from the concrete determinations of social existence. However, neither those determinations nor those structures can allow for experiences (that is, for understandings of a certain type, for rules of a certain form, for a certain mode of consciousness of oneself and of others) except through thought. There is no experience which is not a

> way of thinking, and which cannot be analyzed from the point of view of the history of thought; this is what might be called the principle of irriducibility of thought.
>
> (Foucault 1984c: 335)

Thus, for the analysis of changing forms of subjectivity in the course of Western history, Foucault does not rely on a general theory of subjectivity or human nature. On the contrary, general theories of the subject, in so far as they are products of knowledge, are themselves to be studied as part of a history of thought. Aside from this well-known negative starting-point, however, Foucault also offers a positive key for reading how forms of subjectivity have changed in the course of Western history. Subjectivity is 'that which constitutes and transforms itself through the relationship with its own truth. No theory of the subject is independent of a relationship with truth' (Foucault 1981a, unpublished). We can therefore study 'subjectivity' through and via the 'truth' that is its counterpoint. Crucial to this suggestion, naturally, is the status of the concept of truth. This is not defined as the content of universally valid knowledge, nor by any formal criterion, but rather as a 'system of obligations': truth is what obligates. This definition allows the notion of truth to be historicized and to serve as an inherently flexible, empirical reference for the study of how subjectivities emerge. To this I shall come back in due course.

Homo Clausus as the product of psychogenesis

Elias' theory of the civilizing process describes a trajectory of transformations in the sphere of subjective experience that culminates in the modern form he calls *Homo Clausus*. Here I shall survey only this aspect of Elias' comprehensive and multi-faceted historical argument. I shall therefore neglect all but the most general features of his theory of state formation and his detailed descriptions of developing networks of interdependence. In 'Civilization and its discontents' (1930), Freud proposed that the development of civilization involves an increasing transformation of external constraints into self-restraints. Despite the ways in which Elias can be set apart from Freud (ways indicated by Elias himself and to which I shall return below), this also constitutes the theme of *The Civilizing Process* (1978b). Changes in conduct and sentiment in a civilizing direction, according to Elias, stand in close relationship with the growing monopolization of physical force on the part of emerging state apparatuses. The monopolization process allows for, but also enforces, different forms of interaction between people. Within the newly pacified social spaces, interactions become less susceptible to the whims and fluctuations of individual tempers, but human beings face new and different dangers and pressures. The threat of random and unpredictable violence is gradually replaced by:

> intrigue, conflicts in which careers and social success are contested with words . . . . Continuous reflection, foresight and calculation, self-control, precise and articulate regulation of one's own effects . . . become more and more indispensable preconditions of human success.
>
> (Elias 1982a: 271)

While in the simpler societies of the medieval world 'affect directly engages affect' (ibid.: 273), in the early modern world the modes of mutual engagement become more abstract, more subtle, and more complicated. This complexity reflects the lengthening of chains of social interdependence and a corresponding increase in the differentiation of social functions. Both of these require growing measures of 'foresight' (ibid.: 281) and of affective restraint.

As Elias remarks in the preface to his essay on time, it is a mistaken vulgarization to regard the civilizing process as consisting 'solely [in] a continuous increase and reinforcement of self-restraint' (Elias 1992: 25). The difference between patterns of self-restraint in people within simpler and more complex societies is qualitative rather than merely quantitative. In more complex societies, these patterns are remarkable for their evenness and calculability. They are more moderate than the severe ascetism that existed earlier, but also more uniform and inescapable. Thus, the type of self-control expressed in medieval ascetism is paradoxically *passionate*, in its deliberateness and superfluousness, by comparison with the 'more dispassionate' type of self-control required by ordinary life in the societies of later stages. With the monopolization of physical violence, 'the controlling agency forming itself as part of the individual's personality structure corresponds to the controlling agency forming itself in society at large' (Elias 1982a: 240). It no longer corresponds, therefore, to the specificity of an individual choice or vocation.

Like in Freud's well-known model for the development of the super-ego, in Elias the process of external pacification is complemented by a process of internalization of tension and conflict. In his own words, 'the battlefield is, in a sense, moved within' (Elias 1982: 242). The chief source of danger faced by individuals is no longer directly physical or external. Instead, it lies in their own loss of self-control. To illustrate this, Elias contrasts the typical road system of a warrior society with that of a modern city. The greatest danger in the medieval setting is represented by the high probability of sudden, violent attacks on the part of bandits. Such attacks would require of individuals a readiness to respond immediately with equal or superior violence. In a modern city, on the other hand, the probability of attacks of this kind is relatively low, but injury could easily result from collision with other vehicles. Everyone relies on their own and everyone else's self-control to avoid accidents. And, should one occur, any impulse to respond violently must also be controlled for fear of a conviction. Thus, the loss of self-control carries also more long-term and less immediate dangers. The possibility of acquiring or maintaining a position within the network of interdependencies increasingly comes to rely on individuals' ability to monitor and regulate their own behaviour. Correspondingly, the fear of an external threat becomes fear of a threat which is posed to the individual by aspects of his or her own self (Elias 1982a).

As Freud remarked, with internalization 'the distinction between doing something bad and wishing to do it disappears entirely, since nothing can be hidden from the super-ego, not even thoughts' (Freud 1930: 125). This can serve to clarify further the difference between the ascetism of less developed societies and the self-restraint demanded by later stages of civilization. At later stages, according to Freud, 'instinctual renunciation no longer has a completely liberating effect' (ibid.: 127–8). More civilized individuals are therefore internally split and permanently engaged in a semi-automatic struggle with themselves, a struggle that, Elias agrees, 'does not always find a happy resolution' (Elias 1982a: 242). Freud's assertion that 'it is not merely a question of the *existence* of a super-ego but of its relative strength and sphere of influence' (Freud 1930: 125, note 2) applies even more markedly for Elias. For both thinkers there is no zero-point before which one could say that the super-ego did not exist; it is rather a matter of gradual transitions and changing nuances. While Freud entirely neglected the historical details of this process, they were the object of Elias' empirical scrutiny in the first volume of *The Civilizing Process*.

A key word for the description of changes in personality structure across the societal stages examined by Elias, and one which aptly catches the gradual nature of the process, is the term 'psychologization'. Elias initially defines it as a form of foresight that develops among the circles of court life in the sixteenth century. It is the product of,

> a more precise observation of others and oneself in terms of longer series of motives and causal connections, because it is here [at court] that vigilant self-control and perpetual observation of others are among the elementary prerequisites for the preservation of one's social position.
>
> (Elias 1982a: 274)

'Psychologization' describes a mode of perception of oneself and others that increasingly involves the assumption, on the part of the actors, that they possess an *interiority* that may be in contrast with an appearance or a *mask*. In the cognitive space or gap that comes into being through the process of psychologization, a new order of relationship becomes possible and is constantly being negotiated: the relationship between self and role, between the socially visible and the socially invisible aspects of the individual.[1] The constant activity of negotiation is still fully perceptible on the part of the actor within the context of court society, where the new restraints make themselves felt as an awkward and uncomfortable armour, as a mask that each and everyone is fully conscious of wearing. It is a declaredly 'hypocritical' stage, characterized by two-facedness and double play, where 'the awareness that this control is exercised for social reasons is more alive' (Elias 1982a: 272). At further stages in the process, as the socially visible and invisible aspects of oneself become increasingly distant and estranged from each other, a 'wall of forgetfulness' gradually consolidates between them, making each oblivious to the other. To the individual, they no longer appear as distinct opposites that are mostly in conflict. The mask merges with the face: it can no longer be removed at will. Self-controls thus acquire the universal appearance of a 'psychological' phenomenon that refers to the inner qualities of the person rather than to the dimension of the social. 'Hypocrisy' is no longer so clearly detectable at an interpersonal level because it has gradually become a form of self-deception, as Freud 'discovered' in due course. There is no longer as great a need deliberately to conceal one's feelings, for the very capacity to feel has been moulded to let only appropriate feelings emerge to consciousness at appropriate times. Individuals come to resemble increasingly 'watertight compartments from which no internal substance – be it mucus, saliva, urine or tears – is allowed to come out except within rigidly regulated circumstances (often "in private"), just as the emission of words and sentiments is strictly monitored' (Eve 1983: 405).

Homo Clausus is the name Elias offers for the provisional end-product of this long-term pattern of transformation. As a form of self-consciousness, *Homo Clausus* is characterized by 'an attitude of being alone, with an inner, "true" self, a pure "I" and an outward costume' (Elias 1991: 28). Elias takes his distance from Freud on the basis of his demonstration that *Homo Clausus* – and the strict juxtaposition of 'inside' and 'outside', of a natural 'core' surrounded by a social 'shell' – is the result of a historical process, and not an extra-temporal human characteristic. Freud, according to Elias, discovered the peculiar features of the personality structure of people in his own time and mistakenly ascribed them to an unchanging human nature. He therefore failed to realize that what he took to be immutable human attributes, especially the strict division between unconscious and conscious mental functions, are only a relatively recent development. They are an *effect* rather than a precondition of the figurations formed by people, and of the people forming those figurations (Elias 1982a: 286). Elias levels this same criticism, the adoption of *Homo Clausus* as a self-evident image of man, as an 'eternal, fundamental experience of all human beings accessible to no further explanation', to Descartes, to Weber and Parsons, and to the human sciences. Since Descartes, Elias maintains, many different and sophisticated versions of *Homo Clausus* have appeared in scholarly work. These range from *Homo Philosophicus*, the subject of classical epistemology, to *Homo Oeconomicus*, *Homo Sociologicus* and, last but not least, *Homo Psychiatricus* (Elias 1978b: 245–9; see also 1969).

Elias is keen to stress how far the influence of *Homo Clausus* as an ideal image of man spreads. Most importantly, he is very explicit in pointing out that *Homo Clausus* as a self-perception carries with it postulates and assumptions concerning a number of other categories, such as 'nature', 'truth', and 'individuality'. 'The advance . . . of civilization at certain stages', Elias writes,

> is . . . increasingly accompanied by the feeling in individuals that in order to maintain their positions in the human network they must allow their true nature to whither. They feel constantly impelled by the social structure to violate their 'inner truth'.
>
> (Elias 1991: 30)

Similarly, to the modern subject, 'only that part of himself which [he] can explain by his "nature" seems entirely his own' (ibid.: 57). However, Elias maintains, we are at a loss when trying to discern the 'truth contained' – that allegedly holds priority in accounting for the real nature of human beings – from the less true 'container' in which the subject is supposedly trapped: for 'is the body the vessel which holds the true self locked within it? Is the skin the frontier between "inside" and "outside"? What in man is the capsule, and what the encapsulated?' (Elias 1978b: 249). The crux of Elias' battle against *Homo Clausus* as a self-perception is to highlight that what is experienced as a wall between subject and object, between self and society, are nothing but the 'civilizational self-controls' whose development he documents in volume one of *The Civilizing Process* (1978b). The argument comes full circle with the demonstration that instinct controls are not any less natural or primary to the human being than are instinctive impulses themselves. Indeed, given the nature of 'nature' in a human context, 'there is no structural feature that justifies our calling one thing the core of man and another the shell' (Elias 1978b: 259; on human nature see Elias 1987).

In his studies, Elias thus shows that the notion of an uncontaminated 'inner truth' of the subject is a historically generated fiction. However, he does so by replacing this fiction with a more fundamental and more general 'truth'. This more fundamental truth is one according to which there is an intrinsic opposition between individual impulses (identifiable as the 'instinct functions') and social demands (identifiable as the 'ego' and 'super-ego functions') (Elias 1991: 9, 55). The separate poles of 'self' and 'society' are in fact structural to his account of *Homo Clausus*: the motor of civilization is the irreducible distinction between an individual principle (affect, or libidinal energy) and a social one (affect-control), *both* of which are equally rooted in human nature and whose contrast increases with the civilizing process itself. For Elias, the notion that subjects hold a pure truth within themselves that makes them 'individuals', a truth menaced and opposed by the supposedly unnatural demands of society, is a fiction because the opposition itself is the natural, and supra-historical, truth of the subject. Ultimately, following Elias' own logic, the self-perception of individuals as *Homini Clausi* appears necessary and inescapable at least as much as it is illusory. For this reason, there is a certain ambiguity in Elias' use of concepts such as 'ego', 'instinct' and 'super-ego'. On the one hand, they are objects of his description: as concepts and words, they are products of a historically determined way of thinking; they are not static substances, Elias warns us, and they do not exist in the same way as the stomach or the skull (Elias 1991: 34). On the other hand, however, these concepts can be adopted by him as interpretive devices because they refer to an objective opposition between affects and their controls. It is not a matter of disputing the referential adequacy of these concepts to an empirical datum. Rather, it is a matter of refining their use in accordance with the historical changes that the datum itself undergoes. This ultimately leads to an impasse. Elias' thesis as it stands can only rely and be derived from the same historical form of self-consciousness that is the object of his diagnosis and of his critique. Like the figure of *Homo Clausus*, Elias is not immune from the search for a 'deeper' truth to be opposed to the contingency of appearance or illusion: this search is simply transposed to a more general and remote level.

We can now see how the theory of the civilizing process is relevant to a sociogenetic explanation for the prevalence and incidence of 'psychosomatic illness' in modern society. It is indeed possible to argue that the development of an increasingly effective monopoly on violence by the state has modified what outlets are available for the discharge of alarm reactions on the part of the vegetative nervous system. It certainly appears to be the case that individuals, for the most part, now refrain from discharging such reactions into motor activity. And, as Elias himself suggested,

> in societies in which one is forbidden to inflict physical pain on others, the incidence of those who instead inflict physical pain upon themselves is likely to be high. Inflicting pain on others is strictly forbidden. Inflicting pain upon oneself is not forbidden and not punishable.
>
> (1982b, unpublished transcript)

Psychosomatic disorders, in this line of argument, stem from the,

> difficulties of members of specific societies, of representatives of a particular stage in their development. If one likes, one may call them 'disorders of a period'.
>
> (ibid.)

The prevalence of 'psychosomatic illness' in modernity may be thus regarded as the price modern subjects pay, in the form of redirecting violence towards themselves, for the relative protection from external violence afforded by the process of pacification. This constitutes a plausible account of the sociogenesis of certain types of illness that can be further developed as a complement, for example, to strictly biological perspectives. For our purposes, however, Elias' explanation presents a problematic overlap with the propositions of psychosomatics, resting as it does on a similar conception of the psychophysiological structure of human beings. His framework is inadequate to address the question of what accounts for the emergence of psychosomatics as a way of posing the problem of illness. Or rather, it appears able to address this question only in terms of an untenable correspondence-theory of reality, according to which a change in the biological substratum of disease would automatically call for alternative forms of knowledge.

Homo Clausus as a correlate of technology

We can fruitfully refer to Elias' diagnosis of *Homo Clausus* without resorting to either the notion of drives or controls as ultimate principles that articulate the relations to oneself and to others. Following Foucault, we may instead resort to a historicized notion of truth as the *shifting*, discursive ground for a diagnostics of subjectivity. Western history, Foucault maintains, has been characterized by the documentable persistence, albeit taking on a variety of forms, of an 'obligation of truth' (Foucault 1988c: 15). The analysis of objectifying and subjectifying 'technologies' informed by games of truth is Foucault's chosen strategy to dispense with a preconstituted theory of the subject as a starting-point for inquiry. In Foucault's account, the search for a true theory of the subject is itself a phenomenon liable to historicization. Foucault argues that the tendency to search for a positive theory of man as a foundation for the 'self' emerged in political, philosophical and epistemological theory in the seventeenth century, and that it is an effect linked to the heritage of Christianity (Foucault 1980c: 19; see also 1988d: 48).[2]

The following discussion is set in an explicitly comparative framework, starting with the juxtaposition of each author's characterization of 'individuality' and the 'self'. Let us begin with Elias, who maintains that:

> What we call a person's 'individuality' is, first of all, a peculiarity of his or her *psychical* functions, a structural quality of his or her self-regulation in relation to other persons and things.
>
> (Elias 1991: 57)

In contrast, Foucault argues:

> It may be that the problem about the self does not have to do with discovering what it is, but maybe has to do with discovering that the self is nothing more than a correlate of technology built into our history.
>
> (Foucault 1993: 222)

The key words I would like to isolate for comparison are 'self-regulation' and 'technologies'. Both formulations presuppose the notion that the subject is never quite complete and finished – that in order to function socially individuals must somehow work on themselves to *turn* themselves into subjects – but they do so in a rather different sense. For Elias, the conscious and unconscious patterns of self-regulation, as we have seen, are traced back to the working balance of opposite 'functions'. This balance in each case corresponds to the quality and quantity of danger faced by individuals in any particular historical configuration. Elias' theory of state-formation accounts for the changing character of social demands. But it is impossible to account for different forms of subjectivity without recourse to a (psychobiological) function of compliance with those demands. This function is presumed to be inherent in human beings, on account of their peculiarly 'social' nature. The notion of technologies of the self, on the other hand, eschews any prior assumptions about the inherent qualities of human beings. On the contrary, it makes room for a number of questions to be investigated historically. Such questions are, for example: Where and how do individuals come to perceive themselves as 'inadequate' or in need of perfecting? And therefore: what is the point of application for intervention of any kind? It is by considering these questions that the crucial methodological link with the concept of truth becomes apparent. The (self-)fashioning of the subject always involves and/or implies a *diagnosis*: an articulation in thought of the present state of affairs, and of what the subject should do or should be in relation to it. And therefore this fashioning implies the reference to a form of 'truth', to propositions deemed to have a certain authority. Foucault's endeavour arises from the reversal of a question which Elias shared with Max Weber:

> Max Weber posed the question: If one wants to behave rationally and regulate one's actions according to true principles, what part of one's self should one renounce? What is the ascetic price of reason? . . . I posed the opposite question: How have certain interdictions required the price of certain kinds of knowledge about oneself? *What must one know about oneself in order to be willing to renounce anything?*
>
> (Foucault 1988d: 17, added emphasis)

This is the reason why subjectivity is conceived as 'that which constitutes and transforms itself through the relationship with its own truth' (Foucault 1981a).

The notion of technologies informed by games of truth offers the opportunity for a detailed analysis of the sites and methods whereby certain effects on the subject are brought about. 'Objectifying' technologies of control are for example those devised in conformity with the forms of self-understanding provided by medicine, penology and psychiatry – to name only the three domains investigated by Foucault. These are deployed within concrete institutional settings whose very architecture testifies to the 'truth' of the objects they contain. The possibilities of self-experience on the part of the subject are intrinsically affected by the presence of someone who has the authority to claim that they are 'truly' ill, or mad, or a criminal. 'Subjectifying' technologies of self-control are those through which individuals:

> effect by their own means or with the help of others a certain number of operations on their own bodies and souls, thoughts, conduct and way of being, so as to transform themselves in order to attain a certain state of happiness, purity, wisdom, perfection or immortality.
>
> (Foucault 1988d: 18)

These are similarly linked to 'truthful' formulations of the task or the problem that certain domains of experience and activity pose, in this case for individuals themselves. The parameters of self-experience change with every acquisition, on the part of individuals, of a possibility, or a right, or an obligation, to state a certain 'truth' about themselves. Thus, the recourse to the notion of technologies is capable of accommodating the complexity of the 'subject' who, as a form, 'is not above all or always identical to itself. You do not have towards yourself the same kind of relationship when you constitute yourself as a political subject . . . and when you try to fulfil your desires in a sexual relationship' (Foucault 1988a: 10).

Although Foucault maintained the distinction between the so-called technologies of power or domination and the technologies of the self, these should not be regarded as acting in opposition to or in isolation from each other. Indeed, Foucault repeatedly stressed the importance of considering the two in their interaction and interdependence, by identifying in concrete examples 'the point where the technologies of domination of individuals over one another have recourse to processes by which the individual acts upon himself and, conversely, the points where the techniques of the self are integrated into structures of coercion' (Foucault 1993: 203). For exactly this intersection between subjectifying and objectifying technologies, Foucault coined the well-known term 'governmentality'. The distinction should therefore be considered as something more than a mere heuristic device, and yet not as the representation or the expression of two separate and conflicting sets of interests or demands (social and individual), such as we find them in Elias. To reiterate a well-known point concerning Foucault's conception of power, the theme of subjective constitution through practices of control and self-control should not be opposed to a theme of 'liberation' of the true nature of human beings. This is not to suggest that Elias could be counted among the advocates of liberation as a solution to the ills of civilization, in the sense of Wilhelm Reich or Herbert Marcuse. As we have seen, Elias does not identify the true foundation of human beings solely in the function that is repressed. He does however preserve a dichotomous structure wherein control, discipline and calculability stand opposed to raw affect and are never geared towards its creation or its release as such (see e.g. Elias 1982: 242). In Foucault, the analytical difference between technologies of power and technologies of the self does not refer to an opposition, but rather to the relative importance assumed by various forms of veridiction (or truth-telling) within different domains of experience. For example, the main feature of true discourse concerning madness, crime and disease consists in its being 'held from the outside'. Subjects can speak of madness to the extent that they themselves are not mad. In contrast, the domain of sexuality is for Foucault an example of a different domain of veridiction characterized, since the advent of Christianity, by hermeneutical practices that elicit a truth spoken by the subject about him or herself (Foucault 1981a).

On the basis of this methodological framework, we can approach the task of accounting for the self-experience of modern subjects as *Homini Clausi* in a different way. I propose to do so in terms of a 'dynamic of truthfulness'[3] that informs the relationship to one's self and that changes and unfolds in the course of Western history. To produce this account I shall recast some elements of Elias' description on the basis of arguments adopted from Foucault. To begin with, this recasting involves modifying our stance in respect to the figure of *Homo Clausus*. To acknowledge the historical contingency of *Homo Clausus* as a mode of self-perception does not imply that it should be regarded and discarded as the illusory byproduct of a history. Rather it is an effective element of that history, an element that contributes to the structuring of it in a circular feedback process. As a first move, therefore, the self-perception of *Homo Clausus* must be taken seriously and somewhat at face-value, since it makes a difference to the practices through which forms of subjective experience materially constitute themselves. As Elias pointed out, one of the main features of this self-perception is a sense of violation of, and longing for, one's own unique 'inner truth'.

Foucault's comparative studies of late antiquity have highlighted how the 'forms' of the truth (as opposed to the 'contents'), and hence the models of relationship between the subject and truth, have historically been not singular but multiple. Different 'forms' of truth underlie practices which, despite any superficial similarities, are very dissimilar in their consequences. To illustrate the point we may take the contrast Foucault draws between the Stoic and the Christian examination of conscience. In the case of the Stoics, truth is understood as being not in or of oneself but in the *logoi*: a collection of rules of conduct based on the teaching of the teachers. As such, truth cannot lie 'hidden' within the subject but can be forgotten by the subject through a fault of practice. For the Stoics, the examination of conscience measures the distance between what has been done and what should have been done, and evaluates the adjustment between aims and means in the sequence of actions performed during the day. For Seneca, Foucault writes, 'the subject constitutes the intersection between acts which have to be regulated and rules for what ought to be done' (Foucault 1988d: 34; 1993: 209). The Christian examination of conscience, on the other hand, is an entirely different truth-game. It is geared towards disclosing a hidden secrecy, towards detecting the presence of unacknowledged desires. It elicits truth as a personal quality of the individual – not of impersonal actions – for a task of purification.

Christianity instituted practices of self-observation coupled with obligations of voluntary self-disclosure and self-exposure (Foucault 1993: 211). It is to these that we may trace the perception that 'there is something hidden in ourselves and that we are always in a self-illusion which hides the secret' (Foucault 1988d: 46). This confessional tradition envisages the truth as a desire-to-be-renounced, whose renouncement involves the will to reveal what is hidden. This 'will to self-revelation' can be regarded as an important dynamic principle in the changing forms of Western perceptions of self. Unlike what can be said for the extra-historical concept of 'instinct', a will to self-revelation can be shown historically to have been called into being, to have been patiently nurtured and fostered, through a variety of practices and techniques. We can therefore presume it to have provided quite a strong bias in the development of different forms of subjectivity. Foucault indeed maintains that the aim of the human sciences and of medical, psychological and psychiatric institutions since the eighteenth century has been to found a hermeneutics of the self that would substitute a 'positive' self for the self-sacrifice imposed by the Christian imperative of renunciation (see the discussion of *exomologesis* – or *publicatio sui* – and *exagoreusis* in Foucault 1988d: 41–8, 1993: 213–20). For Foucault, this new use of techniques of verbalization represents a significant break from the past. Their genealogy, however, both leads us and entitles us to formulate the question: 'Is this hermeneutics of the self worthy of saving? . . . Do we need a positive man who serves as the foundation of these hermeneutics of the self?' (Foucault 1980c: 20).

If we accept the development of a 'will to self-revelation' as a working historical hypothesis, it is no longer relevant whether or not the hidden truth exists as a material or as a purely discursive reality. It is no longer relevant whether or not the hidden desire gains a claim to legitimacy, and thereby to 'positivity', on the basis of shifting metaphysics. The historical will to reveal the self produces effects autonomously: effects that are independent of the truth it addresses. The dynamic of these effects, I propose, leads to the configuration Elias describes as *Homo Clausus*. Let us then return to the key concept of 'psychologization' in order to rewrite the movement it describes starting with the passage from warrior to court society. This movement can be envisaged as a dynamic propelled, on the part of the subject (i.e. *not* exclusively), by an underlying will to self-revelation.

In line with Elias' description, the process of 'psychologization' involves the opening of a distance, or a gap, between what is shown and what is not shown, what is felt and what is made out to be felt. We can read this as a multiplication of the truths of reference that are available to the individual about him- or herself within different situations.[4] As we have seen, the Christian conception of truth identifies what is worth knowing as true with what is worth hiding,[5] and construes truth as a predicate of the person rather than of situations or roles. It is only by an implicit but constant reference to this Christian conception that the multiplication of truths about the self can be experienced as a contradiction – a contradiction that is not mere duality, but also a *fraud*: a fraud, because one pole of the duality is experienced as truer, and truer precisely on account of being *hidden*. This argument implies a reversal in the order of explanation for the origin of 'repression' as a mechanism that favours collective interest at the expense of individual fulfilment. It is not on account of the essential truth of drives, and of their incompatibility with social demands, that they exist as hidden (at first only from others and eventually also from the subject's own consciousness). It is rather on account of their being hidden that certain human features, behaviours, and thoughts, acquire priority in attesting for what is essentially true about the individual. In the reversal from Christian renunciation to scientific 'positivity', these features become represented as the self-interested principle of a desire which must find an outlet or a means of affirmation, if the self is to be whole and sound.

On this basis, we can provide an alternative account of the manner whereby the perceived conflict between individual needs and social demands intensifies in the course of the civilizing process. It is a story that can be told with a heuristic reference to the notion of 'hypocrisy'. Still without contradicting Elias, we can say that the extent to which this multiple character of the self's truths is consciously experienced as hypocritical depends on the length of chains of interdependence and the consequent amount and quality of foresight implicit in social interaction. In the setting of court society, self-control consists in the conscious putting on of a mask, in the playing of a nearly theatrical role in which the actors never forget themselves as such. In such a setting, foresightful behaviour involves a clear fore-thought, a deliberate practice of *ad hoc* fabrication in which specific parts are devised towards specific ends. Here the contrast between a hidden and a manifest 'truth' about the self is blatant and conspicuous to the subject of action. Yet, at this obviously hypocritical stage the 'will to self-revelation' is not foiled in such a way that the individual can feel socially deprived of his or her own truer self. The reason for this is that the opportunity for self-revelation remains available as an option, albeit as a theoretical and probably inconvenient one. It remains available to the extent that the individual can still directly address and identify with a hidden truth that it could be worth telling, a truth whose disclosure would make a difference to the status and being of the subject him- or herself.

By way of a seeming paradox, it is only at a later stage in the historical process that we contemplate the pandemic experience of a loss or lack on the part of the subject. This only happens when foresightful behaviour has become effortless and second-nature to the adult human being, through an inter-generational force of habit and practice linked to the further lengthening of chains of interdependence. It is when, in other words, there is no longer consciously anything to hide in order to perform adequately on the social stage. What is lost then, what is sacrificed to the social, are not one's immediate impulses but their worthiness of being hidden/revealed.[6] At this later stage, when the self has become a 'positive' matter for knowledge, the will to self-revelation addresses an overabundance of truths of reference. Such truths are increasingly provided by expertise, through technology, and within institutions. None of these truths, however, has the secret unforseeable quality that would make it feel true enough – that is, worthy enough as a truth to be revealed – for and by each individual. The will to self-revelation is frustrated in the original, etymological sense of the word: it is 'in vain', it is made redundant, while it continues to have a value for the self-recognition of individuals.

The proposition that a 'will to self-revelation' has undergone a historical process of frustration could easily meet with an objection based on one of Foucault's best known books. In his first volume of the *History of Sexuality* (1978), Foucault mounted a powerful critique of the 'repressive hypothesis'. He showed not only how it is flawed to presume that the society that emerged in the nineteenth century had confronted sex with a fundamental refusal of recognition, but also that the discursive explosion that has produced 'sexuality' since the eighteenth century can be regarded as continuous with the technologies of confession developed in the Christian West as a means for the production of the truth of individuals. Confessional technology became gradually disengaged from the destiny of Christian spirituality and its sacrament of penance; the development of what Foucault termed the new form of 'pastoral power', with its focus on 'population' and 'individuals' as political and economic problems, provided confessional technology with a new *raison d'être*, with new means of support and new relay mechanisms that enabled it to spread out into the whole social body through a multitude of institutions (Foucault 1978: 23–6, 1982: 213–15). It would therefore seem that, from the rituals of early Christian penance to the deployment of pedagogy, medicine and psychiatry, any will to self-revelation has been met with an unbroken crescendo of opportunities pivoting around sex as the fundamental secret to be revealed. Accordingly, our perception that 'truth, lodged in our most secret nature, "demands" only to surface; that if it fails to do so, this is because a constraint holds it in place' is univocally attributed by Foucault to the cumulative pervasiveness of the obligation to confess. This, he writes, has become 'so deeply ingrained in us, that we no longer perceive it as the effect of a power that constrains us' (Foucault 1978: 60). Hence the objection: if it is questionable to presume that our sexuality has undergone a process of repression over the last three-hundred years, it seems equally questionable to displace a 'repressive hypothesis' onto the will to self-revelation implanted in individuals with the advent of Christianity.

The first volume of *The History of Sexuality* (1978), however, antedates

Foucault's analytical distinction between 'objectifying' technologies of power and 'subjectifying' technologies of the self. In that book, as we can see retrospectively, an undiscriminating reference to 'confessional technology' conflates these two viewpoints, with a marked emphasis on the coercive and objectifying aspects of confession. As its French title indicates, the book was concerned more with the 'will to know' than with the will to be known. In the unpublished preface to the second volume, Foucault justified his turn to antiquity by saying that it was easier to distinguish in that period the specificity of the domain of 'relations to the self' from the domains of knowledge and of normative systems:

> the very important role played at the end of the eighteenth and in the nineteenth century by the formation of domains of knowledge about sexuality from the points of view of biology, medicine, psychopathology, sociology, and ethnology; the determining role also played by the normative systems imposed on sexual behavior through the intermediary of education, medicine, and justice made it hard to distinguish the forms and effects of the relation to the self as particular elements in the constitution of this experience. There was always the risk of reproducing, with regard of sexuality, forms of analysis focused on the organization of a domain of learning or on the techniques of control and coercion, as in my previous work on sickness and criminality.
>
> (Foucault 1984c: 338)

The first volume of *The History of Sexuality* (1978) does in fact point to the sort of project from which Foucault here is explicitly taking distance. It is therefore important to allow for ways in which the specific domain of 'relations to the self' may have been affected by the emergence of a new regime of discourses wherein 'things were said in a different way; it was different people who said them, from different points of view, and in order to obtain different results' (Foucault 1978: 27). In other words, we can suppose that the relation to the self that pivots on a singular quest for truth changes as it meets with the newly established domain of scientific, 'positive' truth-games. It is very significant, from the point of view of the subject, that,

> [f]or a long time [the] archive [of the pleasures of sex] dematerialized as it was formed. It regularly disappeared without a trace (thus suiting the purposes of the Christian pastoral) until medicine, psychiatry, and pedagogy began to solidify it.
>
> (Foucault 1978: 63)

The solidification of the truth of sex into scientific knowledge allowed for the specification of individuals into types, for the indexing of identities in relation to 'normal' measures. The stakes of the incitement to discourse there lay not so much in an inherently therapeutic act of self-revelation, where a transitory truth is the unique expression of an individuality about to be transformed. On the contrary, a truth exacted in the name of science served to fix that individuality onto a permanent category without residue, without scope for any further revelation:

> The nineteenth-century homosexual became a personage . . . . Nothing that went into his total composition was unaffected by his sexuality . . . . It was cosubstantial with him, less as a habitual sin than as a singular nature . . . . The sodomite had been a temporary aberration; the homosexual was now a species.
>
> (Foucault 1978: 43)

Thus, objectifying technologies of power have produced sexuality as the secret of our common nature. But precisely for this reason that secret could no longer function, by itself, as the hidden reference upon which the constitution and the transformation of a unique self has been predicated since the advent of Christianity. The repressed self as a modern form of self-perception may thus be regarded as plausible even and precisely in the face of the discursive explosion that has produced sexuality rather than confined it to silence. We should consider it as the effect of a discontinuity, a gap, an emerging lack, in the history of technologies of the self.

In this account, the advent of psychoanalysis represents a significant threshold. It is significant not in regard to the history of 'sexuality' (where it is perhaps a point of culmination), and therefore not for having highlighted the sexual aetiology of neuroses. It is significant, rather, in respect to this history of relations to one's hidden truth – and therefore, for having affirmed the logic of the unconscious (Foucault 1980a: 213). The logic of the unconscious reinstates the fundamental truth of the subject as one that is permanently hidden, recessed, inaccessible. The truth to be known is never there where anyone can expect, predict, calculate to see it: the more obvious and plausible it appears, the more deceptive it is likely to be. The manifestation of this truth cannot be forced out of the subject but only elicited gently through a unique, irrepeatable process of free association. The notion of an inevitable 'return of the repressed', moreover, ascribes a new value to symptoms as episodes in which the truth surfaces despite the subject's own self.[7] This preempts even the need for a therapeutic setting in which to experience the effects of truth, provided a degree of 'proto-professionalization' is in place (De Swaan 1981). 'Pathological' products among which, since Freud, we must count dreams, slips of the tongue and even jokes, are certainly not transparent manifestations of the unconscious, but they are enough to testify to the existence of a truth which is unique, and in regard to which the subject has a privileged relationship. The neurotic symptom, a 'compromise formation', has a twofold significance. It is an instance of self-revelation but it is also, at the same time, concrete evidence that the subject has complied with the canons of 'normality' and of civilized existence. As in the rituals of penance, the development of a symptom is at once an act of manifestation and an act of renouncement of a socially untenable inner 'desire'.

Conclusion: the body as a vessel of truth

In conclusion to this narrative, let us explore a further turn that takes us to psychosomatics as a form of (self-)questioning. We can now begin to see, by way of a negative logic, how the body and *its* symptoms may historically have come to be probed as a privileged site for the truth of the self, and as a new opportunity for self-revelation – the 'body' that is mute, the 'body' that we have been accustomed to think of as a machine. Well, it is precisely on account of this exclusion of the body's internal functioning from the domain of purposeful agency that the body itself, the anatomical body, is perfectly inconspicuous from a *socio-* and *psycho*-pathological point of view. As such, it represents the most hidden, unlikely place in which to look for the truth of an unruly desire; it is on account of being so hidden, so improbable as a site of truth, that the body is liable to being newly problematized in this sense.

The development of anatomo-clinical medicine in the eighteenth century conferred to the human body an unprecedented visibility. This visibility, however, should also be regarded as a profound invisibility of the body in other respects. The anatomo-clinical structure:

> constitutes the historical condition of a medicine that is given and accepted as positive. Positive here should be taken in the strong sense. Disease breaks away from the metaphysics of evil, to which it had been related for centuries.
>
> (Foucault 1973: 196)

Foucault here rightly emphasizes the moral and normative dimension of this development. With it, all disease that pertains to one's body in its concrete objectivity, is beyond the threshold of relevance as the expression of a subjectivity, as evidence of a relation between the subject and truth. This is what changes, what is newly problematized, in modern psychosomatic discourse. The ways of this discourse are quite specific to this historical conjuncture, and do not simply reproduce an age-old question. How, then, is the modern problematic of psychosomatics rooted in a specific configuration of subjectivity? Not, or at least not only, in the causal sense that is suggested by Elias, that psychosomatic illnesses appear as a consequence of the psychic tension to which modern individuals must submit in order to be civilized.

As I have stressed throughout this chapter, this book does not intend to contribute to an understanding of the aetiology of 'psychosomatic illness', whatever is understood by this expression. Instead, my task has been to highlight some of the conditions of possibility for psychosomatics as a form of problematization, as a way of posing the *question* of illness. These conditions of possibility, we may say, inflect this question in a particular direction. Modern subjects (both the subjects of knowledge, and those of action) seek a hiding place for the truth-to-be-revealed, a truth that expresses the compromise made by the subject in favour of sociability. At the same time, the body culturally represents the best hiding place, a hiding place that remains inconspicuous as such until the advent of psychosomatics. Thereafter, to describe it as the locus of a hidden truth is not uncontroversial, but it becomes possible.

We may also ask how this problematic modifies the possibilities for the constitution and transformation of the self as a subject. In other words, what are the likely effects of this problematization, in this respect, given its conditions of possibility? At a most general level, the answer here follows the logical form of the question. Subjective relations to the self will be affected to the extent that psychosomatics confronts individuals with the proposition that this subjective truth – the truth of their relation to themselves and to others – may be revealed by their bodies. If this general hypothesis is tenable, we may anticipate that through psychosomatics the problematic of illness rejoins the sphere of ethics, in modernity, through the back door. By ethics here I mean, in line with Foucault, the 'deliberate practice of liberty . . . the deliberate form assumed by liberty' (Foucault 1988c: 4). Illness as problematized in the discourse of psychosomatics will again belong to the strategic margin, the space for 'play', that the individual embodies as the subject of purposeful action. To say that someone is (psychosomatically) ill will be to say something more than that the pressures of civilization have taken their toll. It will imply regarding the pathological manifestations of the body under the aspect of strategic performance, as the visible sign of the compromise subjects have made in order to constitute themselves as the social person they are. Accordingly, while confronting an illness may involve a deliberate practice of self-transformation, self-transformation thereafter must pass through a learning about the self from the truth told by illness. This is what we glean as a hypothesis, by building abstractly on historical arguments that chart the development of a privileged relationship between the self and its truth. In the following chapters I examine whether and how the different aspects of these conditions of possibility organize the actual propositions of psychosomatic discourse.

2

HIDE AND SEEK

Medicine and 'somatization'

> The pride of a doctor who has caught a malingerer is akin to that of a fisherman who has landed an enormous fish.
>
> (Asher 1972: 145, in Cunnien 1988: 24)

Chapter one ended with the claim that in order to understand what is at stake in the modern problematic of psychosomatics we must first recognize a number of features of the modern context of experience, a context that embraces both the modern subjects of action and the modern subjects of knowledge. First, we must recognize the force of the idea that what is proper to the 'self' is an irreducible kernel of truth that violates (and is violated by) the requirements of social coexistence. Second, we must recognize the force of the imperative to seek this truth in hidden places. And third, we must recognize that the most hidden of these places in the modern context is the physiological and anatomical body, precisely because it is the most unthinkable in this respect. To illustrate this last point, let us briefly return to Elias' theory of the civilizing process. What, according to that theory, counts as a visible failure to comply with the requirements of civilized behaviour? What counts as the sign of an 'individual civilizing process that is considered . . . unsuccessful' (Elias 1982a: 245)?: certainly not a physical medical condition. On the other hand, psychotic and neurotic symptoms might well do, if not necessarily in expert discourse at least in the context of social interaction. In other words, 'civilized' existence is structured around a normative separation of the 'mental' from the 'physical'. Normative here means simply that 'physical' attributes or conditions are evaluated quite differently from 'mental' ones. The normative weight of this separation has important consequences for the possibility of articulating a 'psychosomatic' way of thinking about disease, as I shall argue later in this book.

In this chapter, my task is to illustrate the effects of this normativity at the level of institutional and discursive practices that are currently dominant. As a platform to set off the discussion, I shall begin with an extended review of Edward Shorter's *From Paralysis to Fatigue: A History of Psychosomatic Illness in the Modern Era* (1992). Shorter's influential book emerges among a striking paucity of historiographical and sociological works purporting to engage critically with the questions of psychosomatics. Furthermore, Shorter is the rare example of a historian that has published, and has been reviewed, in journals of psychosomatic research. Finally, and more importantly for our purposes, Shorter's thesis may be regarded as an argument in support of the idea that the body in modernity represents the 'best hiding place' for those aspects of the self that are perceived as socially maladaptive or deviant. In what follows, I shall argue that Shorter does not simply expose this as a cultural assumption of his informants, but also uses it as a guiding principle for his research. This is why we cannot take his work as the basis for an analysis of psychosomatics as a form of knowledge, much in the same way as we had to abandon Elias on this front. Futher in the chapter, I shall turn from Shorter to medical/psychiatric literature where the problem of deceptive, 'false' illnesses is addressed. This will illustrate how bodily evidence indeed functions as a precious 'guarantor' of the good intentions of the subject in relation to the social. When clear physical evidence is lacking, it is as if a guarantee of these intentions were missing. I shall highlight what questions are raised and must be answered in such cases, that would otherwise remain implicit and whose answers would be taken for granted. And, finally, I shall ask what role this plays in making 'false' illnesses a socially preferable option to other thinkable alternatives.[1]

How history reveals the body as a disguise: a critique

Let us then turn to Shorter's argument. How, first of all, does he see his task? Historians, Shorter maintains, can make an independent contribution to the great scientific debates that have never ceased to surround the phenomenon of hysteria. They can lend new support, through historical evidence, to certain explanations of what goes on in the 'mysterious leap from the mind to the body'.[2] Thus his goal is not simply to illustrate what medicine already knows about this controversial subject, but explicitly to '[use] the past to illuminate today's problems' (Shorter 1992: xi; see also 1984). Historical evidence can show 'how the body's response to stress or unhappiness is orchestrated by the unconscious' (ibid.: ix). Clear sociocultural changes, Shorter argues, run in parallel with the changing symptomatology of what he calls 'psychosomatic disorders', and may well explain it. Before looking at this thesis in more detail, let me point out that Shorter in this book assumes a semantic equivalence and interchangeability between the terms 'somatoform', 'somatization', 'psychogenic', 'hysterical', and 'psychosomatic'. In reconstructing his argument I have maintained his terminological usage (until otherwise specified), although I fundamentally disagree with it for reasons that will become apparent.

The argument opens with the question: 'why [do] the kinds of psychosomatic symptoms that patients perceive change so much over the ages?' (Shorter 1992: ix). Shorter begins by saying that the symptoms of organic disease (like 'coughing up sputum if one has pneumonia') have remained historically invariant. Unlike these, psychogenic symptoms 'have a history of their own' (ibid.: 1). In particular, he continues, it is since the first decades of the nineteenth century that psychosomatic illnesses have assumed a variety of typical forms. These have changed in rapid succession over time and have ranged from the now uncommon symptoms of 'hysterical paralysis' to those of 'chronic fatigue'. These changes, according to Shorter, are understandable in view of the nature of the symptoms themselves. They are symptoms produced by the unconscious mind, rather than by an organic cause, and – this is the crux of Shorter's thesis – they are produced in accordance with a 'template' provided by the surrounding culture. Such templates embody 'the culture's collective memory of how to behave when ill' (ibid.: 2). They constitute, in other words, 'pools' of symptoms that are considered legitimate evidence of disease by the medical profession at any particular time.

The role of an official medical theory is central to Shorter's argument and provides the rationale for saying that 'psychosomatic symptoms changed relatively little before the second half of the eighteenth century' (1992: xi). The diagnosis of spinal irritation in the 1820s offers 'the first modern instance of a cultural shaping of patients' symptoms, in this case with the doctor acting as the agent of the culture' (ibid.: 25). The historical correspondence between sociocultural changes and the changing symptoms of psychosomatic illness should therefore be understood in quite a literal, and linear, sense:

> The unconscious mind desires to be taken seriously and not be ridiculed. It will therefore strive to present symptoms that always seem, to the surrounding culture, legitimate evidence of organic disease. This striving introduces a historical dimension. As the culture changes its mind about what is legitimate disease and what is not, the pattern of psychosomatic illness changes.
>
> (Shorter 1992: x)

Given this as its main theoretical premise, the bulk of Shorter's book presents a wealth of illustrations of how symptoms have evolved following a number of medical 'paradigms': from the doctrines of spinal irritation and of the reflex arc, to the theories of motor hysteria and dissociation, to the central nervous paradigm with its model diagnosis of neurasthenia.

The role of the last medical paradigm Shorter considers – the 'psychological' paradigm – is crucial to his discussion. Shorter describes it as the predominant explanation of psychosomatic symptoms from the 1920s to the 1970s. Despite its popularity among doctors during that period, the psychological paradigm failed to persuade the general public according to Shorter. This failure had the effect of shifting the main source of inspiration for the 'unconscious mind' from the authority of medical knowledge to the 'authority' of the media. The picture of somatoform illness in the twentieth century might have been very different, Shorter maintains, if insights about psychogenesis had penetrated the public in the same way as they infiltrated the medical profession. But why did the psychological paradigm fail to gain this wider credence? As reasons, Shorter gives the following: first, the early association of the psychological paradigm with psychoanalysis ('consultation with a psychiatrist for the symptoms of somatization now became tantamount to "seeing a shrink"') (ibid.: 261); then, the idea that the public as a whole is 'refractory to any notion of "nerves" smacking of psychology or the action of the mind' (ibid.: 263); and further, the conclusion that 'the advocates of all these [psychological] therapies underestimated the deep terror with which patients contemplate physical symptoms. No therapeutic approach would succeed that did not reassure patients of the reality of their symptoms' (ibid.: 266). Briefly, the bottom cause for this failure is the fact that somatoform symptoms were subsumed under the heading of psychiatry, as opposed to that of neurology. Shorter squarely imputes this to the 'hijacking' of psychotherapy by psychoanalysis. He gives here a crucial clue: psychoanalysis made psychotherapy explicit as such, as opposed to performing it while letting patients believe that they were receiving organic treatment. Unfortunately, he does not elaborate on this point other than to say that this marked the end of,

> any hope of achieving public enlightenment about somatoform illness . . . . Psychoanalysis, which had set out to inform the public, correctly or incorrectly, about the unconscious roots of neurosis, thus achieved the paradoxical result of strengthening the public's conviction of organicity.
>
> (Shorter 1992: 261)

Shorter's story therefore offers a vast amount of evidence to suggest that the body does represent a good 'hiding place', at least in the sense that it is thus regarded by what he calls the public 'unconscious mind'. But is this story believable, in the way it is told? It seems paradoxical that a work whose aim is to highlight the normative force of illness concepts should fail to reflect upon its own relationship to medical knowledge, and to realize what this relationship contributes to the narrative. For instance, Shorter maintains in his preface that 'psychosomatic illnesses have always existed' (Shorter 1992: x). Have they? If 'psychosomatic illness' is the fabrication of physical symptoms to suit cultural templates of 'legitimate' disease, as Shorter maintains, this must mean one of two things. Either it is simply false to claim that 'psychosomatic illnesses' have always existed. Or, to say so presupposes that 'organicity' is a universal criterion upon which the legitimacy of illness is predicated – which is equally evidently false. We can still maintain that 'psychosomatic illnesses' have always existed only if we grossly reduce the meaning of the expression to signify 'false' or 'deceptive' illness. Let us pursue this for a moment. It means we must be flexible as to what types of symptoms count as 'psychosomatic' in the first place, in order to suit culturally diverse templates of 'true' illness. But in this case, a 'somatoform' illness need not present itself somatically at all. Finally, even this dubious exercise begs the question of cultural specificity. This is because the relevance (or the 'function') of ascertaining the legitimacy of illness through 'objective' parameters is indissociable from the structure of therapeutic relationships, and ultimately from the value ascribed to illness episodes within any given culture. The sick-role itself, in other words, is culturally specific in its predicament of excusing the patient for his or her condition; and presumably the same applies to the 'secondary gain' whose role in substantiating psychosomatic illness is paramount in Shorter's definition. It follows that the value of (consciously or unconsciously) producing, and of detecting, false or deceptive illnesses is itself a highly relative phenomenon.

In sum, while it is axiomatic to Shorter's thesis that culture 'changes its mind' about what constitutes legitimate illness, it seems clear that, for him, such changes do not impinge on his definition of what a true illness is. And his definition is a naive endorsement of biomedical epistemology (Fabrega 1990). As Freidson wrote in 1970, the normative import of medical authority is not confined to 'the power to legitimize one's acting sick by conceding that he is really sick' (1970: 205). Rather, 'by virtue of being the authority on what illness "really" is, medicine creates the social possibilities for acting sick' (ibid.: 206). Shorter, contrary to all appearances, fails to regard the phenomenon of somatoform illness critically, in terms of how knowledge contributes to the possibility of its existence. He fails to ask why we are so concerned to speak of illness in these terms, and what this says about the condition of the present. Like Elias, Shorter takes this concern for granted, never loses familiarity with it, and can only address it in terms of a correspondence-theory of reality: we are concerned because these illnesses have increased, or worsened, in recent history. Shorter imputes the current prevalence of somatoform symptoms to the condition of 'postmodernity', which he identifies with 'the solitude and sense of precariousness arising from ruptures in intimate relationships' (Shorter 1992: 320). As in Elias, this is a socio-aetiological explanation, based on the idea that these symptoms are 'a patient's way of saying that he cannot cope with the society in which he finds himself' (Review in *The Economist* 1992).

As a result of these important shortcomings, the 'failure' of the psychological paradigm to persuade the general public lacks an adequate explanation in Shorter's book. The fact that the public is refractory to psychology and to psychotherapy is clearly part of what is to be explained, and merely reinstates the question rather than answering it. But where does Shorter himself stand on this question? The psychological paradigm offers what for him is the correct explanation of somatoform symptoms only in the negative sense of revealing that they are not truly physical, not in the positive sense of defining them as legitimate pathologies. Shorter seems to endorse Alfred Schofield's reminder that 'a disease of the imagination is not an imaginary disease'

(Shorter 1992a: 291), but also stresses that it is only 'from the patient's viewpoint' that somatoform problems 'qualify as genuine diseases' (ibid.: ix). His position coincides with the dominant view in Western medicine that 'somatizing patients may be regarded as ill, but their illnesses are nonmedical, or "existential"' (Jennings 1986, in Lipowski 1988: 1362). Thus, Shorter adopts a double-standard with regard to biomedical and to psychological explanations, despite heavily relying on concepts like the 'unconscious' in his account. Similarly, he appears to reproduce within his argument the cultural prejudice that regards only 'physical' illness as fully legitimate illness, and 'mental' illness as always ambiguously placed between illness and deviance. This, again, should be clearly part of what his critical account addresses, and not one of its premises.

Shorter, then, shares with his informants the common understanding that 'psychosomatic illness', once it is revealed for what it is, is not clearly identifiable as a legitimate 'health' problem. Given these premises, a crucial question arises: what can logically be expected to happen as a result of a 'public enlightenment' on the question of psychosomatic illness as Shorter understands it? Is it so surprising that, by his own account, the psychological paradigm fails to persuade? Let us suppose, for a moment, that such a public enlightenment could turn 'existential suffering' into a legitimate type of illness. If this were to happen, it follows that these disorders should logically disappear, since existential suffering would no longer need to emerge socially in a disguised form. This argument can be maintained in a 'hard' sense, implying that people would actually somatize less and report, and receive treatment for, existential complaints instead. Or it can be maintained in a 'soft' sense, implying that they would somatize just as much but not insist on the organic nature of their symptoms, since their pathological relevance would not be put into question. In either case, 'somatoform disorders' as such would no longer (be said to) exist. But let us now end this thought-experiment and come back to more likely prospects. To the extent that announcing the presence of a 'somatoform illness' is equivalent to *denouncing* its equivocal status, the failure of the psychological paradigm to persuade the public at large is only tautological. This failure only reflects the conditions that give rise to 'somatoform illness' in the first place.

We can make this point even if we don't agree with Shorter that the psychological paradigm has failed to persuade members of the general public. For example, we could look at some of the explanations that have been produced within medical circles for an alleged decline in the prevalence of 'hysteria'. One of these is precisely the 'argument from psychological literacy'. As a result of the popularization of concepts such as unconscious motivation, the argument goes,

> laypersons began to comprehend the psychodynamics behind hysterical conversion symptoms, which thereafter failed to elicit the desired

> social response and subjective gratification. For secondary gain to work, it must remain unconscious in the mind of the patient. As a result . . . people have been forced to develop subtler and more sophisticated mental mechanisms for coping with the stresses of life.
> (Micale 1993: 499)[3]

This line of analysis is supported by cross-cultural epidemiological data arguing for the fact that somatoform disorders currently prevail mostly in lower-class, rural, or third-world environments. Their decline within industrialized and Western(ized) populations has allegedly been accompanied by an increase in depressive and narcissistic disorders (see e.g. Chodoff 1954; Schimel *et al.* 1973; Stefansson *et al.* 1976; Krohn 1978; Swartz *et al.* 1986). This evidence suggests that public enlightenment about somatoform illness has indeed had an effect. Significantly, however, this effect is to be noted among those who can culturally and materially afford to act upon their psychological distress in terms of a veritable illness. To the extent that somatoform disorders persist in our society, they constitute a demand for care whose form points to the ambiguities, conflicts and contradictions that surround the status of suffering that is not demonstrably 'physical', or even demonstrably real.

The remainder of this chapter is devoted to these ambiguities, conflicts, and contradictions. I will look at 'somatizing disorders' as these are debated in the specialized press. This will serve to illustrate what issues are raised in relation to conditions, and patients, that appear 'false' from a biomedical point of view. This will also make it clearer for us what issues are *not* raised when, on the contrary, the source of a demand for care is a demonstrable physical condition. Before I go on to do this, however, I briefly want to return to Shorter on a last but crucial point. Is Shorter justified in treating terms like 'somatoform', 'psychosomatic', 'psychogenic' and 'hysterical' as synonymous and interchangeable? And is he justified in treating them as qualifying adjectives for discrete 'disorders' rather than, say, to qualify medical perspectives? Shorter's rather casual attitude towards medical knowledge is reflected in his very casual use of these controversial terms – a point that has not gone unnoticed among his medical readers (Lask 1996). As I shall use (and have used) some of these terms myself, it is convenient now to introduce them in more detail.

Questions of definition

The main distinction I want to draw attention to is between two general terms: 'psychosomatic', and 'somatization'. Ideally this distinction should be warranted by clear, consensual definitions of either term, and yet these are not available. The term 'psychosomatic' is sometimes applied to 'functional' disturbances whose organic aetiology is not clearly established (e.g. irritable bowel syndrome, non-ulcer dyspepsia). At other times, the term is applied to organic pathology with demonstrable lesions in which psychological factors are reputed to play a necessary role (e.g. ulcerative colitis). In yet another use, the term is extended to include a wide range of diseases that are traditionally accounted for in organic terms (e.g. neoplasms and diabetes). A 1964 report of the World Health Organization denounced the restrictive application of the adjective 'psychosomatic' to only a subset of conditions as a latent contradiction and a paradox. The same report suggested that the line of demarcation between 'psychosomatic' and 'non-psychosomatic' diseases may be shifted to different positions depending on whether the task of prevention, therapy, or diagnosis is under consideration (WHO Expert Committee on Mental Health 1964). Thus, while no agreed-upon definition can be found in the literature as a whole, the ambiguity and polysemy of the concept are abundantly remarked upon (see e.g. Engel 1967; Fava 1992; Fava and Wise 1987; Lipowski 1986, 1988). Conceptual ambivalence and confusion are also acknowledged in internationally accredited manuals of psychosomatics for the use of clinicians (e.g. Luban-Plozza and Pöldinger 1977). I shall follow Todarello and Porcelli (1992) in suggesting that it is possible to identify two broad and distinct meanings for the term 'psychosomatic' amid conceptual overcrowding and confusion:

> in a *wide* sense, it refers to the holistic unity of the individual. In this view, it is never possible to separate the physical from the mental, and therefore everything is psychosomatic. From this perspective, since any disease is psychosomatic, it is perfectly identical whether we speak of psychosomatic conditions *and* of organic, physical or somatic conditions.
>
> (1992: 15)

Authoritative representatives of this position include Lipowski (1986) and Engel (1967), both of whom are critical of the notion of 'psychosomatic disorder' in that it implies a separate category of conditions and therefore, by inference, the absence of psychosomatic interface in other diseases. This wider sense of the term reflects the growing *programmatic* consensus as to how it should be used, in the wake of developments in systemic and multi-factoral thinking. Conversely, in a narrow sense, the adjective 'psychosomatic' refers to 'the possibility of identifying particular psychic factors or personality structures to be regarded as primary aetiological data for the disease' (Todarello and Porcelli 1992: 16). The best-known reference figure for this still widespread way of using the word is Franz Alexander (1943, 1950, Alexander *et al.*1968). For Alexander the adjective applied to a clearly circumscribed pathological subgroup, which he opposed both to classic neuroses and to purely somatic conditions. Most authors occupy intermediate (and often unclear) positions between these two extremes and offer more nuanced definitions of the task of psychosomatics as a field of inquiry. Positions, needless to say, vary greatly according to the context of each author's practice and disciplinary location.

In terms of its clinical application, it must be stressed that the term 'psychosomatic' has practical currency mostly only for a residue of leftover conditions that biomedicine fails to manage adequately – for instance, when a condition becomes chronic as a consequence of a negative response to organic treatment, or when no clear organic cause is established for the presence of a clear functional alteration. These situations provide virtually the only criteria for a 'psychosomatic' diagnosis that are met with nearly unanimous consensus on the part of medical practitioners and psychoanalysts alike (Todarello and Porcelli 1992). Thus, despite the programmatic value of regarding all disease as 'psychosomatic', authors like Todarello and Porcelli regret that acknowledging this dimension of disease is by no means a practical reality. They attribute this to the dominance of biomedicine in setting the sequence of diagnostic inferences that follow the presentation of a physical complaint (1992: 14; see also Furlan and Mancini 1980; Todarello 1988). Physicians are consulted in the first place, and only if the standard diagnostic or treatment procedures fail do 'psychosomatic' approaches rise to the status of formal statements, usually by referral to a consultation-liaison psychiatric practice. Before then, the presence accorded to psychosomatics in the context of institutional settings remains within the margin of activity that is left to the discretion of single practitioners.

In any case, no definition, however provisional or contradictory of others, warrants confusion between the expression 'psychosomatic' and the notion of 'somatization'. Unlike the term 'psychosomatic', the term 'somatization' does appear as a specific disorder in the *Diagnostic and Statistical Manual* (DSM-IV) of the American Psychiatric Association, alongside others (e.g. hypochondriasis, conversion disorder, pain disorder, body dysmorphic disorder, etc.) that are classified under the broader heading of 'somatoform disorders'. The DSM-IV 'decision tree' for differential diagnosis further links this group to the categories of 'factitious disorder' and 'malingering', both of which must be ruled out for a somatoform disorder to be diagnosed, but both of which can figure as hypotheses in the process of making that decision. In the next section, I follow Ford (1983) in using the expressions 'somatizing disorders' and 'somatization' in a generic sense, to embrace the DSM-IV categories of 'somatoform disorders', 'factitious disorders', and 'malingering', on account of the fact that these may all come into play in the process of settling on a diagnosis. Taken as a whole, all these labels refer to conditions that appear 'false' from a biomedical point of view. As a minimum common denominator between all of them, we have the following situation: a patient reports somatic symptoms which they attribute to a physical disease. Doctors, on the other hand, repeatedly fail to find that there is anything wrong – except for, crucially, the patient's own persistence in seeking medical help.

The paradox of health

The contemporary debate surrounding somatizing disorders reflects a wider societal concern about what Barsky has called the 'paradox of health': a rising preoccupation with sickness and disability despite objective improvement in health status and overall declining mortality (Barsky 1988a; 1988b). A clear unifying theme in the specialized literature is the perception that somatizing patients account for a disproportionately high fraction of medical care costs. The socioeconomic impact of somatization (including disability payments, time lost from work, and so on) is claimed to amount to a worldwide problem of major dimensions (Ford 1983: 3; see also Barsky *et al.* 1986; Bass and Benjamin 1993; Bass and Murphy 1990; Blackwell 1992; Katon *et al.* 1990; Osterweis *et al.* 1987; Shaw and Creed 1991). Some authors argue that this economic aspect of the problem alone is enough to warrant generating further research efforts into these conditions (Lipowski 1988). The cost of somatizing disorders is thus not only high, but also claimed to be unjustified:

> The point is that a large portion of medical care services are directed toward persons without a disease and/or are overutilized by some persons who may or may not have evidence of disease. These services are offered in a fashion consistent with the disease model; but because these patients do not have organic disease it is not unreasonable to propose that the treatment they receive is not very effective.
>
> (Ford 1983: 4)

Let us ignore at present whether Ford is right in ruling out any use for the biomedical treatment of patients who do not have a biomedical disease.[4] What is more fundamentally at stake is whether somatizing disorders should be regarded as *medical* conditions in the first place, justifying the attribution of the sick-role and of its corollaries. The boundaries between preventing a disease and preventing the unlawful abuse of a public service become blurred: somatizing disorders seem to put into question the very basis of this distinction.

Somatization thus calls attention to the 'external' system of institutional relations of which medicine is a part. In so doing, it also generates 'internal' reflection on the consequences of this system of relations for medical practice. The traditional doctor–patient relationship is said to have been eroded by the presence of competing demands linked to insurance practices, or by patients' rights in relation to 'malpractice'. Given these recent changes in the provision of health care, it is argued that clinicians can no longer assume that patients will not deliberately distort their clinical presentations (see Rogers 1988; also McGregor and Duncan 1988). On the other hand, the traditional structure of the doctor–patient relationship has also been posited as a possible source for the perpetuation of unjustified treatment, on account of the therapist's desire to ally with the patient and gratify his or her dependency needs (Turco 1991).

The outcome of this dynamic is described often to be 'chronic incompetence with loss of any expectation of recovery and a new role of being honorably disabled' (Sturges, in Turco 1991: 36). At the root allegedly lies the 'faulty concept that the treating physician best knows the condition of the claimant' (ibid.). This, in fact, is the premise that underlies the compensation system as a whole.

Deception is central to the way the problem of somatizing disorders is articulated. All patients in this category allegedly perpetrate deception, whether consciously or unconsciously, sometimes clearly in pursuit of a 'secondary gain'. The precept that 'the treating physician best knows the condition of the patient' is thus put into question by introducing the possibility that the patient may 'know better' than the physician. In contemporary Western societies, secondary benefits represent a natural corollary of the sick-role (*bona fide* sick people get them as well). But it remains understood that the primary benefit or goal is the restoring of health, and therefore the fact of relinquishing the sick status itself. In order to maintain this specific hierarchy between primary and secondary benefits the demand arises for an 'objective' and visible measure of suffering or disadvantage. 'Evidence' of disease, where disease is understood as a biochemically measurable phenomenon, is as a rule what fulfils this requirement in the current functioning of Western medicine. Evidence of disease thus understood is also 'evidence' that the system of resource allocation is being used rather than abused; it is a guarantee that an individual actually has the right to enjoy the dignity that all disease confers. Some might object to this characterization by saying that 'evidence' of this kind is certainly not in place for the production of most psychiatric diagnoses. But the exception of mental illness is only an apparent one. Consider simply that 'organicist' psychiatry treats the visible disruption in the social and personal life of the patient as evidence of a physical defect that is not yet detectable, but probably to be inferred from the effects of drugs (Kramer 1994). And when classical anti-psychiatry rejects the postulate of biochemical aetiology it also explicitly rejects the pathological label that medicine attaches to the individual (Fabrega 1976; 1980).

The main sense in which somatizing disorders constitute a broad single category is in that they render the issue of 'evidence' in one way or another problematic. Either such evidence is lacking altogether (as in conversion disorder or hypochondriasis), or it cannot guarantee that the person involved is in good faith (as with self-induced factitious illness and malingering). Moreover, somatizing patients are characterized specifically by the fact that they do *not* experience or report psychological symptoms (Lipowski 1988: 1359), so that the only 'evidence' of a psychiatric condition is their abnormal illness behaviour. The concept of 'abnormal illness behavior' was first presented by Pilowski in 1969 and later supplemented by a diagnostic scale for it, the Illness Behavior Questionnaire (Pilowski 1969, 1975; for a critical review of the questionnaire, see Zonderman *et al.* 1985). Sociological analysis had previously formulated the notion of 'illness behavior' with the explicit intent of distinguishing disease from 'what people do about it'. As a sociological tool, it served to acknowledge and to promote the study of a separate domain of 'lay' conceptualizations of illness (Gerhardt 1989; Mechanic and Volkart 1960; Zola 1966, 1973). Pilowski's endeavour, however, follows the medical proposal advocated by A.J. Lewis (1934) for the systematic study of what he called the 'psychopathology of insight' (patients' distorted perceptions and understanding of their own symptoms, whether mental, physical or both). Lewis and Pilowski both presuppose that medical perception provides the objective and accurate standard for assessing health status. Somatizing disorders imply 'a discrepancy between subjective and objective health' (Lipowski 1988: 1361) which parallels the discrepancy between the concepts of *illness* and *disease*. In biomedical epistemology, the phenomena of disease and illness are presumed to be overlapping and coextensive, on the assumption that illness is caused by and follows the onset of disease. This 'correspondence postulate' involves assumptions about the presentation of illness, which include the 'culturally appropriate degrees and forms of worry', and it is normative in that it 'validates how disease changes affect behavior' (Fabrega 1990: 654; see also Fava 1992; Kirmayer 1984, 1986).

The discrepancy between subjective and objective health is what justifies a psychiatric diagnosis of somatization. This is what provides the otherwise missing evidence that something out of the ordinary is indeed going on. The difference between doctors' and patients' assessments of the situation is therefore a crucial feature of the phenomenon. In itself, however, it cannot determine that an individual is 'ill' rather than 'deviant'. To achieve this, specific guidelines in DSM-IV help clinicians to establish the status of this discrepancy of judgements – its status either as a sign of deviance or as a sign of (psycho)-pathology. These guidelines can be read as answers to the following questions: do the doctor and patient really disagree, or is their disagreement, like the physical symptom itself, a false one? In other words, is the patient deliberately pretending to be ill, or are they deceiving themselves as well as the doctor? And if they they are deliberately pretending, what are their reasons for doing so? These questions represent the hermeneutical grid through which the elusive 'evidence' of this disagreement is sorted into different diagnostic subgroups associated with what I have generically called 'somatization'. How, then, are the questions answered, and what diagnoses do they give rise to? The first question, concerning whether the disagreement is genuine or false, is answered in terms of the opposite concepts 'intentional' and 'not intentional' (DSM-IV: 445). If symptoms are intentionally produced to deceive the doctor, then the patient must have known to begin with that they were not truly ill, and the disagreement between doctor and patient is fundamentally false. Vice versa if they are not intentionally produced, then the patient is a victim of this (self-)deception at least as much as the doctor. The disagreement is genuine, hence there are genuine grounds for a psychiatric diagnosis. In terms of diagnostic labelling, the 'intentional' *vs.* 'not intentional' axis neatly opposes the DSM-IV categories of 'somatoform disorders', on the one hand, and those of 'factitious disorders' and 'malingering', on the other. A second set of opposite concepts comes into play when the disagreement between doctor and patient is shown or assumed to be simulated. This set describes the nature of the secondary gain deception can be presumed to serve, which can be either 'external', or not externally recognizable and therefore, by inference, 'psychological' (DSM-IV: 471, 683). These concepts lead respectively to the labels of 'malingering' and of 'factitious disorders': 'the patient who simulates pain in order to obtain drugs is a malingerer, and the patient who simulates pain in order to draw attention to a difficult home situation is factitiously ill' (Cunnien 1988: 14). But 'malingering' and 'factitious disorder' do not equally grant a right of entry into the sick-role. The factitiously ill person only imperfectly fulfils the requirements of this role in that he or she obviously does not hold the restoring of health as a primary goal. Yet, this is rendered as the notion that he or she is a 'problem *patient*' (for a case report, see Feldman and Escalona 1991). On the other hand, it is not entirely clear whether malingering calls for therapeutic help or entirely different forms of social action (e.g. legal sanctioning); whether it should be defined as an illegal act rather than a mental status (Gorman 1982), or as a maladaptive coping strategy (Rogers and Cavanaugh 1983).

It is little wonder that the practical application of such criteria is reported as difficult and controversial (Cunnien 1988; Jonas and Pope 1985), for the task of assessing the status of a deception is itself something of a scientific paradox. Clinicians are in the double position of subject and object of their own judgement. They must adjudicate between their own perception and the patient's with regards to the patient's degree of consciousness and motivations. Yes, the doctor's perception is aided by technology, but how useful is that in this case? In Cunnien's words,

> An act may be so clearly deceptive as to obviate any debate about its veracity, but motivations for deceptive acts are highly complex and are not amenable to simple categorizations of conscious versus unconscious or environmental versus internal and psychological.
>
> (Cunnien 1988: 14)

It is certainly not in their position as a scientist that the clinician is competent to make this type of assessment, although it is as a scientist that he or she has authority over the situation. Rather, the assessment is made by the clinician in another of his or her capacities, namely as an agent of social, moral, or even economic norms. This is the crux of Szasz's argument against the 'diagnosis' of malingering, which he equates with a form of social or moral condemnation (Szasz 1956; see also Trimble 1995). Others have drawn attention to the possibility that the pursuit of a secondary gain on the part of the doctor may play a role in the 'psychologization of illness' (Goudsmit and Gadd 1991). In a similar vein, Ford (1983) has suggested that identical psychological dynamics may be at work in the psychopathological development of somatic symptoms and in the choice of medicine as a career. All these suggestions are useful in problematizing the assumed neutrality of the clinician when faced with assessing presentations that potentially undermine the position from where he or she speaks.

Calling into question the neutrality of the clinician in his or her judging capacity remains for the most part a purely theoretical exercise. The point remains, however, that the phenomenon of somatization stands in a peculiar relationship to the epistemology of biomedicine, a purely negative one. When someone presents somatic symptoms, and yet there are no organic findings to corroborate them and when, moreover, none of the typical characteristics of a psychiatric disorder are present (other than the discrepancy between medical judgement and the reported symptoms), then it must be a case of somatization. For the patient, undergoing all the evaluative judgments surveyed above (concerning the purpose illness serves and the relative gain obtained through it) may prove to be a route into categories of deviance rather than pathology. Conversely, when the presence of biochemical or tissue alterations is established, this preemptively excludes patients from being assessed in all these social and moral respects, and potentially as legally accountable for their condition. It seems obvious that this predicament itself should play a role in creating the opportunity for somatization as a behaviour, if not also as a genuine experience. Somatizing disorders are 'irreducibly tied to a social situation in which the validity of the person's suffering is called into question' (Kirmayer *et al.* 1994: 133), a social and *historical* situation where a demand for care is not in itself sufficient to signify an actual need (see Jewson 1976). Accordingly, it seems plausible to suggest that:

> [patients'] opposition to psychological explanations may reflect defensiveness about emotional problems, but it may also be a realistic appraisal of the deleterious social consequences of psychiatric labelling. Some of what is attributed to psychopathology in somatization may be better understood as individuals' response to this threat of psychiatric stigma.
>
> (Kirmayer *et al.* 1994: 133)

The tendency to attribute these patients' problems to 'inner' characteristics of psychopathology, Kirmayer *et al.* suggest, is:

> consistent with a general European-American cultural bias for attributing others' behavior to their individual characteristics rather than to the social situation . . . . From these attributions of responsibility, it is a short step to viewing the patient as morally culpable.
>
> (1994: 133)

Thus, the concern is apparent even in the clinical disciplines that the (conscious or unconscious) 'choice' of somatic symptoms on the part of somatizing patients may not bear a psychopathological feature, but a form of adaptation or conformity to culturally predominant value standards. But note that even as the focus shifts to a sociological perspective that acknowledges the effects of labelling, still no account of the reality of somatization as a form of suffering is provided. On the contrary, the very possibility of such an account seems to recede further and further into the background, as 'somatizers' appear only to behave logically after all: the conclusion remains that there is nothing wrong with them. What this means is that some fundamental questions are still not being asked, or that they are still asked in the wrong way. Is it really a matter of understanding the aetiology of somatization, as either mental or physical or social, or even as a combination of these? Is it really a problem of insufficient knowledge, or of the wrong epistemology being in place? Is it not rather a question of understanding what values are at stake – operational, financial, moral, and health values – in regarding 'existential suffering' as a veritable problem of health?

Conclusion: resistance or cooperation?

To begin to offer an alternative, we may suggest that somatizing patients' insistence on the physical nature of their complaint reflects more than fear of psychiatric stigma. For, given that they do not allegedly perceive and certainly do not report their distress psychologically, it is only on account of their resistance to psychological explanations that they appear able to command some recognition of need – albeit at a considerable cost both to themselves and to the medical establishment. Somatizing patients with unexplained medical symptoms are said to benefit from psychological (rather than biomedical) treatment. Yet in order to be recognized as a 'somatizer' worthy of such treatment it is first necessary to have reached a point of contradiction and conflict with medical opinion – an opinion that still perceives itself primarily as failing to reassure the patient of the non-reality of their problem, giving rise to the reality of the 'problem patient'. A very similar point is put forward by Salmon and May, who argue that doctors' reliance on conventional biological expertise as a general default option is what traps them into becoming an 'instrument of somatization' (1995: 325). A recent paper by Speckens *et al.* (1995) also suggests that somatizing patients are probably more willing to accept psychological treatment than they are generally assumed to be by the medical profession. All this points to a certain number of questions. If these patients did not resist psychological explanations, we may ask, what sort of problem would they pose for medical practice? At present, would patients be taken seriously if, as so many authors advocate, they learned to voice their demands in psychological or in social terms? And, if they were taken seriously, what sort of problems would medicine be compelled to regard as pertinent to its concerns and part of its formal responsibilities? Would it be a manageable situation? Would it be a desirable situation?

For the purposes of a sociological inquiry, patients' resistance to psychological explanations of their condition is of particular relevance. This resistance does present a management problem for current medicine (Bass and Benjamin 1993; Creed and Guthrie 1993). But this management problem is still relatively minor when compared with the theoretical possibility of acknowledging the psychosocial issues at root as truly medical problems. Such issues apply widely across the population, and may well also underlie, undetected, many more straightforward medical conditions that at present are treated biomedically and that do not give rise to conflict or antagonism. To identify the reality of disease with what is 'objectively' present in the body practically and theoretically creates the possibility for somatizing disorders, as I have illustrated. But it also protects medicine from the public expectation that it should generally count aspects other than somatic ones in the explanation and management of medical conditions. Thus, if the body is the 'best hiding place' for maladaptive individuals, it is such also for the medical profession and for society as a whole, who are thereby shielded from confronting their ambivalence towards the status of psychosocial problems as either illness or deviance. For the vast majority of conditions, medicine can afford to function not in spite of, but because of the persistence of this ambivalence. To conclude, then, while somatizing patients' resistance is discussed in the literature precisely in terms of what makes them 'unmanageable', this same resistance is probably an asset for the management capacities of current medicine.

3

THE VITAL AND THE SOCIAL

In the course of the last chapter I argued that the construct of 'somatization' is the product of a certain configuration of knowledge and practices and that, as a phenomenon, it highlights how the distinction between 'body' and 'mind' is both normative and powerful. It is easier to take sides with either term than it is to transcend their difference without denying it. This is particularly the case when it comes to conceiving the reality of illness, where accounts seem to be trapped between the 'objectivism' of bodily evidence that is predominant in medicine, and the 'relativism' of many sociological perspectives that draw attention to the connection between illness and social norms. What does it mean to say that illness is a 'normative', value-laden concept? In this chapter I shall approach this question with a specific purpose. My purpose is, most generally, to show that it can be answered at a variety of levels and from a variety of angles. And specifically, that we can acknowledge the norm-related character of illness from a *medical* perspective, that is, without adopting relativism in relation to the problem of knowledge (except in so far as this knowledge allows for it). The reason for doing so is to show that 'objectivism' is not a necessary stance, epistemologically speaking, from the viewpoint of medicine itself (and not only from the viewpoint of the critics of medicine). The discussion will revolve around the problem of somatization, with which readers will by now be familiar.

The social

To think of 'somatizing disorders' as a form of adaptation or conformity to the values of a stigmatizing culture might represent the beginning of a reflexive attitude on medical practice, in the sense that this practice is not seen simply as a neutral agent encountering an independent phenomenon. On the contrary, medicine is seen to uphold and promote the very values to which 'somatizers' conform, only then to denounce these individuals as problematic cases. This does not tell us, however, whether there is anything more to 'somatization' than an act of labelling. This problem is not new in the context of medical sociology. The numerous issues involved in addressing it can be introduced through what has been termed, within labelling-theory approaches to mental illness, the problem of 'primary deviation' (see Gerhardt 1989; Gove 1970, 1974). This starts from the premise that 'illness' means deviation from normative standards and that becoming ill is to be characterized accordingly. The question then becomes whether categorization focuses on actually strange or impaired behaviour, or whether the behaviour in question falls within the range of what is ordinary and normal. Labelling theorists cluster around two different positions in this respect: positions which Uta Gerhardt has characterized respectively as the 'non-conspicuousness' and the 'life-problem' approaches. According to the first approach, 'what distinguishes normal from symptomatic behaviour is not its contents – what the person, in fact, does – but its *context*' (Gerhardt 1989: 94). Somatizing 'disorders' superficially would seem to offer a case in point of this hypothesis, since by definition they cannot arise outside a medical context within which the conflict between doctors' and patients' accounts of the situation takes place. Indeed, physical symptoms not accounted for by demonstrable disease appear to be ubiquitous in the population (Lipowski 1988; Mayou 1993; Von Korff *et al*. 1988). Similarly, the tendency to experience and communicate distress in a somatic rather than a psychological mode is acknowledged as widespread with variations in most societies (Kirmayer 1984). Yet it is only when this communication occurs within a medical setting that a 'societal reaction' takes place through which 'somatization' as such becomes manifest. In line with this hypothesis, one could argue that diagnoses of somatization perfectly exemplify the instance where 'the act of labelling [is] the only homogeneous aspect of the heterogeneous symptoms' (Gerhardt 1989: 94, citing Goffman 1961b).

The 'somatizing patients' that worry the doctors, however, are individuals who deliberately and repeatedly seek confrontation with the context within which they are thus labelled. It is this behaviour that at least in part defines their diagnosis. Their persistence in seeking biomedical help despite doctors' reassurances offers the grounds for arguing that their way of acting is indeed anomalous, and this leads us to what Gerhardt terms the 'life-problem' approach. This approach maintains that '"primary deviation" exists but may be analysed as rational behaviour occurring in an irrational environment' (Gerhardt 1989: 93). Critics such as Szasz, Lemert and Laing have contested that certain behaviours, which they acknowledge to be conspicuous and 'deviant', should receive a pathological label. This is on grounds that such behaviours 'may offer temporarily or relatively stable solutions to life problems despite the fact that they represent a lower order of human existence' (Lemert 1967: 48, in Gerhardt 1989: 96). In this view somatization could be interpreted as an actual (psychological and/or physical) process taking place within the individual, independently of an act of labelling (although not independently of the social environment). The 'societal reaction' precipitated by the absence of organic findings in this case merely detects (and labels) the anomaly accordingly.

To the extent that somatizing disorders can be conceived as the product of a (conscious or unconscious) 'choice' of somatic suffering as opposed to, and instead of, psychosocial suffering, they confront our ethical system with the proposition that such a choice is, in principle, possible as a solution to 'problems in living'. By saying this I do not mean to convey any facile assumptions about the genesis of somatic symptoms themselves, an issue that for the moment should be left within brackets. I mean rather to suggest that the sociocultural context, on its part, makes this a possibility first by differentiating between physical and mental illness, and second by attaching different values to these notions.[1] But even having said this, the problem remains: how can this choice be possible from the point of view of the embodied individual? Does our culture have the conceptual means to envisage this possibility other than by saying that it is 'all in the mind'?

Somatization thus poses a conceptual problem that is in some respects analogous to the broader questions of mental illness – a classic issue in medical sociological discussion. The problem of somatization recalls the anti-psychiatric critique of mental illness to the extent that its status as a form of medical pathology is also not warranted by objective evidence of disease. It differs from the case of mental illness, however, to the extent that the initiative in demanding treatment comes from patients themselves, who arguably experience and report their condition in somatic terms because it would not otherwise be held to require or justify a medical response. Peter Sedgwick (1972) championed the cause of rendering the illness concept both critical and yet available to psychiatric patients, in the wake of the impact of the anti-psychiatry movement. Against proponents of this movement whom he termed 'immanentists', Sedgwick proposed a 'relativist' solution to redeem and retrieve the concept of mental illness without its stigmatizing connotations. His strategy was to show that the concept of physical illness is equally not objective but value-laden, and that no diseases exist as such in nature prior to the cultural meanings that are attached to certain sectors of human experience. He appealed both to variations across cultures and to plant and animal pathology to argue that all sickness is essentially deviancy from a normative alternative state. The weakness in Sedgwick's argument is that it is highly unlikely to persuade anyone who does not already agree with him. He leaves us with a concept of illness that is totally emptied of any specific content, with the implication that the only rationale for its use must be political. On the basis of this argument Sedgwick claims that 'mental illness *is* illness' but others might equally well claim that 'physical illness *is not* illness', leaving the choice between these conclusions as a matter of political or ethical preference. This weakness appears particularly relevant in relation to phenomena, such as somatization, that do not immediately present with clear or striking evidence of psychological suffering or impairment, while failing to meet the standard 'objective' requirements to qualify as a genuine disease. Briefly, the case of somatization invites a concrete and specifiable account of the 'pathological' as a domain of experience that is not reductively identifiable with objective parameters.

The vital

The work of Georges Canguilhem is uniquely helpful here. In *The Normal and the Pathological* (1989) he exposes the fallacy underlying the notion that health and disease are value-free and objectively definable conditions. Yet Canguilhem's work also provides a powerful counterweight to the equation of health normativism with relativism. Three points from *The Normal and the Pathological* highlight the contrast between Canguilhem's position and the relativist position exemplified in Sedgwick's work. First, the norms on the basis of which a state of illness can be said to exist are not arbitrary, despite the fact that they cannot be established by scientific methods and independently of value judgements. Second, such norms are not social but organic, in the sense that they are posited by the organism itself and are immanent to it. Third, what distinguishes health from illness is not conformity to given norms or their violation, but the range of circumstances in which an organism can afford to function normally – that is, its ability to institute new norms in accordance with changing circumstances. These are all well-rehearsed aspects of Canguilhem's thesis. Let us see how they relate to the problem of relativism.

The first point enables us to pinpoint the specificity of illness among the totality of norm-governed categories. Despite their subjective character, norms of health and illness are 'rooted not in the whims or idiosyncrasies of the individual organism, but in its essential nature as the sort of organism it is' (Gutting 1989: 49). If the norms which define the presence of illness are not interchangeable with all other norms, then the concept of illness has a specific value over and above its instrumental value in a political context. There are 'objective' reasons to preserve its use despite the fact that the term does not refer to an objective set of facts. Relativist accounts do not make this point with sufficient clarity, although Sedgwick recognizes the need 'to discern a common structural element which distinguishes the notion of illness from other attributions of social failure' (1972: 216). For Canguilhem, the salient feature of 'organic norms' is not that they are relative to a body but to something which is *alive*. Life, Canguilhem argues, endows the organism with an intrinsic finality proper to it as a whole which cannot equally be ascribed to social organizations. Canguilhem's use of the the term 'norm' implies an opposition between the 'organic' and the 'social', *not* between the 'organic' and the 'mental'. Hence the relevance of the second point, which distinguishes between social and organic norms and refers the concept of illness specifically to the latter. Sedgwick's account by definition fails to elaborate this distinction and, as a result, his search for the common logical features between states of illness lapses into a quest for the common elements in all accounts of illness. This common element he identifies in the individual human being:

> Each culturally specific account of illness must involve a theory of the person . . . if the current theory of the person is positivistic and physical, the agencies of illness will be seen as arising from factors within (or at the boundaries of) his body.
>
> (1972: 216)

Descriptions and explanations of illness all appear to depend on some theory of the person which is, inescapably, culturally relative. Thus neither the social norm which attributes causes to illness nor the social act of attribution itself can provide unity to the concept, since such norms – as Sedgwick powerfully illustrates – vary so greatly. In Canguilhem's account, on the other hand, what provides the norm of health or illness is not a theory of the individual, but the vitality of the individual organism itself. This does not exclude its being a norm of what we call 'emotional' or 'psychological' functioning, but maintains that the phenomenon of disease is logically prior to cultural differences and, more specifically, prior to the scientific expertise that claims sole authority over its definition. Canguilhem, let us recall, refers approvingly to the 'technician' Leriche, according to whom 'physiology is the collection of solutions to problems posed by sick men through their illnesses' (1989: 100). We might contrast this with a passage from Christopher Boorse (1975) that seems exemplary of a typical objection: 'The corollary of [a normativist] position', Boorse writes, 'will be that writers of medical texts must do an empirical survey of human preferences to be sure that a condition is a disease. No such considerations seem to enter into human physiological research' (1975: 53). In this passage Boorse seems to forget that the clinic, as Leriche points out, constitutes precisely such a survey of human preferences.

The third point asserts that what distinguishes health from illness is the range of circumstances in which an organism can afford to function normally. This leads us to reconsider illness in relation to deviance. In Sedgwick's relativist account there is a tendency to conflate what happens in the social context (the 'societal reaction') with what happens in the sick individual (the 'primary deviation'). For Canguilhem, the state of illness does not consist of a deviation from or an infringement of healthy norms. A diseased state is also regulated by norms, although these are different from healthy ones and inferior to them, in that they leave the organism 'a smaller margin of tolerance for the inconstancies of the environment' (Canguilhem 1989: 197). It is plausible, of course, that what we call illness, what we collectively recognize as such, is what deviates from a given range of social norms which varies across cultures. It might also be suggested that the extent to which someone suffers from being in a pathological state – the extent to which the condition is undesired by him or her – is determined, at least in part, by the exent to which and by the sense in which that state does constitute deviance from such social norms. But these points, to which I shall return below, should be regarded as a predicate of the interrelatedness of different types of norms. They are not, for Canguilhem, what constitutes the specificity of the pathological as such.

Let me now return first to the problem of mental illness, and then to the issue of somatization. This requires a more detailed consideration of the distinction and of the interaction between social and organic norms. The fact that the norms of health or pathology are 'organic' rather than 'social' should not lead to the inference that the organism is conceived in a reductively physical sense. It does not require us to deny that 'organisms' are culturally and socially bound, and in a sense culturally and socially created. An organism is more than, and different from, merely a physical body. The notion that organic norms are rooted in the 'essential nature [of the individual organism] as the sort of organism it is' (Gutting 1989: 49) is premised upon the understanding that human beings, as the sort of organism they are, are exceptionally open to cultural moulding and specifically required to function in a meaning-laden cultural environment. The line Canguilhem is keen to draw between organic norms and social norms refers to the analogy so often posited between organism and organization. Canguilhem wants to preclude the ascription of a teleological finality to the latter while asserting it for the former. This demarcation, however, by no means excludes the possibility of an interaction between the two:

> Relating physiological norms to man to show up cultural norms, is naturally extended by the study of specifically human pathogenic situations. In man, unlike in laboratory animals, the pathogenic stimuli or agents are never received by the organism as brute physical facts, but are lived by the consciousness as signs of tasks or tests.
>
> (1989: 270)

This is the reason why Canguilhem asserts explicitly that we must look beyond the body in order to discern what is normal and what is pathological even for the body itself. To discern the normal and the pathological we must adopt the point of view of a body inserted within an environment understood as being historically and culturally structured with respect to the possibilities it offers and the capacities it normally requires. If by 'organism' we understand a decontextualized, ahistorical entity, the point must indeed be made that 'man, even physical man, is not limited to his organism' (Canguilhem 1989: 200).

The question of mental illness can be approached from this perspective. The realm of 'life' in which the living being partakes is understood to include more than the physical dimension. The needs and the ideals that must be accessible in order to 'feel normal' refer not only to physical activities but also to the cognitive, affective and behavioural demands set by a social and moral environment. What is (mentally) pathological is not relative to the social and/or moral norms themselves; it is not merely a deviation from them. Rather, what is pathological is immanent to the living being as a subjective norm of functioning that defines not its degree of *adaptation* but its degree of *adaptability*. As with physical illness, 'the [mentally] sick living being is normalized in well-defined conditions of existence and has lost its normative capacity, the capacity to establish other norms in other conditions' (Canguilhem 1989: 183). Canguilhem's account of the distinction between the normal and the pathological enables us therefore to formulate a dynamic notion of mental illness indexed not to specific types of behaviour or descriptive contents, but rather to a mode of being experienced as problematic, in the first instance, by the organism itself. In this view, eccentricity or deviant behaviour as such cannot be regarded as pathological, to the extent that the eccentric or deviant individual is potentially able to institute different norms of behaviour for him- or herself. The normative alternative state to mental, as to physical, pathology is relative to the individual in a prior state and refers not to specific acts but to the margin of agency, immanent to the individual, from which the acts arise:

> the normal and abnormal are determined less by the encounter of two independent causal series, the organism and the environment, than by the quantity of energy at the disposal of the organic agent for delimiting and structuring this field of experiences and practices, called its environment. But, you will ask, where is the measure of this quantity of energy? It is to be sought nowhere other than in the history of each of us.
>
> (Canguilhem 1989: 283–4)

In the question of mental illness it is therefore imperative and crucial to distinguish between the dynamic and the static senses of the term 'adaptation'. This distinction as it applies to organic norms precludes the theoretical assimilation of health normativism with social normativism in the notion that conformity to social norms can be regarded as psychic health – and that deviation from them is what defines psychological pathology. The concept of adaptation, therefore, 'can only be used in the most critical spirit' precisely on account of the applications it has received in the contexts of psychology and sociology, both of which define normality from perspectives which are entirely other or only partial with respect to that of the living being. For this reason, Canguilhem writes,

> we are taking care not to define the normal and the pathological in terms of their simple relation to the phenomenon of adaptation . . . . The psychosocial definition of the normal in terms of adaptedness implies a concept of society which surreptitiously and wrongly assimilates it to an environment, that is, to a system of determinisms when it is a system of constraints which, already and before all relations between it and the environment, contains collective norms for

> evaluating the qualities of those relations. To define abnormality in terms of social maladaptation is more or less to accept the idea that the individual must subscribe to the fact of such a society, hence must accommodate himself to it as to a reality which is at the same time a good . . . . If societies are badly unified sets of means, they can be denied the right to define normality in terms of the attitude of instrumental subordination which they valorize under the name of adaptation.
>
> (Canguilhem 1989: 282–3)

The distinction between organic and social norms entails a number of important consequences that will lead us back to the problem of somatizing disorders. We have seen how, for Canguilhem, social and moral normality and abnormality cannot be said to represent values of existence in the same sense that the notions of health and disease express such values. This proposition stems from the fact that no teleology can be ascribed to social organizations in the same way as to an organism. It is crucial to stress the difference between an environment (understood as a system of determinisms) and society (understood as a system of constraints, in regard to which the living being has in principle a choice) in order to preclude the facile and politically dangerous assimilation of adaptedness to health and deviance to pathology. An individual may be socially deviant or maladaptive without being any less healthy; the same socially maladaptive behaviour may in fact represent, from the point of view of the living being, an expression of its vitality or health. Theft and murder for survival provide apt examples of relations between the living being and its environment whose qualities are already evaluated in the relationship between the living being and society. They might be biologically healthy in so far as they ensure survival, but as social options they are unavailable except at possibly unbearable costs.

When the social becomes vital

On the basis of what has been said so far, I want to introduce a possibility that appears relevant to the context of somatization, but that remains unthematized in Canguilhem's work. I have already said enough about his distinction between social and organic norms, and something about the way in which they interact. Let us now imagine a hypothetical situation in which social and moral demands are experienced as 'determinisms' rather than 'constraints' by the living being. A situation whereby certain social and moral demands are apprehended by the individual as the qualities of an 'environment' and not of a social context. Let us imagine that these social and moral demands are literally 'incorporated', mistaken by the organism for vital norms as opposed to social ones. I say 'mistaken' to suggest that the very sense of any difference between them is lost. This situation is not inconceivable in the light of the specificity of human physiology (see Canguilhem 1989: 165–72). How might such a situation interfere, if at all, with the singular teleology of the organism? I can only be very tentative here, but will nonetheless offer an interpretation based on Canguilhem. If the difference is lost between given social/moral values and vital values, what this means is that the organism has lost, or rather 'delegated' some of its normative capacity. On account of this delegation, the organism may pursue 'needs' that do not correspond to its own evaluation of itself in relation to the environment, but correspond instead to the social norms that already evaluate its relationship with the environment. This 'too perfect' coincidence between vital and social norms could presumably originate in the uncritical, unreflexive, or preemptive endorsement of social values themselves; this way of 'endorsing' before even 'encountering' would itself have been learned, at some stage, and the practices of certain cultures might well generate it more than others.[2] Such a situation would provide a powerful illustration of the interaction and co-relativity of social and organic norms. It could arise as an effect of assimilating as 'natural' the psychosocial definition of 'normality' – a definition which, as we have seen, is too partial and static from the point of view of the total living being. To the extent that a social or moral norm is stubbornly pursued because it is apprehended as vital, and when this pursuit contradicts the vital needs of the organism (because it is superfluous, unnecessary, or excessive), it is literally as if 'the organism aimed badly, calculated badly' (Canguilhem 1989: 98). If such a line of reasoning is defensible, it represents an extension and a generalization of pathology conceived as *error*, a notion used by pathologists 'to designate a disturbance whose origin is to be sought in the physiological function itself and not in the external agent' (ibid.). In this sense, the experience of social and moral demands as determinisms is not unlike an inherited 'error of metabolism' and like it, at bottom, a form of 'misunderstanding' (ibid.: 275–9).

The avoidance of social and moral 'abnormality' *per se* could thus emerge as a physiological automatic activity, as a functional norm of life, within the gap that separates social from organic norms, and through the socially enforced denial of that gap. Through this denial, the possibility arises for what we may call a 're-evaluation of the value of dis-ease' on the part of the living being. Adaptation to social and moral demands need not contradict the vital needs of the organism. The proposition is not that what is done in favour of social life must be to the detriment of organic life, or vice versa (see last note). Rather, if and when such a conflict arises, disease may come to derive its value for the individual on the basis of the fact that it is a mode of relating to the environment that – like any such mode – is already evaluated by social norms. Within such a setting, it seems no longer paradoxical to suggest that the presence of bodily dis-ease may represent a superior norm of life with respect to its absence: a norm of life that includes both what the absence of dis-ease permits and what it forbids. The clear correspondence between 'health' and 'superiority', on the one hand, or 'disease' and 'inferiority' on the other, may be altered for the human organism when the cultural distinction between two forms of 'normality', mental and physical, is apprehended as 'natural'. Within such a configuration, dis-ease remains indeed a 'worse' condition from the point of view of the body: but this point of view no longer entirely coincides with that of the living being. The dis-eased body may represent a more suitable tool or means of action towards certain ends than the healthy body itself. The foreclosing of certain possibilities may be the precondition for others to become accessible.

In the literature on 'somatization' social and moral adaptedness are not questioned as to their normality or healthfulness. Neither are they reported as problems by patients. This is so even when this 'adaptation' reflects the static sense of the term as specialization and rigidity, as the inability to 'live otherwise', as the organism's lack of normative power, and therefore as an ultimately *pathological* state. The adequation of fact and norm that is valorized under the name of adaptation is not health to the extent that it is not the result of a choice, but the result of an incapacity to envisage oneself differently. The being who perceives social and moral values or demands as determinisms may also be confronted by the notion that, in principle, he or she has a choice with respect to meeting or not meeting those demands or values. In societies where this is the case, the act of choosing represents one such value and one such demand. If the exercise of this choice is preempted by the perception that adequation to the rule is a vital necessity beyond questioning, then existence in accordance to the rule is devalued existence. This is true not only in a biological sense but also, in some contexts, in an ethical sense: there is no merit in an act that is not freely chosen. In a being for whom 'goodness' is among the conditions to be permanently fulfilled in order to permit life, the adaptive effort can never be sufficient to its purpose; it may even be regarded as self-defeating in that it circumvents the choice from whence the value of the act arises. Within a consciousness that is thus morally and socially informed, the loss in the experience of agency is retranscribed in terms of permanent guilt or as a permanent sense of inadequacy, both calling for greater adaptive efforts. It seems therefore no accident that feelings of guilt and inadequacy are described as primary symptoms of clinical depression, while a growing body of literature exists on the relation between depression, somatization, and physical illness (for an example and further references, see Katon *et al.* 1982a; 1982b).

Conclusion: evaluating values

Through Canguilhem I have argued that it is possible to envisage a reality of 'somatization' that does not depend for its clinical recognition either on objective parameters or on the patient's resistance to psychological explanations. On the contrary, this hypothetical reality makes sense of such resistance as a logical, perhaps necessary concomitant of the mode of life that is expressed in 'somatization'. The account I have provided synthesizes the challenge facing contemporary attempts to rethink health and medicine in their 'biopsychosocial' dimensions. The contradiction of values that might give rise to 'somatization' in an individual cannot be disjoined from the contradictory functions medicine is currently expected to perform: to cure, on the one hand, and to sanction, on the other; to empathize and ally with the patient, while also policing and regulating their behaviour. For medicine, to acknowledge the reality of 'somatization' as I have described it would imply a public revision of the psychosocial definition of 'normality' as adaptedness. And even if this were to happen, 'adaptation' is intrinsically linked to existential choices that within plural, democratic societies cannot simply be prescribed or proscribed, supposedly even in the name of health. Nor is there any guarantee that, if prescribed, these 'existential' remedies would produce the desired effects, for reasons that should be obvious. What is called into question is the vocation of medicine as it is shaped by its integration within a larger network of institutions and values.

The problem of 'somatization' surveyed in the last two chapters illustrates in precise and immediate terms how, as soon as we search for a truth of illness beyond the static object-ness of the body, we trespass into a problematic that oscillates between the poles of ethics and politics, between the individual and the collective exercise of freedom. The discourse of psychosomatics, where this search more generally takes place, is profoundly structured by this predicament.

4

DOES PSYCHOSOMATICS EXIST?

An introduction

Any approach proposing to address 'psychosomatics' as a unitary field of discourse and practices is bound to attract dissent from a variety of positions. As I have already shown, there is no clear consensus as to the meaning of the term 'psychosomatic' and as to how it should be correctly employed: the term is bedevilled by ambiguity and semantic confusion (Lask 1996; Lipowski 1986). When we consider that the published literature on psychosomatics expresses an extreme heterogeneity of hypotheses, investigative methods and contexts of application, this confusion does not appear surprising. For this reason, the task of approaching 'psychosomatics' with a view to raising questions of general relevance requires careful methodological specification. What frequently safeguards legitimacy in writing, in or on psychosomatics, are implicit or explicit references to a theoretical affiliation or to disciplinary boundaries. Therefore, even when the term is apparently employed generally in fact it refers to something quite specific and possibly exclusive of other existing options. This is especially clear when comparing the psychoanalytic branch of psychosomatics with psychosomatics as researched and practised in the domain of the experimental sciences.

The comfort and safety afforded by this type of methodological restriction are foregone here. Rather than resting with one of the accepted definitions of the term and of the problem, I shall take the confusion itself as the starting-point of my approach to the field as a whole. I shall not exclude any specific enunciative position on an a priori basis in my attempt to articulate the problem of psychosomatics. Such an approach cannot fail to recognize how each of the existing positions produces its own account of the meaning of psychosomatic concepts, and thereby also its own account of what the field is doing and where it is going. This includes decisions as to what counts as progressive within it and what should or should not legitimately be included. Some authors refer to recent developments in immunology and related areas of experimental research to show that the psychosomatic ambition is near to crossing the threshold of scientificity (Levin and Solomon 1990). Others regard these very developments as just one among many different and incommensurable projects that adopt the name of 'psychosomatics', and as relatively marginal regarding the possibility of addressing fundamental questions (Morelli 1982). It is not easy to glean the coordinates of 'psychosomatics' as a whole, when it appears that the field is riddled with so much cross-purpose communication. The immediate impression one has when attempting to approach the field comprehensively is that there is no 'psychosomatics' as such. And indeed, at a recent conference entitled *Psychosomatics Today*, there was an entire symposium devoted to the question: 'Does psychosomatics exist?'.[1]

If it is so difficult to pinpoint what 'psychosomatics' refers to, it is clearly because each of the branches of psychosomatic research can be traced to an autonomous line of development that does not necessarily communicate with all the others. What I hope to show in the next two chapters, however, is that these lines of development are only relatively, or superficially autonomous. They all stem from the same background: a historical conjuncture that makes certain questions askable and certain thoughts thinkable. A historical conjuncture that also 'sorts' the answers to these questions into a hierarchy of values: a hierarchy that makes some types of answers more readily acceptable than others. We can only approach the general problematic of psychosomatics if we begin by addressing this historical conjuncture, and the system of dispersion it gives rise to. In order to do so, we must suspend all the customary ways in which positions are delimited and given orders of priority. Such orders of priority only come into effect on the basis of more general, historical conditions of possibility. And it is these that I now set out to explore.

Acknowledging dispersion

To approach the field of psychosomatics in this way means to regard it in terms of what Foucault called a 'discursive formation' (1972b). The analysis of 'discursive formations' is the result of a certain way of envisaging historical work, for which Foucault used the terms 'archaeology' and 'genealogy'. Archaeology and genealogy contrast with 'history' understood as the repository of a pure, inherently truthful 'memory' that is simply there to be retrieved and reconstituted. On the contrary, 'history' is regarded as the product of work applied to material documentation (Foucault 1972b; for 'archaeology' and 'genealogy' see also Cousins and Hussain 1984; Dean 1994; Dreyfus and Rabinow 1982; Gutting 1989; Kusch 1991). This corresponds to a phenomenological position in terms of the epistemology and ontology of historical truth (Dreyfus and Rabinow 1982). But Foucault goes beyond this phenomenological position by suggesting that we shift the question we pose in regard to history and truth. Instead of asking whether or how we can determine historical truth, we may ask how 'truth' is determined in historical practices, and how 'truth' in turn generates effects by virtue of its normative weight. This position rests on the idea that 'truth' is never neutral, but always implicated in relations of power, and hence always partial. This does not therefore mean for Foucault that these historically produced 'truths' are not 'truths', for archaeology and genealogy do not have a 'truer' truth to propose in their place. The purpose of archaeology and genealogy is to retrieve the possibilities of discourse that disappear from view as a result of the sign-posts through which we ordinarily sort and order our experience. It follows that in order to approach these possibilities we must momentarily suspend our trust in all these sign-posts: we must ignore their value to ask how they have come to function as sign-posts in the first place.

'Archaeology' is the activity of dismantling the customary 'unities of discourse' (or sign-posts) through which any particular problem is addressed. In relation to psychosomatics this means, for example, that we cannot approach the field with an *a priori* definition of what 'psychosomatic' means or should mean. Similarly, it is not a question of choosing between available definitions, theories, disciplines or concepts on grounds of their greater truthfulness, applicability, or scientificity. All these norms, including scientificity, are among the sign-posts that archaeology suspends (Foucault 1972b: 178–95). The task is not to debunk one plausibility in favour of another, but rather to ask: what is being problematized, and how? Archaeology thus 'frees' the field of discursive possibilities by bracketing the customary values through which these possibilities are ordered and ranked. Archaeological description makes these possibilities look more neutral with respect to each other than they actually are in historical practice. What might have happened is momentarily given equal weight as what did happen, to retrieve the sense that what did happen was not as necessary, as inevitable as it may appear now. The 'genealogical' aspect of this work, then, injects the dimension of value back into the picture, so to speak. After having lost familiarity with the rankings, with the different weight carried by each position, we can return to them and ask: what do these weightings permit, and what do they forbid? Why this particular pattern, and not another one? What is at stake in this problem, in terms of what its modes of articulation suggest?

This will also make it clear why, from this perspective, it makes no sense to speak of psychosomatics as addressing an old or timeless question, or as returning to a 'holism' that modernity allegedly lost to the strictures of science and its dualist predicament. There is no *essential* question of psychosomatics, outside relations of power/knowledge that are always historically contingent and specific. There are instead 'statements' of psychosomatics whose exact import arises from their conditions of coexistence within a network of other statements. Dreyfus and Rabinow propose to substitute the expression 'serious speech acts' for the easily misleading 'statement'. This makes it somewhat easier to clarify what Foucault means:

> any culture in which methods allow privileged speakers to speak with authority beyond the range of their personal situation and power could be the subject of an archaeological study. In any such speech act

> an authorized subject asserts (writes, paints, says) what – on the basis of an accepted method – is a serious truth claim. This systematic, institutionalized justification of the claim of certain speech acts to be true of reality takes place in a context in which truth and falsity have serious social consequences.
>
> (1982: 48)

On account of the shifting forms of 'seriousness', what Foucault means by 'statements' can only be identified by and through the system of relations they inhabit, and not by their grammatical structure, by their logical or material form, or by the meaning of the words they contain. As Foucault writes,

> The affirmation that the earth is round or that species evolve does not constitute the same statement before and after Copernicus, before and after Darwin; it is not, for such simple formulations, that the meaning of words has changed; what has changed is the relation of these affirmations to other propositions, their conditions of use and reinvestment, the field of experience, of possible verifications, of problems to be resolved, to which they can be referred. The sentence 'dreams fulfil desires' may have been repeated throughout the centuries; it is not the same statement in Plato and Freud.
>
> (1972b: 27)

In the field of psychosomatics perhaps more than in others, the narratives that call upon timeless values or distant traditions are especially rife. More generally, what is rife is a search for the distant or essential origins of psychosomatics, origins that are claimed and reclaimed on the part of different groups. This search interweaves with the sense of a historical 'mission' that invests researchers in this field, although the contents of this mission also vary between groups. The remainder of this chapter is devoted to dismantling such narratives in so far as they invite us to regard 'psychosomatics' either as essentially in line with a history of Western progress, or as vindicating old wisdom that this progress has neglected. I will do so by looking at how psychosomatic discourse describes itself through its relation to two specific categories: the category of 'tradition' and the category of 'biomedicine'. Further in the chapter I shall offer an alternative account of the nature of relationships between biomedicine and psychosomatics, based on Foucault's archaeologies of 'madness' and the 'clinic'.

Unsorting values: the old and the new

Most general overviews of the project of psychosomatics, such as we find them in editorials and especially in the introductions to clinical manuals aimed at generalists and medical students, are replete with references to 'tradition'.

This could be the continuing tradition of Western rationalism and progress, as opposed to the blindness of ignorance which it leaves behind. Or it could be the tradition of a past that Western 'progress' has already left behind, only to regret the consequences. The reference to 'tradition' serves to establish a sense of continuity or of rupture, in the name of a better value upheld or promised through psychosomatics. It is of little relevance whether this value refers to the scientificity of theory, to the effectiveness of practice, or its humaneness. Something very similar can be said for the term 'biomedicine', which also often appears in such general overviews, with the difference that it always refers to something psychosomatics is said to oppose or to overcome. These categories ('tradition' and 'biomedicine') have an important role to play in the self-descriptions of psychosomatics. This is not only in terms of what is explicitly advocated through their use, but also in terms of their function in the internal economy of psychosomatics understood as a system of dispersion. In other words, they are 'speech-acts' through which tensions and difficulties that are intrinsic to psychosomatics in its present conditions of existence are superficially resolved or effaced. Let me turn to some examples. In a well-known critical review of psychosomatic concepts, Roy Grinker (1973) notes that soon after the publication of Flanders Dunbar's *Emotions and Bodily Changes* in 1935:

> the historically curious began to trace the roots of ideas that seemed so new and startling to this generation. Much evidence accumulated to indicate that many outstanding thinkers, investigators, and clinicians had, in the long past, touched on many fundamental and tangential aspects of what we now call psychosomatic medicine . . . . Some cynically contend by a process of retrospective reinterpretation of what was meant by writers in the past (Bernard, 1865; Darwin, 1871; Jennings, 1905, 1906), in terms of what we now know, that there is nothing new under the sun. Others contend that such complete accreditation of priority to historical work can only be the result of incorrectly loose and liberal interpretations. The truth probably lies somewhere in between.
>
> (Grinker 1973: 19–20)

Grinker's is already a reflexive account of the relationship of psychosomatic medicine to the question of 'tradition'. His compromise suggestion that 'the truth probably lies somewhere in between', however, equally does not escape this category. It is merely a corrective to enable the author to claim that, given the existence of a psychosomatic tradition, this should not prevent us from acknowledging that there is indeed something new under the sun. What is new is 'the attempt at systematization of these ideas, formulation of specific hypotheses, and a methodology applicable for fresh investigations' (ibid.: 20). The emergence of psychosomatic medicine is thus portrayed as a re-ordering, along scientific principles, of the same set of ideas and observations made by past clinicians. Discontinuity is claimed at the level of methods and degrees of scientific accuracy, but continuity is not questioned at the more fundamental level of problems. The difference is presented as one between naive, or intuitive, and informed psychosomatics. Therefore Grinker's suggestion expresses, and is fully compatible with, the widely held opinion that psychosomatics 'continues a long tradition in Western thought and medicine, one concerned with the reciprocal relationships of mind and body as two integral aspects of the human organism' (Lipowski 1986: 2). Here too discontinuity is reduced to the idea that 'what used to be personal convictions, anecdotes, and medical folklore, [became] a subject of rigorous empirical research' (ibid.: 5). The list of 'precursors', not surprisingly, extends as far back as the Hippocratic school of Kos and includes most leading names in the history of Western medicine. Another implication of fundamental continuity is at work in the claim that psychosomatics expresses a '*revival* of interest in the psychosomatic approach' (Rees 1983: 157, added emphasis). It is often presumed that such a revival was made inevitable by the dehumanizing effects of scientific medicine, in which case the claim may form part of a general critique of modernity. Alternatively, when science or technology as such are not the target of critique, the need to look back is justified as a logical response to the pressure of conditions that biomedical theory has proved unable to explain. In this case, a continuity is assumed not only between the past and the present, but also between the reality of phenomena and their eventual representation within scientific theory: knowledge changes as it becomes more exhaustive with respect to representing the totality of the real.

But the input of tradition, the continuity with tradition, is also made responsible for the existence of tensions, contradictions and disagreements within the discourse of psychosomatic. Modern psychosomatics is often described as the result of a flowing together of different traditions concerning the relationship between body and mind in health and disease. The two most important of these, it is said, are the 'psychogenetic' and the 'holistic' traditions (Lipowski 1986). The term 'psychosomatic', in its different uses, can be coloured by either of these connotations. The 'psychogenetic' tradition understands the term to mean that certain physical diseases are actually caused by psychological factors. This tradition is described as 'obsolete' and 'misleading'. Its persisting popularity (itself attributed to the influence of tradition) allegedly explains why the field of psychosomatics is replete with confusion and constantly misrepresented (ibid.: 12). Here, the category of tradition performs the function of containing within itself, and relegating to a past we feel entitled to forget except as memory, what in fact should be regarded as an inherent tension in psychosomatics, a tension that stems from its contemporary conditions of existence. Psychogenetic hypotheses can be said to be 'obsolete' only to the extent that aetiological thinking as a whole is obsolete, which is clearly a highly disputable claim (see Todarello and Porcelli

1992: 130–4). It is probably more correct to say that aetiological thinking may be more or less 'obsolete' in relation to different contexts of practice and research.

The vanguard of medical theorizing, following general developments in scientific thinking, has indeed relinquished simple causal models for the explanation of any disease. But aetiological thinking still provides the basic working-model for most therapeutic institutions: institutions through which, for which, and in which psychosomatic hypotheses are formulated and used. Psychogenetic hypotheses, whether or not they are endorsed, come into being as a result of a contemporary network of discursive relations where a definite space exists for them in which to emerge. This space is the discursive space of linear causality, which these hypotheses occupy alongside many others that are not equally disputed in practice. Thus, blaming the persistence of the wrong 'tradition' obscures the extent to which we cannot simply 'do away' with psychogenesis as an idea. This idea is firmly rooted, not within tradition or history, but in the contemporary configuration of explanatory and management models for disease. We cannot reduce the contradictions and complexities of the field of psychosomatics to the noxious influence of tradition; we cannot dismiss them as we may dismiss the category of tradition itself.

The retrospective attribution of psychosomatic ideas, concepts and theories to medical writers in the past should therefore be regarded as misleading, both as a reconstruction of past statements and as a clarification of contemporary ones. Acts of restrospective attribution should themselves be studied in terms of what they make possible within the current configuration of psychosomatic discourse. A rare example of such a study is Theodore Brown's (1985) investigation of what he calls a 'shared mythology and literary convention' that existed within early US psychosomatic literature. According to this widely shared mythology, Descartes' dualism was directly and overwhelmingly responsible for the disruption of a prior 'holistic' medicine. As Brown convincingly shows, the historical Descartes had hardly any direct impact on contemporary medical theory, whose allegedly 'holistic' features persisted for over a century after the publication of his writings. The function of that literary convention, Brown argues, was to simplify and superficially resolve an internal conflict and latent contradiction in the situation of early psychosomatic practitioners themselves. How? Through 'projection of one symbolic polar representation of the simplified conflict on to an external object' (Brown 1985: 57). The claims of these early practitioners, including their advocacy of a holistic approach, could only be voiced under specific conditions defined by an entire context. They spoke and practised as *psychological* experts and consultants to somatic practitioners within a dualistically organized medical field. This field determined both the possibilities and the limits of what they could seriously do or say. In such a context, Descartes and his dualism represented 'unquestionably safe targets for disdain' (ibid.). On the contrary, the dualistic role structure that gave such experts their very *raison d'être*, and furnished them with a site from which to speak, was clearly not an equally 'safe' or even thinkable target. Brown's general analysis validly supports the idea that historical descriptions and reconstructions, within the discourse of psychosomatics as elsewhere, should be read as a function of the set of speakers' positions that are available in any given discursive formation.

It is also necessary to distance ourselves from other misconceptions that arise from an incautious reference to tradition, this time concerning not medical theory and concepts but medical practice. There are many variants of the proposition that medical practice, independently of medical theory, has always been 'psychosomatic' (e.g. Margetts 1950). The implication is often that the goal of modern psychosomatic medicine is to restore to medicine the 'artful' element it gradually lost to science. The fallacy here lies in the failure to acknowledge the gulf which separates the 'serious' from the everyday or commonsense use of concepts. The philosopher of science Gaston Bachelard (1951) employed the expression of 'epistemological break' to suggest that the work of science, its reorganization of experience through experiment and new technology, is inseparable from a reformulation of ordinary concepts and their displacement from customary meanings. For Bachelard it is precisely the *refusal* to receive concepts as given that distinguishes science as a cognitive realm. Scientific work is a threshold of conceptual transformation (Bachelard 1951; for a discussion see Canguilhem 1975). Bachelard, of course, is concerned with norms of scientificity that are precisely avoided as criteria in an archaeological approach. However, the 'seriousness' of archaeological statements involves a similar distance with respect to the individual and contingent use of concepts. And not only concepts undergo a transformation in the process of acquiring a claim to seriousness. Practices themselves, to the extent that they are organized and legitimized by serious discourse, differ from practices that are not thus organized. We cannot therefore assume continuity between a practice of medicine where so-called psychosomatic perspectives are implicitly taken into account by individual doctors, and a practice of medicine structured by the 'serious' endorsement of a psychosomatic problematic. Edward Margetts commented unfavourably on his contemporaries' persistence 'in regarding the flood of publications in this branch of medicine as something new' (1950: 402). Psychosomatic medicine, he wrote, 'to me has never meant anything new, and has merely implied *good* medicine' (ibid.). In mid-century USA, Margetts was thus among those who claimed that there was nothing new under the sun. But his claim was quite different from those addressed in Grinker's text of the same year. Margetts does not refer to the more or less distant past to find evidence of a psychosomatic approach: he refers to the current practice of *good* medicine. The very term 'psychosomatic', Margetts maintained, 'should be superfluous' (ibid.). This comment is precious because it logically invites the question: if the term should be superfluous, why then does it stop going without saying? What does it mean that Margetts should have to write an entire article to dismiss it? In what sense did it become a necessary term?

The reference to a difference between 'good' and 'bad' medicine is clearly a politically charged one. It leads us to consider the second trope that is most frequently met with in the self-descriptions of psychosomatics, where psychosomatics is opposed to 'biomedicine'. Sociologist N.D. Jewson has offered an aptly synthetic definition for the charges held against biomedicine, through the thesis of a 'disappearance of the sick-man from medical cosmology' (Jewson 1976; see also Figlio 1977). This expression provides a useful shorthand for what appears to be the result of a complex historical development exceeding the boundaries of medicine alone. Descriptions of psychosomatics as an endeavour to restore the patient 'as a whole' or the patient 'as a person' to the attention of an allegedly dehumanizing medicine are so numerous and ubiquitous that we can forgo mentioning specific examples. What is of more interest is the implicit suggestion that psychosomatics may represent an expert form of anti-medicine, offering the promise of a fundamental rupture with respect to the model of functioning of 'biomedicine'. How should we read this suggestion? The following point argued by Thomas Osborne offers important clues:

> It is commonly supposed that 'bio-medicine' has at its origin a neglect of the mental or emotional component of disease. In a sense . . . this is true; the clinic was certainly, in *diagnostic* terms, lesion-centred, concerned as far as possible to localize pathology within the body, to give it a singular organic form. Nevertheless . . . the aetiological emphases of the clinic opened up 'for the gaze' an endlessly heterogeneous variety of components, by no means excluding in principle those that we would now classify as 'emotional' or whatever . . . . For the notion of disease *aetiology* basic to clinical medicine is also a dynamic and open one; indeed, one could say that it provides a certain latitude for a variety of perspectives without the basic rationality being disturbed.
>
> (Osborne 1992: 84–5)

Osborne's point shows that the relationship between psychosomatics and biomedicine cannot be thought of as one of simple opposition or linear discontinuity. It is important, on the contrary, to acknowledge that biomedicine is part of the conditions of possibility for the emergence of modern psychosomatics. As I shall argue in more detail in the next chapter, the discourse of psychosomatics owes its configuration to having biomedicine as an epistemic precedent and as an epistemic contemporary.

What do 'psychosomatics' and 'biomedicine' have in common? In what sense are they both part of the same context of emergence? This is what I will explore in the remainder of this chapter in a genealogy of psychosomatic questions. I should stress at the outset that this brief genealogy should not be read in a historiographical spirit: a spirit that might aim to 'do justice' to the detail of events as they happened. My purpose here is to reconstruct the discursive space of a problem, the figures that delimit its contour and that make room for new questions to become conspicuous.

A noso-political context of emergence

In *The Birth of the Clinic* (1973) and elsewhere, Foucault argued that the emergence of anatomo-clinical medicine was made possible not by the cumulative advance of observations, nor by the foundation of the first European clinics as such, but rather by the 'clinic' as a special space where medical knowledge was articulated through therapeutic efficiency. The process whereby the clinic came to occupy this central position cannot be understood except with reference to a broader context of societal transformations, pivoting on the emergence of the 'population' as 'an object of surveillance, analysis, intervention, modification, etc.' (Foucault 1980d: 171). A number of more specific processes can be identified under this general heading.

One sub-process that appears of particular relevance for the subsequent development of psychosomatics is what Foucault called the 'progressive dislocation of [the] mixed and polyvalent procedures of assistance' that had been prevalent until the end of the seventeenth century (Foucault 1980d: 169; see also Foucault 1972a, especially part III). In the 'Classical age', the collective means of dealing with disease coincided with institutions for the assistance of 'necessitous paupers', the general and undifferentiated category forming the idle population of hospitals. These populations were qualified by a range of diverse factors including infirmity, old age, inability to find work and destitution. The role of therapeutics was only a marginal component of assistance in the working of hospitals, where provision of material assistance and administrative structures were comparatively more important. Foucault maintains that the eighteenth century saw the call for a dismantling of this polyvalent concept of assistance, as the product of a general re-examination of modes of investment and capitalization. The actual process of dismantling involved a specific instance of the analysis of population in general, an instance Foucault calls the 'analysis of idleness'. This analysis was a type of work through which fine distinctions were drawn between categories of unfortunates. As a result of it, the polymorphous figure of the pauper disappears,

> giving way to a whole series of functional discriminations (the good poor and the bad poor, the wilfully idle and the involuntarily unemployed, those who can do some kind of work and those who cannot) . . . . This analysis has as its practical objective at best to make poverty useful by fixing it to the apparatus of production, at

worst to lighten as much as possible the burden it imposes on the rest of society.

(Foucault 1980d: 169)

This transformation is relevant to the development both of biomedicine and of psychosomatics, although in different and not equally direct ways. Let us look at biomedicine first. The 'analysis of idleness' produced the disengagement of public concern with disease from the provision of economic assistance. This process mirrors the emergence of a 'noso-politics' addressed to the health of the population as a whole and as a sum of distinct individuals, following a logic of *omnes et singulatim* (Foucault 1981c; see also 1988e). Thus, illness was isolated from the societal problems of poverty and other multiple forms of misery, and this was one of the central preconditions for the medicalization of the hospital. On this basis the hospital specialized as a place of therapeutic activity (a *machine à guerir*), as a supporting structure for the permanent medical staffing of the population, and as the ideal setting for medical teaching and training. The features of 'clinical rationality' – which set the stage for the medicine of the nineteenth and twentieth centuries – were made possible by this medicalization of hospitals: this is how the production of medical knowledge was spatio-temporally aligned with the medical treatment of patients.[2]

The relevance of this process to the development of psychosomatics, on the other hand, can be appreciated only via a detour through psychiatry. Within the analytical economy of assistance, the 'sick' and the 'criminal' appeared as newly distinct categories. As such, both figures remained excluded from the processes of production, circulation and accumulation of riches, on grounds that were specific to each and justified for each. Other individuals did not present with equally clear reasons for their exclusion. The analysis of idleness thus highlighted the singularity of these individuals, who fell into the residual category of the 'mad'. In this new context, their exclusion became positively defined by comparison and contrast with the other categories of exclusion. This conjuncture, Foucault argues, was crucial for the framing of madness in terms of 'mental illness' and hence for the development of modern psychiatry. In seeking to justify the unbroken internment of madmen, but also to allow for their difference from criminals, knowledge came to distinguish madness from crime on psychopathological grounds. The new knowledge spoke of forms of pathology relating to the capacity to will, to act, to make decisions, and ultimately to be free: 'the disappearance of freedom that was the consequence of madness becomes its foundation, its secret, its essence' (Foucault 1972a: 459).

The 'psychologization' of madness, and the possibility of a purely psychological medicine, therefore appear as the result of the strange kinship relations madness bears, on account of its history, to other categories met within the space of the 'great confinement' (Foucault 1972a: 470–1). On this basis,

Foucault reinterprets the meaning of Pinel's 'freeing of the insane'. This freedom became, for knowledge, a principle of verification. Unchaining the insane would let them appear objectively for what they were; the truth of their condition would no longer be distorted by persecutions and by the rages to which these give rise (ibid.: 491). This freedom would reveal madness veritably as *pathology*, as an underlying condition liable to scientific description, as opposed to the freedom of the criminal that is obedient to their own intact will. Charcot's hysteric is, for Foucault, the paradigmatic example of this function of verification:

> The hysteric was the perfect patient, since she *provided material for knowledge {donnait à connaître}*: she herself would retranscribe the effects of medical power into the forms that the physician could describe according to a scientifically acceptable discourse. As for the power relation that made this whole operation possible, how could it have been detected in its decisive role, since – supreme virtue of hysteria, unparalleled docility, veritable epistemological sanctity – the patients themselves took charge of it and accepted responsibility for it: it appeared in the symptomatology as morbid suggestibility.
>
> (Foucault 1997: 44–5)

This is the general background against which it is possible to appreciate why the problem of 'simulation' became so central to psychiatric theory and practice in the second half of the nineteenth century, and widely investigated through techniques of hypnosis and suggestion (Foucault 1987; see Ellenberger 1970). Simulation becomes a significant question precisely in view of the fine line that both links and distinguishes madness and crime.

The hysteric notoriously failed to sustain Charcot's attempt to provide a psychiatry that would simply overlap with neuropathology. On the contrary, her symptoms were 'unmasked' by Freud to be simulations of real anatomical lesions. This crucial watershed marks the beginning of psychoanalysis as an independent science of the mind and as a first form of anti-psychiatry. But this episode is also a watershed in the history of psychosomatics, and in a sense it marks its inauguration as a modern problematic. As Franz Alexander wrote in 1925,

> The hysteric played a mean trick on the physician by showing that the physio-chemical apparatus could serve her desires and that she could use her whole body as a means of expression. The physician could only save himself before the problem of hysteria by closing his eyes and denying its existence . . . . It has rightly been suggested that this would deal the fatal blow to materialistic medicine, and to the whole materialistic conception of the nineteenth century.
>
> (1925: 446)

The earliest propositions of modern psychosomatics, exemplified in the writings of Freud's immediate followers, sought to extend the model of hysterical conversion to all pathological manifestations of the body. This attempt was based on the assumption that any physical condition could be 'unmasked', just like hysteria, to reveal a hidden psychological truth. As Georg Groddeck wrote in 1917, '[t]he assumption that only the hysterical personality is capable of producing an illness for certain purposes I consider to be a fundamental and dangerous error. Every person has this ability and everybody makes extensive use of it' (Groddeck 1977a [1917]: 112). Let us suspend, for the moment, the fact that we now know these propositions to be mostly discredited, even ridiculed. Let us dwell instead on what they imply in terms of reorganizing the relationship between illness, madness, and crime. Through the 'analysis of idleness', the notion of illness had broken 'away from the metaphysics of evil' (Foucault 1973: 196), at the same time as madness was gaining a new relationship with evil through its ambiguous association with crime. Now physical illness itself gains a relationship with 'madness', through the proposition that it is possible to interrogate the body to reveal a truth of the mind. Through this new kinship, the notion of physical illness inherits some of the associations of madness, including its uneasy distinction from ordinary deviance.

As Alexander's pronouncement indicates, it is only with the advent of psychoanalysis that we may speak of a psychosomatic problematic in the modern sense. This does not mean that psychoanalysis, or forms of psychosomatic medicine based on it, have sole claim over the historical project of psychosomatics. The configuration of medical knowledge and institutions does not so easily lend itself to the confounding of categories so painstakingly delineated in the course of a long historical process – a confounding of categories that psychosomatics initially suggested on the basis of psychoanalysis. The dialogue initiated between psychoanalysis and biomedicine under the aegis of 'psychosomatic medicine' has entailed a process of constant mutual readjustment, often in a confrontational mode. Freud himself anticipated the possibility of antagonism and was extremely careful to avoid it, precisely by putting a ban on psychoanalytic concern with organic disease. His position on this issue and its effects on the development of psychosomatics will be discussed in the next chapter.

In this overview, I have reproposed Foucault's well-known argument that the emergence of clinical medicine is linked to the development of a multifaceted project of a technology of population. Beside the maintenance of order and the organization of enrichment, this project instituted the health of the population as a major concern of the state. Until the mid-twentieth century this task was understood as serving the upkeep of the national labour force and military capacity: the individual should be in good health in order to be able to serve the state (Foucault 1976). We have here a supplementary meaning for the expression 'docile bodies' first introduced in *Discipline and Punish* (1979);

the securing of health was a vital component in ensuring the 'docility' of bodies, as bodies that could be counted upon for economic and political purposes. From this perspective, psychosomatics can be read as a problematization of this docility. Who or what do bodies really obey? Can illness be produced at will? Can it be a site of resistance? The unmasking of the hysteric revealed the counter-power that illness can be to those who wanted to see it: the power of 'madness' or deviance to disguise itself in the form of an ordinary organic condition. The problematic of psychosomatics is historically linked to the will to know, to define, to spell out the possibilities of this newly perceived power, and to the questions that this task generated.

This genealogy of 'psychosomatic illness' appears clearly from the empirical contexts in relation to which it was debated as a new and urgent problem for knowledge: contexts that I can only refer to very briefly here, but that have been widely investigated. What are these contexts? One is the field of rapidly expanding practices of insurance and indemnification related to the hazards of industrial work, especially conspicuous from the second half of the nineteenth century and into the early twentieth. An even more significant context is the field of practices of military drafting for the two World Wars (for both contexts, see Ewald 1986; Figlio 1982, 1985, 1987; Harrington 1996; Krasner 1985; Harrington 1996; Sass and Crook 1981). The settings of modern industrial work and modern war both entailed historically new experiences and possibly historically new pathologies. But they also both entailed a historically new relevance for questions around the reliability of certification for incapacity and about who should be held responsible for the burden of illness. This entire background is what gives proper denseness to the probing of illness and its cure in terms of individual 'styles' and 'strategies': response strategies, coping strategies, behavioural strategies, cognitive strategies. Whether such strategies are understood as devised in consciousness or by the unconscious, and whether the individual appears to be their master or their victim, are less fundamental questions. The possibility of shifting from one to the other of these polar opposites, of turning 'style' into 'strategy' and vice versa, is intrinsic to the terms in which the problem is addressed.

Conclusion: psychosomatics between words and things

A history which 'we must presume to be "alive" and present within each of us' – a history whose figures still echo in our contemporary perception of the mad, the criminal and the ill – is thus reactivated in psychosomatics as a form of problematization (Chiozza 1981: 67; see also Entralgo 1955). This history does not only provide the epistemic conditions for the development of psychosomatics as a discourse. If we join this discourse to imagine that a culturally informed, embodied subjectivity – a subjectivity that partakes in the differential evaluation of physical and mental illness – plays an active role in the pathogenesis of disease, then this history is literally reactivated in and through the individual who falls ill. In this sense, the conditions of possibility for psychosomatics as a form of knowledge also would be the conditions of possibility for a way of falling ill that we might call 'psychosomatic'. We must be careful to distinguish this claim from the idea that knowledge produces its own objects through an act of labelling. We are here in a space of analysis that is literally – and paradigmatically – between words and things, a space that eschews the simple alternative between a static realism and a fleeting nominalism. Psychosomatics from this perspective is not simply one among many possible ways of speaking about what we culturally designate as pathology (although, of course, it is that too). On the other hand, it is not simply an adequation of medical knowledge to 'new' pathological phenomena produced by processes (e.g. raised levels of 'stress') that are imagined to be independent from knowledge itself. Rather, as we acknowledge that categories of perception are constructed through historical and cultural evaluations of existence, we are also led to acknowledge the correctness of psychosomatic hypotheses which thematize a historical mutation in the individual pathogenetic process on account of the role of cultural evaluations. The history which 'we must presume to be "alive" and present within each of us', is alive and present in us both as *subjects* and *objects* of knowledge. This is why we cannot reduce, assimilate, or confuse the problematic of psychosomatics with the problematic of a physiology of emotions. What is central to the problem of psychosomatics is a self-reflexive, circular movement that shifts and reallocates the positions of the subject–object dyad. Consider the following proposition, according to which the task of psychosomatics is to:

> interpret, from a psychological perspective, the fact that psychosomatic patients appear inconspicuous from a psychopathological point of view, and that they share this inconspicuousness with organic patients. [Psychosomatic medicine] must, in other words, interpret this as an intentional psychic saving and provide it with a sociological foundation by referring it to the social control of norm-transgressive behavior.
>
> (Brede 1972: 65)

This statement can be read as a 'distillate' of the genealogy I have proposed. It implies a new type of reciprocity between the subject and the object of medical knowledge, a reciprocity that pivots on the effects of their mutual in/visibility. At the core of what biomedicine cannot see lies the fact that its object knows what it can see, and will behave accordingly. The problematization of illness as a work of thought pulls medical thought into the work of illness. Yet we would be mistaken to regard this as a radical discontinuity with respect to the epistemological foundation of biomedicine. In the emergence of psychosomatics we have something analogous to a 'return of the repressed' for biomedicine. Let us briefly see how this is the case.

The experience of clinical medicine, the focus on the actual patient, was made possible by a passage through 'the stable, visible, legible basis of death' (Foucault 1973: 196): a visibility significantly connected to death's 'primary passivity' (ibid.: xiv). It is this primary passivity, granting sovereign power to the 'empirical gaze', that allowed Western man to constitute himself as an object, and thereby as an object of science. Thus Foucault speaks of the status of object as an 'acquisition' rather than a 'reduction' of the individual. In the earlier medicine of species the actual patient had to be 'subtracted' from the account in order to lay bare the essence of the disease. By contrast, the 'primary passivity' of the individual understood as an object allowed for a 'perpetual and objectively based correlation between the visible and the expressible' (ibid.: 196). Concrete cases could become visible in their unique and irreducible quality for medical attention. This point may well be raised against simplistic readings of lesion-centred medicine as instrinsically reductive of the individual in his or her singularity (Osborne 1992).

Nonetheless, the constant and implicit reference to the primary passivity of the corpse is what accounts for the legibility and visibility of the individual case: a visibility where what one sees exhausts what one has to say. The consequence of this is that for positive medicine and its clinical experience 'the *object* of discourse may equally well be a *subject*, without the figures of objectivity being in any way altered' (Foucault 1973: xiv). This means that the subjective dimension of individuality is preemptively made irrelevant by what is read as the teeming presence of death in the living person: death is already there in and as 'disease' (Foucault 1973: 140ff; 156–9). Anatomo-clinical rationality operates thanks to the ability to ignore the relation between life and death that disease might express, by focusing on the visible outcome of that relation. Therefore, positive medicine effectively relates to the sick individual as the anticipation of a corpse. By identifying the reality of the disease with the lesion that is its sign, the 'dotted outline of the future autopsy' is projected onto the living body (ibid.: 162). In this sense biomedical rationality is indeed reductive. It projects the 'truth' of illness onto what it can see, but this static visibility is only partial with respect to the relation between life and death that makes 'visibility' itself possible. It is partial on the side of death, or in considering the truth of an outcome exhaustive with respect to the truth of a relation: 'that which is not on the scale of the gaze falls outside the domain of possible knowledge' (Foucault 1973: 166). Only on this basis is it possible to sever the continuity between the 'symptom' and the 'sign', and no longer to see it. Only on this basis is it possible to devalue the 'symptom' as to its powers of truth, and to establish within medical discourse a distinction between subjective and objective health, between the concepts of 'illness' and 'disease'.

If I have drawn attention to this reductiveness of biomedical rationality it is not in order to reiterate well-known accusations against biomedicine. My purpose has been to point to where the continuity and the discontinuity between biomedicine and psychosomatics lie at an epistemological level. The vantage-point of death, of the body-as-object, is the source of knowledge for positive medicine. For this very reason, it is also the horizon beyond which it can neither see nor say. Biomedicine can speak positively about the body that is *of* the individual, but not of the body that *is* the individual. The figures of positive knowledge are literally held in place by this full presence of the body, acting like a solid dam against the flowing of the patient's subjectivity and its overflowing into the subject of knowledge. Only in the absence of a lesion does medicine literally see that it cannot see; only then does it acknowledge that its notion of the pathological may be correct, but only ever partial.

'Psychosomatic medicine' receives the dignity of institutional recognition and of large-scale research funding mostly in connection with so-called 'functional disorders'. These are conditions, like irritable bowel syndrome or non-ulcer dyspepsia, that are acknowledged as genuine pathologies but that present no lesions. However, in admitting the need to develop a 'psychosomatic' approach for certain diseases, biomedicine by no means renounces the privileges of positivity. Rather it extends them speculatively to the possibility of making 'visible' the psychological components of disease. In this sense, and only in this sense, may we agree with Osborne (1992) in rejecting the common supposition that biomedicine neglects the mental or emotional side of things. Yet the 'mental' or the 'emotional' can only be envisaged, from this perspective, precisely as discrete 'components' that are logically not dissimilar from chemical ingredients, viruses, or genes. When their presence is established, such components may be added to an aetiological picture. But there is no displacement of the notion that disease is ultimately a bodily truth, a truth whose complete and fully graspable expression is given as an outcome in the body (Armstrong 1987).

In admitting the 'psychological' in terms of aetiological *components* biomedicine fills the absence which it cannot think of except as the negativity of disease. The biomedical 'gaze' thus operates a reduction to the same of what is other, with respect to its own rationality, in pathological life. This implies that when concepts like the 'unconscious' are employed from within this horizon, they do not refer to a 'perpetual principle of dissatisfaction' with whatever presents itself as 'visible' in experience (Foucault 1970: 373). They refer instead to a principle of localization of the psychic to be made visible. In the chapters that follow, I shall argue that the possibility of this reduction, of this misunderstanding, is a principle that structures the variety of psychosomatics as a 'system of dispersion'.

5

THE DISPERSION OF PSYCHOSOMATICS

Where and how can we locate the point at which psychosomatics becomes a 'problematization', if we look at the actual propositions of psychosomatic discourse? What are the instances that introduce something different in what can be seriously thought about disease? And what do these instances reveal about psychosomatic statements as functions of their mutual relationships? In this chapter I approach these questions by focusing on a number of 'textual episodes' in the history of psychosomatic medicine. The first of these episodes is a paper that Viktor Von Weiszäcker delivered at the fifty-fifth conference of the German Society for Internal Medicine, held in Wiesbaden in 1949. Von Weizsäcker, a physiologist, clinician and philosopher, was a prominent figure in the debates surrounding the establishment of psychosomatic research in Germany. He is often credited with being a 'pioneer' of psychosomatic ideas and even the 'founder' of psychosomatic medicine in that national context. But this is not the reason why his work is approached here; on the contrary, we should deliberately refrain from treating it as a point of origin, not least because what followed historically bears only a marginal relationship with what he advocated. The reason to turn to Von Weiszäcker's work in this context is that some of his propositions represent 'governing statements' in the sense that they enable us to read psychosomatics as a system of dispersion. What Foucault means by this expression is:

> those [statements] that concern the definition of observable structures and the field of possible objects, those that prescribe the forms of description and the perceptual codes that it can use, those that reveal the most general possibilities of characterization, and thus open up a whole domain of concepts to be constructed, and, lastly, those that, while constituting a strategic choice, leave room for the greatest number of subsequent options.
>
> (Foucault 1972b: 147)

'Governing statements' are thus characterized by a level of generality and not by the degree of consensus they enjoy or represent. They too constitute a strategic, partial choice. But, unlike 'derived statements', 'governing statements' point to fundamental rather than local regularities and distinctions. The acceptance or rejection of a derived statement always occurs within the field of possibilities made available by a set of governing statements.

It is important to stress that the relationship between the two types of statements is not one of chronological order. In this case, the year 1949 is already well into the course of psychosomatics as a historical phenomenon. The psychoanalytical treatment of organic diseases had been performed and written about in German since the first decades of the century by analysts from Freud's Viennese circle such as Sándor Ferenczi and Felix Deutsch, and by Georg Groddeck in his well-known 'Satanarium' at Baden-Baden. By 1949 the call for a 'psychosomatic' reform in the agenda of medical teaching and research was well established in Germany, where 'psychosomatic medicine' was institutionalized as a university chair earlier than anywhere else.[1] Perhaps even more importantly, 'psychosomatic medicine' had developed to a considerable degree in the USA. This development stemmed partly from what has been described as an indigenous form of psychoanalysis, under the auspices of Adolf Meyer, William Alanson White, Smith Ely Jelliffe and others. And partly it stemmed from the establishment of the 'Chicago School', centred on the psychoanalytic institute founded by the Berlin-trained Franz Alexander (Krasner 1985; Powell 1977). The first large-scale programme of psychosomatic research had been organized by Flanders Dunbar between 1934 and 1938, involving the psychosomatic evaluation of over 1,600 serial admissions to Columbia-Presbyterian Hospital in New York. In 1935 Dunbar first published *Emotions and Bodily Changes*, which was followed by three updated editions between 1938 and 1954. Still in the USA, a scientific journal entitled *Psychosomatic Medicine* had existed since 1939; the board of editors included practitioners and researchers from the disciplines of psychoanalysis, internal medicine, physiology, neurology, psychiatry, psychology, comparative physiology and paediatrics; the advisory board to the journal included thirty-eight additional persons whose names 'read like a Who's Who of American Medicine' (Jenkins 1985: 4). A US psychosomatic society had been founded in 1942; in 1943 it had appointed a committee on psychosomatic research comprising ten subcommittees devoted to specific areas of investigation. The functions of these subcommittees included promoting and presenting research in annual reports, suggesting problems for joint sessions with other medical societies, and conducting scientific conferences. In 1950, Hans Selye proposed a redefined concept of 'stress' and named it the 'General Adaptation Syndrome'. This would open the scope for an entire field of research, experimental as well as epidemiological, thereafter often identified with the endeavours of 'psychosomatics' (Mason 1975a, 1975b). In the UK, James Halliday's *Psychosocial Medicine: A Study of the Sick Society* had appeared in 1948. This work drew general conclusions and programmatic suggestions from Halliday's experience as a public health official in Scotland. Halliday advocated coining the expression 'psychosomatic affections' to underline the role of a pathological social environment in the development of individual disease. In 1949 the second edition of the first internationally accredited textbook of psychosomatic medicine for general practitioners was published (Weiss and English 1949).

By the time Von Weizsäcker addressed the German Society for Internal Medicine in May 1949, a field of psychosomatic discourse had therefore already developed with evident success. This field was already articulated into a variety of positions and counter-positions, theories and counter-theories, and it had at its disposal a whole arsenal of concepts to be applied and revised. A vast number of precedents that were to shape future research and institutional agendas had been set in place. At this time Von Weizsäcker confronted the medical profession with the question of whether this flourishing, this success, did in fact make any difference to the fundamental aims of a medical reform in a 'psychosomatic' direction. His way of posing the question was to step back from the specific items of dissent that preoccupied his contemporaries in order to ask again, more generally: what are we saying when we advocate the creation of a psychosomatic medicine? What exactly are we saying we want? What do we understand by the 'psychological' dimension of disease, and what should we understand by this idea in order to make a difference?

A child before the snake of Aesculapius

The search for the so-called psychological aspects of disease, Von Weizsäcker explained, should be regarded as the symptom of a more fundamental change concerning the 'conception of man, of diseased man, of disease and of therapy' (Von Weizsäcker 1986 [1949]: 451). The kernel of this transformation could be described as the introduction of the subject within medicine. This meant, he argued, that the task of psychosomatics was not simply to admit the existence and the influence of an entity, the 'psyche' or the 'mind', different and separate from the body. This might give rise to investigations as to the relationship and interaction between these two objects ('body' and 'mind') in a causal or logical sense, and for certain diseases more than for others. On the contrary, the question for psychosomatics should be how to cease considering the event of disease as an 'objective event' in the first place, as an event occurring primarily in or to an object. The new medicine, according to Von Weizsäcker, should operate a shift in the types of questions to be asked of all pathological phenomena: a shift whereby the questions that can only be asked of a subject become of paramount relevance. This is why for him the problematic of psychosomatics must be distinguished from the problematic of psychophysiology. The efforts of psychophysiology are all aimed towards methodically excluding the aims, motives and values that are inherent in psychological, that is 'subjective', events:

> If someone limits themselves to recording the vasomotor reaction to an artificially provoked fright or pleasure, then they are merely doing psychophysiology . . . . On the other hand, if someone tries to understand what *meaning this* specific fright may have, what *value this* pleasure may have (which is also recorded by vasomotor nerves), then they will already have admitted and recognized the role of the subject. We must therefore distinguish between a naturalistic psychosomatics and an anthropological psychosomatics, and I shall attribute the capacity to reform medicine only to the latter.
>
> (Von Weizsäcker 1986 [1949]: 453–4)

Von Weizsäcker then goes on to say that the most conspicuous threat to the possibility of a medical reform does not come, as one might superficially expect, from the type of medical thinking that is indifferent to the psychic domain. It comes instead from psychosomatic medicine itself, when it adopts the highly sophisticated methods of natural science in relation to somatic events, while it is satisfied to treat the psychological aspect in a non-analytical, acritical and purely phenomenalistical manner, through recourse to 'any sort of triviality' (Von Weizsäcker 1986 [1949]: 455). In 1949 psychosomatic medicine was still a child, but it must already fight with the snake of Aesculapius and it stood already before a dilemma. Yet, Von Weizsäcker underlined, the already vast German and US literatures appeared oblivious to this fundamental alternative and displayed an unreflexive mixture of two irreconcilable tendencies, the naturalistic and the anthropological. Whatever had hitherto constituted itself as 'psychosomatic medicine', according to Von Weizsäcker, was therefore prey to a dangerous self-misunderstanding.

The fundamental distinction that Von Weizsäcker addresses, and its misrecognition or denial, organize psychosomatic discourse as a 'system of dispersion'. This denial should not be regarded as the consequence of individual or intentional shortcomings. On the contrary, it should be understood as the outcome of a network of relations that make psychosomatics possible for what it is at present. Readers will note that what Von Weizsäcker calls 'naturalistic' psychosomatics represents the activation of the possibilities for envisaging the 'psychological' that are made available by the rationality of biomedicine (see chapter four). What is the relation between these possibilities and those Von Weizsäcker advocates? In its present conditions of existence, we may say that psychosomatics as a discursive formation is governed by a fundamental tension. This tension is between, on the one hand, the need to comply with the prescriptions of objectivizing science; and, on the other hand, the need to transcend these prescriptions in order to address the dimension of the 'subject'. This tension has been inherent in the field since its inception, from the moment psychosomatic propositions acquired a claim to serious meaning, and by the very moves through which such a claim was acquired. Psychosomatic propositions derive their specificity from the type of compromise they represent with respect to this fundamental tension, as this chapter will begin to show.

Nearly fifty years later, Von Weizsäcker is not alone in lamenting this contradictory outcome in the development of psychosomatic medicine. But his formulation remains among the most lucid and significant because it addresses the root level of the issue rather than its more peripheral or derivative branches. To illustrate a more 'peripheral' way of approaching the problem we may turn to the work of Todarello and Porcelli (1992). These authors have offered a clear diagnosis for the situation of psychosomatics, argued in epistemological terms. They describe psychosomatics as a 'paradox': as a project (or set of projects) rooted in logically contradictory premises. This is their argument: while the link between the 'psychic' and the 'somatic' dimensions of disease may appear strikingly real in clinical experience, this link is never and can never be *true* in a theoretical sense. We can easily enough intuit that human beings are anthropological wholes, and we can regard this as a matter of fact. But this 'matter of fact' can only be articulated in thought on the basis of available scientific parameters, and these parameters are predicated on the dualism of *psyche* and *soma*. For this reason, short of an entire restructuring of scientific thinking and practices, the field of psychosomatics is doomed to facing situations of 'epistemological imperialism' – doomed to producing what are ultimately 'somatogenetic' or 'psychogenetic' accounts that are epistemologically reductive either on the side of the 'psychic' or on the side of the 'somatic'. Both models are grounded in an aetiological, causal conception that still provides the strongest canon of medical scientificity. In the absence of a meta-language capable of integrating the different viewpoints expressed in different disciplines (Von Bertalanffy 1964), psychosomatics at its best can remain eclectic and descriptive or, at its worst, be plagued by contradiction and semantic confusion. The consequences of this logical *aporia* are immediately visible, the authors suggest, in the failure to produce operatively useful criteria for the diagnosis and treatment of illness as 'psychosomatic'. The paradoxical result is that, in the face of a growing consensus over the multifactoral aetiology of all diseases, in practice only those illnesses that fail to be fully accounted for in organic terms are referred to as 'psychosomatic'.

This epistemological account of the predicament of psychosomatics rests on a very disembodied notion of scientific practice. The paradox it describes is purely logical, necessarily so: how can we provide an adequate psychological approach to the problem of physical disease? It is a contradiction in terms, therefore it is impossible. But where do the terms of this question come from? Why is this the question that is asked? The epistemological argument holds only in so far as we take for granted, as a starting-point, that the 'disease' we are trying to explain psychosomatically is 'disease' as we have hitherto understood it, disease as a condition of the body-as-object. But taking the objectivity of the body as a *sine qua non* is not justified in any absolute sense. It is justified only through an implicit reference to the fact that the organization of medicine as an institutional practice revolves around it. It is justified only to the extent that we presume 'psychosomatics' to be a simple addition to the current functioning of medicine, an addition that should improve this way of functioning without fundamentally altering it (for a similar point, see Armstrong 1987). The 'epistemological argument', therefore, is blind to the fact that the predicament of psychosomatics is given by a situation of tension, a tension that is between the values implied in adopting different epistemological strategies. This is why Von Weizsäcker's way of posing the problem appears more enlightening. Instead of an intrinsic contradiction, Von Weiszäcker invites us to recognize two contradictory empirical 'tendencies'. One tendency is towards preserving the body-as-object as the focal point of medical attention, and as the main criterion that justifies taking medical action. The other tendency is towards shifting the focal point of medical attention onto the embodied subject, which may imply suspending the body-as-object as a relevant criterion for medical practice. This accounts for the situation of psychosomatics not in terms of an abstract epistemological question, but in terms of what we might call a 'situated epistemology'. A 'situated epistemology' would look at what is at stake in activating one strategy of knowledge instead of another. By contrast, Todarello and Porcelli's argument cannot reach this level of the issue. Like science itself, it obeys the constraint of evaluating propositions according to the extent to which they refer to something empirically demonstrable. The two 'tendencies', even when they are acknowledged, are therefore treated with unequal seriousness: the need to take the body-as-object as a starting-point is treated as an incontrovertible fact, while the introduction of the subject within medicine is treated as a fantasy. This state of affairs is the only reason, albeit undoubtedly an important one, why Todarello and Porcelli can suppose that psychosomatics must, in order to be adequate, be able to account for the body-as-object in psychological terms.

These points are worth making in order to render less familiar the ways in which we may evaluate psychosomatics in terms of its 'success' or 'failure'. Where exactly is the failure of psychosomatics? And what might its success look like? Von Weizsäcker's text illustrates the question in precise terms:

> What has clinical psychosomatic medicine accomplished up to now? Whoever frames the question in these terms, and by 'accomplishment' refers to nothing but practical utilization within a modern industrial nation, would have to answer more or less as follows: for the majority of internal diseases it has accomplished nothing at all, for some of them very little, and even here only for isolated cases; only for such cases it would be legitimate to speak of competitiveness with respect to modern biochemical treatments. I would also make a similar judgment if I felt subjected to the business ideal of the

> entrepreneurial state . . . . I believe then that we must make a clarification. The evaluation of theoretical and practical *successes* ultimately depends on the following alternative: whether medicine and doctors subscribe to the value judgment proper to the entrepreneurial state, or whether they locate the value of human life elsewhere.
>
> (Von Weizsäcker 1986 [1949]: 457–8)

This point makes the limits of the 'epistemological argument' even more apparent. According to that argument, it is the theoretical failure of psychosomatics that accounts for the marginal role of these approaches within medical institutions. But if we follow Von Weizsäcker we can reverse this order of explanation. From his perspective, the force of the body-as-object as a medical criterion, in a practical more than a theoretical sense, is primary with respect to the question of theoretical 'success' or 'failure'. The social value of being able to discern illnesses in terms of affected body parts determines in advance the assessment of psychosomatic approaches, by setting the body-as-object as an irrenouncable condition in that assessment itself. The 'epistemological argument' disregards this initial act of evaluation and simply proceeds from it as if it were a necessary given. Thus it prevents us from seeing that the theoretical impasse of psychosomatics is underpinned by a societal impasse, a contradiction that involves different values and different concepts of medical demand and care.

An archaeological perspective allows us to assess the relevance of statements not in terms of the problems they resolve, but in terms of the problems they pose. In other words, it allows us to take propositions seriously independently of the extent to which their claims to truth are practically endorsed, and therefore independently of whether they are 'successful' in that very specific sense. From this perspective, we might speak of a 'majoritarian' and of a 'minoritarian' tendency within psychosomatics. The first begins by regarding the diseased body-as-object as the necessary focus of medical attention. Thus it respects the canons of institutional plausibility, and seeks to devise theoretical models capable of including socio-psychological factors in the aetiology of disease. For this majoritarian tendency Todarello and Porcelli are probably correct in arguing that the project is 'aporetic'. Such a project can undoubtedly yield useful results, but only in the sense of establishing correlations, not in the sense of providing adequately non-reductive explanations. We must count as 'majoritarian' also some instances of psychosomatic discourse that relinquish positivist explanations in favour of psychodynamic ways of accounting for disease. They are 'majoritarian' to the extent that their hypotheses are still addressed to 'disease' understood as what occurs in the body-as-object. The paradigmatic example of these is provided by the indiscriminate application of the 'hysterical conversion' model to account for any physical condition, to be discussed in more detail in the next chapter. The 'minoritarian' tendency, conversely, seeks to elaborate psychosomatic theories that address the dimension of subjectivity, irrespective of the fact that a displacement of the focus of medical attention may occur as a result. Such attempts are 'minoritarian' to the extent that they imply a bracketing of the perceptual categories and distinctions that organize both biomedical theory and practice. This would be the case, for instance, if the explanation and treatment of a clearly identified somatic condition was postponed or subordinated to the task of assessing the meaning or the value of the disease for the individual. Such an approach may clearly result in a normatively weak position. Yet, it would be a mistake to regard it as logically aporetic; it is contradictory of a widely accepted pragmatic principle, and invites reflection on the values at stake in its modification. Finally, to the extent that a 'minoritarian' tendency is also at work in the field of psychosomatics, we should be prepared to look for examples of it in sites other than the traditional medical ones. If this tendency implies a displacement of the medical problem as such, we can expect that the ways and places in which it is articulated will similarly be displaced. As Von Weizsäcker remarked,

> psychosomatic medicine, when it is correctly understood, has a revolutionary character. In such a situation is it often claimed that, before destroying anything, we should have something better to substitute for it. This advice is not entirely incontrovertible, for it is not easy to see how the old *and* the new could remain side by side, within the same place.
>
> (Von Weizsäcker 1986 [1949]: 461–2)

Having outlined the distinction between a 'majoritarian' and a 'minoritarian' tendency within psychosomatics, we must pause to ask in what sense these categories can be used to describe psychosomatics as an empirical field. How, in other words, do they relate to the customary 'sign-posts', to the diversity of disciplines and practices, and to the different theories, concepts, and methods that are employed within them? The distinction between a 'majoritarian' tendency and a 'minoritarian' tendency attempts to specify something which is neither conventionally visible nor hidden. It does not refer to the conservative or non-conservative intentions professed at the level of propositions. It refers instead to the possibilities each statement activates, when read in relation to all others. Still, does the distinction between the two tendencies not overlap with the distribution of disciplinary fields that are involved in psychosomatics? And if it does, should we not ask again whether 'psychosomatics' exists as such? Should we not speak instead of the difference between the natural and the social or human sciences, and of the relationships between them? What does the label 'psychosomatics' add to the sum of descriptions of each of these separate discourses?

Armstrong's critique of biopsychosocial medicine (1987) is useful in highlighting that we cannot assume any direct correspondence or overlap between disciplines and what I called 'tendencies' within psychosomatic discourse. Armstrong argues to warn the social sciences against becoming 'an emasculated, uncritical appendage' of biomedicine (1987: 1217), as a result of endorsing too easily and quickly the proposal for a 'biopsychosocial' alliance. This proposal, he maintains, should be regarded as a palliative offered in response to increasing consumer dissatisfaction with medicine's failure to address patients as persons. It is clear, Armstrong argues, 'that within the biopsychosocial perspective medicine's hegemony is not negotiable . . . . The fact that illness is localised to the lesion inside the body has always ensured medical dominance . . . because only the physician can have access to this truth' (ibid.: 1214). Thus, Armstrong supports the idea that the difference between biomedicine and the social sciences becomes illusory to the extent that these comply with the body-as-object as the single main criterion of pathological 'truth'. But in his polemical focus on medical dominance, Armstrong is perhaps less accurate in describing the extent to which this compliance with the criteria set by the biomedical sciences is not merely imposed on the social sciences from outside. Rather, it is one of the possibilities made available, even probable, by their own epistemic configuration. The critical aspect of the social sciences is only one side of what social scientific work can produce.[2] If this is the case, we will not be able to resort to any easy distinctions along disciplinary lines in order to identify medicine with the 'majoritarian' tendency, and the social sciences with the 'minoritarian' or critical tendency.

We cannot assume, on the other hand, that the 'minoritarian' tendency is necessarily confined to the critical aspect of the human sciences, and entirely absent from natural scientific discourse. Von Weizsäcker, in his description of the implications of an anthropological psychosomatics, stressed how the introduction of the subject within medicine 'will not only mean that depth psychology becomes necessary [to medical thinking]; it will also mean that naturalistic *biology* will thereby find itself modified, whether this will occur gradually or in a revolutionary way' (Von Weizsäcker 1986 [1949]: 457). His own experimental research in neurology and biology yielded the concept of 'gestaltic cycle' (*Gestaltkreis*), whose novelty has been compared to that of Einstein's relativity theory and of Heisenberg's 'uncertainty principle' (Wyss 1957, 1977). More recent descriptions of the field of psychoneuroimmunology claim that a displacement of the body-as-object can be inferred as a probable outcome from the standpoint of experimental science today. We are told that scientists working in this field will be driven by the logic of their own research to 'give up the powerful resources of mechanism' (Levin and Solomon 1990: 521). Medicine and patients alike should therefore be encouraged to relinquish 'counterproductive conceptions of the body' based on 'epistemological assumptions of naive realism' (ibid.: 534) For our purposes, however, it is entirely problematic to approach the 'minoritarian' tendency by pointing to this and similar types of assertions. Like the 'epistemological argument', they lead us to regard psychosomatics in terms of the alternative between an epistemological *status quo* and an allegedly nearing – but as yet projectual and ineffable – transformation. I have already discussed the limits of such an approach. If I mention these developments it is only as a cautionary note against assimilating the 'majoritarian' and 'minoritarian' tendencies respectively to the natural and the human sciences.

Psychosomatic statements are thus dispersed in such a way as to make the distinctions between disciplines less relevant than the modality of their reciprocal engagement. For this reason, the use of the label 'psychosomatics' appears justified to designate a formation that owes its specificity to the coexistence and interrelationship between different types of knowledge. Unlike single scientific disciplines, for which interface relationships are secondary and derived, psychosomatics as a system of dispersion is made possible by the interfaces themselves. The stability of each disciplinary location finds its limit, or its lack, in the necessary reference to what is other with respect to itself. Finally, while different 'tendencies' may describe sub-systems of coherence within the field as a whole, we should not forget that the organizing principle of this field is the tension between them.

Once we take this tension as a guiding principle, and only then, it becomes possible to appreciate the fundamental role of psychoanalysis in the formation and dispersion of psychosomatic statements. The remainder of this chapter is devoted to exploring this fundamental role at two different levels. The first level is epistemological. In this sense psychoanalysis is significant for explicitly addressing (not for resolving) the tension that informs psychosomatics as a form of problematization, as I shall illustrate through Von Weizsäcker's work. The second level is historical. At this level psychoanalysis is significant because Freud banned 'organic disease' as a psychoanalytic concern and built the psychoanalytic edifice around this ban. And yet, Freud's own propositions were the historical starting-points of several 'psychosomatic' projects, despite Freud's prohibition. 'Psychoanalysis' therefore constitutes an ambiguous, double foundation for the modern problematic of psychosomatics. Let us begin to describe this foundation by looking at the epistemological significance of psychoanalysis for psychosomatics.

The 'revolving door' principle

As Paul Ricoeur (1970) has argued, the epistemological problem of Freudianism is to coordinate an 'energetics' (or 'relations of force') with a 'hermeneutics' (or 'relations of meaning'). Ricoeur shows that psychoanalysis in this respect is a mixed discourse that never settles on either of these alternatives; neither does their mixture signify a simple lack of clarity, the use of an outdated vocabulary, or a 'category mistake' (Ricoeur 1974: 167). Rather, it is a discourse where 'the energetics implies the hermeneutics and the hermeneutics discloses an energetics' (Ricoeur 1970: 65). This means that psychoanalysis expresses the very tension that governs the problem of psychosomatics, a tension between the objectivity of matter and the subjectivity of meaning. It expresses this tension by articulating the logic of the unconscious, as 'a perpetual principle of dissatisfaction, of calling into question, of criticism and contestation of what may seem, in other respects, to be established' (Foucault 1970: 373). Von Weizsäcker was a strong advocate of an active role for psychoanalysis in the development of psychosomatics. Significantly, this advocacy rested on his own experimental efforts to redefine the status of biology, rather than on an adaptation of Freud's teachings to the problem of physical illness. Von Weizsäcker was ready to follow to its extreme consequences the subversion of the *cogito* that in Freud's psychoanalysis remained implicit (except with reference to analytic practice itself). In this Von Weizsäcker differed from Freud, who had been careful not to present his endeavour as a 'subversion' to the broader scientific community, by restricting the clinical applicability of psychoanalysis to the problem of neurosis.

Von Weizsäcker's advocacy of psychoanalysis follows a line of reasoning that is quite unusual with respect to the arguments employed by his contemporaries. It rested, as I said, on his biological work, and specifically on the idea that:

> there is no element that can enable us to verify, through observation, what is alive and what is not . . . . I am actually concerned with is what turns out to be researchable and resolvable empirically; and in this case it is clear that the boundaries between the living and the inanimate are not verifiable either in space or in time, either in a dynamic or in a causal sense . . . . [M]odes of relationship have taken the place of substantial essences such as body, soul and spirit. By now, what must count as true is only what can be established at the same time as it is being transformed.
>
> (Von Weizsäcker 1986 [1949]: 455)

For Von Weizsäcker, this is the reason why depth psychology is entirely 'akin' to organic medicine and represents the only adequate complement to it. Both psychic and organic processes are 'unconscious' processes, in so far as they are life processes that operate from a basis that cannot be known objectively as such. Therefore, 'subjectivity' is the mode of being that is proper to all biological acts. Elsewhere, Von Weizsäcker characterized this mode of being also as 'antilogical' in the sense that life, as a form of becoming, is:

> a significant contradiction . . . becoming is the essential determination whereby something neither *is* nor *is not*, but rather, more precisely, loses a being and simultaneously receives one . . . . An antilogical state of things is . . . such that both an assertion and its negation are true . . . . If for instance I say 'I am becoming', and at the

> same time I say 'little by little I am dying', both things are true . . . . *The living is always something permanent that changes – like man.*
> (Von Weizsäcker 1990 [1946]: 181)[3]

The fact of being alive confers to living beings certain peculiarities that make some questions more relevant than others, both for them and about them. What is relevant to life is not so much simply that it is, but rather that it wants, it must, it can, and so on. These, in Von Weizsäcker's vocabulary, are 'pathic' assertions that express an antilogical mode of being. If I say 'I want' something, I imply that what is wanted is not already there; if I say 'I can' it remains implicit that what I can may not come to be. Thus an 'ontic' mode of being must be distinguished from the 'pathic' mode: 'the first [term] expresses pure and simple being, while the second will indicate existence not so much as it is given, but rather as it is *undergone* [*erlitten*]' (Von Weizsäcker 1990 [1946]: 179). Life is experienced and lived as 'life' in the contradiction between the possibilities of being and non-being. The living subject performs its own self-identity through time as a series of biological and antilogical acts, rather than simply 'being' what it 'is'. Von Weizsäcker gave the name of *Gestaltkreis* ('gestaltic' circle or cycle), to 'an indication for the experience of the living', which he attempted to demonstrate experimentally (Von Weizsäcker 1940). In his own words, the *Gestaltkreis*:

> is by no means a reproduction of the figure of life or of life's movement; it is rather, properly speaking, an indication for the experience of the living. We can represent this circle as a traveller following a certain path (it may be someone who is simply strolling, or someone who has a technical means of transport at his disposal: in this case, the scientist).
> (Von Weizsäcker 1990 [1946]: 184)

The concept of *Gestaltkreis* highlights why 'life' in unknowable in any objective sense. The reason is that the observer is not in a position of externality with respect to the condition of other living beings. The only difference between them lies in the availability, to the scientist, of a 'technical means of transport'. This may enable the scientist to run ahead or to look behind, metaphorically speaking, but never to look in all directions simultaneously. Yet this would be what is required in order to grasp the peculiar mode of presence of any living being, a presence that is given as much by what it is no longer or not yet as by where it stands at any particular time. The *Gestaltkreis* is thus a cycle within which the scientist and the living being under observation equally participate, each according to their own trajectory. But how then can the cycle itself be 'known'? It can:

> not be grasped in the full integration of its terms (neither intellectually nor intuitively), but can only be *travelled*, undergoing its

> contrasts in a continuous *losing-sight-of* and a continually renewed *losing-effect*, in order to gain something new.
>
> (Von Weizsäcker 1990 [1946]: 184)

The 'travelling' that characterizes the being of life, the alternation between the possibilities of being and non-being, is circular. This implies that the traveller's gaze, as it moves in one direction in order to make visible what was previously invisible, necessarily blocks out of view the opposite direction. We can infer the cycle precisely from the limits of what we can see from any one perspective. This is what Von Weizsäcker refers to as the 'reciprocal occultation of our beings in the *Gestaltkreis*', or also as the principle of the 'revolving door' (Von Weizsäcker 1990 [1946]: 184). The partial invisibility of any biological act is therefore immanent to such acts themselves; it should not be understood as a result of the provisional incompleteness of scientific biology (ibid.).

What are the consequences of these concepts for psychosomatics? The first consequence is precisely the analogy between organic medicine and psychoanalysis; both 'mind' and 'body' are categories established by consciousness. Pathological life cannot be identified or grasped entirely with either of these terms. The mind–body relationship is an example of the *Gestaltkreis*, whose logic applies to the activity of knowing as to any other biological act. The two perspectives explicate each other reciprocally, in a way that implies the criticism of each by the other: 'each element reveals and manifests the other as something new' (Von Weizsäcker 1990 [1946]: 187). For this reason, it is equally improper either to regard 'body' and 'mind' as two different substances, or to identify them as the same thing. On the contrary,

> The psychic expresses itself in the language of the body, the bodily in that of the psyche: this does not imply a relation of causality. And if we now speak of psychogenesis, we should thereby only mean a historical becoming in the course of which organic changes occur *instead of* [psychic] processes, and viceversa.
>
> (Von Weizsäcker 1986 [1949]: 459–60)

The task of psychosomatics should be, according to Von Weizsäcker, to translate organic language into the comprehensible word of the psyche. This task, once it is understood as a way of producing a movement along the gestaltic cycle, is not merely heuristic. In other words, the activity of translation is itself a *biological act* of some consequence for the living being to whom it applies. Luis Chiozza (1988), who is one of the few systematic practitioners of Von Weizsäcker's proposed method, has argued similar points very clearly. He stresses that: (a) to interpret the meaning of a symptom does not mean postulating a cause; (b) just as understanding the unconscious meaning of a given bodily ailment does not exclude the possibility of explaining it as the effect of a given cause, so establishing a cause does not exclude the possibility of interpreting a meaning; (c) in the same way as the inability to find a cause does not imply having demonstrated its absence, so the inability to discern a meaning does not imply having demonstrated its absence; (d) if we admit that a bodily ailment is a sign expressing a specific unconscious meaning, we must also admit that any transformation of this meaning implies a transformation of the ailment that constituted its sign. Understanding a meaning also inevitably implies changing it, framing it in a context that re-signifies it. A change in signification is also therefore a change of state; the patient whose condition does not change is a patient who has not succeeded in registering what they understand deeply, as a change in what they actually believe (Chiozza 1988).[4]

Von Weizsäcker thus advocated psychoanalysis as a necessary component of psychosomatics because, as a discipline, it acknowledges that subject and object are never entirely separable, and because it accords central importance to what remains unthought in any mode of presence. Yet, if we look at the concrete history of psychosomatics, 'psychoanalytic' perspectives have often failed to provide non-reductive approaches to the problem of physical illness. This can be explained by looking at the legacy Freud left to psychosomatics, or more precisely, at the character of the 'ban' that some of his followers violated in the name of psychosomatic research.

Presenting the unconscious

Freud was very unambiguous in voicing the unilateral character of psychoanalysis when explaining his endeavour to the wider scientific public. He repeatedly invited his followers to refrain from trespassing into the problem of organic illness, since it was 'not within the scope of a purely psychological inquiry to penetrate so far behind the frontiers of physiological research' (Freud 1914: 84; see also 1926). Freud's prohibition has been interpreted as a step made necessary for the survival of psychoanalysis as a science accredited by a scientific community, rather than for reasons of internal coherence (Todarello and Porcelli 1992; Corsi Piacentini *et al.* 1983b). This seems eloquently confirmed in Freud's private correspondence with Georg Groddeck and with Viktor Von Weizsäcker, both of whom saw in Freud's work the opportunity for a reform of general medicine:

> In my article on the unconscious which you mention there is an inconspicuous footnote: 'We are reserving for a different context the mention of another notable privilege of the *Ucs*.' I shall tell you what was not mentioned here: the assumption that the unconscious act exerts an intensive, decisive influence on somatic processes such as conscious acts never do.
>
> (Letter to Groddeck, 5 June, in Groddeck 1977a [1917]: 37)

> I had to keep analysts away from this type of investigations for educational reasons, since innervations, vascular dilatations and nervous pathways would have been exceedingly dangerous temptations for them: they had to learn to limit themselves to a psychological frame of thought.
>
> (Letter to Von Weizsäcker of 1932, quoted in Wyss 1977: 210)

Freud therefore deliberately contained the implications of psychoanalysis with regard to the problem of physical illness. He did so through a series of conceptual moves that defined the perimeter of psychoanalysis in relation to other disciplines, in a way that would allow for their coexistence side by side. In these moves he addressed the physical body, mostly negatively or by default, in order to take distance from it. Two instances in particular articulate the Freudian prohibition: the first is the character of hysterical symptoms, which historically founds the legitimacy of psychoanalysis as an autonomous discipline; the second is the distinction between 'actual neuroses' and 'psychoneuroses'. Each of these instances, taken out of their specific context, acquired enormous relevance for those who produced 'psychoanalytic' hypotheses for the explanation of bodily disease. In order to understand the nature of this relevance, let us look at how each of them works in the context of Freud's writings.

Freud's work on hysteria highlighted that the bodily symptom of the hysteric, like all other subsequent 'analytic material', stood for something else that was fundamentally 'psychic'. The autonomy of psychoanalysis as a scientific enterprise could be claimed and defended precisely on the basis of showing that the hysterical symptom was a *false* one, from an organic point of view (Freud 1893; see also 1926). The lesion of the hysteric was only a *pseudo*-lesion: this offered good evidence for regarding the 'psychological' as an autonomous domain of experience, and therefore of scientific inquiry. It argued for the need to adopt an outlook that, without denying the ultimate rootedness of the psychic in the organic, would 'behave *as if* . . . confronted by psychological factors only' (letter to Fliess, 22 September 1898, in Bonaparte *et al.* 1954: 264). Since the body of the hysteric only behaved *as if* a lesion were present, Freud's own 'as if' in relation to neurophysiology was justified. Freud thus was able to 'translate the language of the body into that of the psyche' on the basis of having shown, first, that the psyche produces peculiar effects of its own. While he stated the 'logic of the unconscious' as a way of reading the relations and correlations between the physical and the mental, in order to do so he implicitly relied on a reified notion of the 'mind' as an independent causal principle for certain specific effects. 'Psychological interpretation' would legitimately apply to effects of that type. It would apply in the presence of psychological symptoms, and to bodily symptoms only to the extent that they could be shown to be truly psychological, that is, organically false. Thus, the dimension of the 'psychological' was effectively reduced by Freud to what manifests itself as such to the scientist, that is, to the psycho-*pathological*. In this way, a double service was being rendered to the epistemological survival of psychoanalysis as a legitimate science: its autonomous value for the explanation and treatment of at least a segment of pathology was being established, whilst a peaceful coexistence with organic medicine could be advocated and defended on the same basis. Psychoanalysis, as Freud reiterated clearly in his 'New introductory lectures on psychoanalysis', had no ambition to replace or to modify the then current scientific *Weltanschauung* (1933, lecture 35).

Let us now turn to the second element of the Freudian prohibition, the distinction between 'actual neuroses' and 'psychoneuroses'. Freud started to outline this distinction in 1894 and never fundamentally revised it, except to include hypochondria among the actual neuroses after much hesitation. The term 'actual neurosis' appears for the first time in Freud's work in 1898, to denote anxiety neurosis and neurasthenia. The idea that these conditions should be set apart from psychoneuroses (which include transference neuroses such as hysteria, and narcissistic neuroses) had been developed much earlier (see Freud 1895). Both nosological categories presented no evidence of organic lesion and so were to be considered part of psychopathology by default. However, while in hysteria the symptom could be a pseudo-lesion, or the somatic representation of a psychic conflict, anxiety neurosis presented different psychological symptoms. These included 'general irritability' or 'anxious expectation' and were accompanied by 'a disturbance of one or more of the bodily functions – such as respiration, heart action, vaso-motor innervation or glandular activity' (Freud 1895: 94). Freud described these as 'equivalents of anxiety attacks' (examples of which are palpitation, dyspnoea, attacks resembling asthma, sweating, tremor and shivering, vertigo and congestions) (ibid.). Freud proposed the two groups should be distinguished aetiologically on account of the difference between the 'actual' sexual life of the subject and the 'representation' of important sexual events of the past. Here the term 'actual' retains the meaning it has in German usage, to signify the temporal dimension of the present. While,

> the cause is definitely sexual in both these types of neurosis . . . in the former case it must be sought in 'a disorder of [the subject's] contemporary sexual life' and not in 'important events of his past life'.
>
> (Laplanche and Pontalis 1988: 10)

The temporal difference implies for Freud a pathogenetic difference. The difference is also one between direct causation as opposed to mediation on the part of the psychic apparatus. The actual neuroses are precipitated directly by a disturbance in the sexual economy of the subject, either due to an accumulation of sexual excitation or to an incomplete satisfaction of it. By contrast the psychoneuroses are precipitated only by a psychic process of symbolic elaboration that mediates between the past, where the initial trauma is to be found, and the present. The 'actual', in other words, 'connotes the absence of the mediations which are to be encountered in the symptom-formation of the psychoneuroses (displacement, condensation, etc.)' (Laplanche and Pontalis 1988: 149). The 'actual' neurotic symptom is the mere somatic equivalent of contingent anxiety, and has no representational value.

The distinction between the two types of neuroses hinges on the Freudian notion of 'instinct'. Instinct for Freud is the condition of possibility for symbolization, whose source, however, is invariably somatic (Freud 1915). The link between force and meaning makes 'instinct' the limit concept at the frontier between the organic and the psychic (Ricoeur 1970); it is what represents the body to the mind on the basis of an 'ideational support'. Thanks to this ideational support or 'representative', instinct undergoes the 'vicissitudes' of repression and symbolic substitution that constitute psychic life (Laplanche and Pontalis 1988: 204). When the temporal process of symbolic elaboration is abstracted from the picture, psychological dynamics remain invisible as such. Affect *prior to* undergoing any 'vicissitudes' is inaccessible to consciousness, and therefore to analysis. We might call this an 'intrinsic occultation' of the psychological dimension, to use Von Weizsäcker's terms. For the purposes of aetiology, however, Freud effectively assimilates this to a simple absence:

> the difference [between hysteria and anxiety neurosis] is merely that in anxiety neurosis the excitation . . . is purely somatic (somatic sexual excitation), whereas in hysteria it is psychical (provoked by conflict).
>
> (Freud 1895: 115)

Hence, actual neuroses are,

> *not further reducible by psychological analysis, nor amenable to psychotherapy*. The mechanism of *substitution*, therefore, does not hold good.
>
> (ibid.: 97)

Unlike transference neuroses such as hysteria, where the ego and its defence apparatus participate in the pathogenesis, there is no such participation in the case of actual neuroses. This means for Freud that they are sterile from a psychological point of view, and devoid of any psychological meaning. They should be considered external to the psychoanalytic endeavour. To explain the pathogenesis of actual neuroses Freud relied on the biomedical models of the reflex arc, on the one hand, and of the phlogistic reaction, on the other. He thus spoke of the 'toxic' character of actual neuroses, in the sense that they are accountable for as an effect of 'sexual toxins' originating in the metabolism of the individual (Freud 1915–17: 387; see Corsi Piacentini *et al.* 1983a; 1983b).

What are the effects of this line of reasoning for psychoanalysis? One effect is to confirm that psychoanalysis is only relevant for properly 'psychological' conditions. A further effect is that the 'psychological' is no longer defined purely by default, as the negative or the absence of a somatic lesion, but becomes identifiable through a specific type of evidence. This is the evidence of functions of representation and symbolization that characterizes psychoneurotic symptoms. It is to these, and to these only, that the 'logic of the unconscious' becomes applicable. The pragmatic appeal of such a move, on Freud's part, is undeniable. In this way, it becomes possible to identify and treat a 'psychodynamic' pathology in terms of whether it is present or absent. Psychoanalysis can operate in a manner that is diametrically opposite, but equivalent to, that of somatic medicine. What are the effects of this line of reasoning for psychosomatics? The most important of these effects is that it becomes improper to speak of the 'unconscious' meaning or dimension of disease in the absence of symptoms of a very specific kind. 'Interpretation' becomes relevant only for psychoneurotic conditions. The absence of psychological symptoms no longer appears meaningful as a mode of pathological presence: there is nothing to interpret in 'actual' or somatic disease.

Conclusion: a matrix for the dispersion of psychosomatics

The psychoanalytic legacy I have described offers a set of coordinates to interpret the dispersion of psychosomatic statements into a series of contradictory and apparently incommensurable positions. These coordinates define a spectrum of wide ranging possibilities that revolve around the following questions: when and how can bodily symptoms be said to reveal (and hide) the functioning of a subject? When is illness amenable to an interpretation as to its meaning, value, and motives? Freud provided relatively clear answers both to the 'when' (when the physical symptom is false as such) and to the 'how' (by deciphering symbolic representations in analytical practice). This resulted in a prohibition for analysts to engage with whatever was truly somatic, even when its superficial manifestation might be psychopathological (actual neuroses). Truly somatic symptoms would remain interpretable within an analytic setting only strictly in a secondary sense. It would still be possible to analyse the patient's fantasies on his or her organic symptom, just as it is possible to thus analyse any material element of the analytic setting (e.g. furniture, the physical appearance of the analyst, etc.); but the fantasies themselves should never be confused with the real thing, with which they are not fundamentally related (Codignola 1977). Short of a revision of the Freudian framework itself, therefore, the application of psychoanalytic method to organic disease was indeed bound to be aporetic.

The early advocacy of psychoanalysis as a foundation for psychosomatics implied directly infringing Freud's prohibition. This could be done in different ways, however, depending on which element of the prohibition was violated. It was possible to violate the 'when', by supposing that psychoanalytic interpretation could be applied not only in the presence of a certain type of symptom, but regardless of the type of symptom. This strategy represents a reduction to the hermeneutic aspect of psychoanalysis. Alternatively, it was possible to violate the 'how', by supposing that identifying psychophysiological 'factors' exhausts the task of a psychological interpretation. This strategy may be described as a reduction to the energetic aspect of psychoanalysis. The different strategies of violation represent different forms of compromise with respect to acknowledging the body-as-object in the medical task. On this basis, it is possible to come back to the details of psychosomatic discourse in order to discuss whether and how this alternative is ever overcome.

6

INTERPRETING THE BODILY SIGN

In the course of the last chapter I proposed that the discourse of psychosomatics is structured by a fundamental tension, on the basis of which we can recognize two tendencies: the 'minoritarian' and the 'majoritarian' tendencies of psychosomatics. I have argued that the difference between them does not correspond clearly to the difference between theoretical disciplines. On the contrary, we find instances of each tendency across the board of psychosomatic research, albeit perhaps unevenly distributed. I have also argued that what makes the tendencies 'minoritarian' or 'majoritarian' is not the degree to which their claims are endorsed, either in theory or in practice, for certain forms of the majoritarian tendency are indeed discredited and marginal in both respects. What distinguishes this majoritarian tendency is the 'paradox' described by Todarello and Porcelli (1992): the attempt to account psychologically for disease understood as an event of the body-as-object. The majoritarian tendency of psychosomatics is what I explore in this chapter. Its possibilities correspond to the two 'paradigms' made available by psychoanalysis through the violation of the Freudian prohibition. The first of these paradigms is the model of hysterical conversion; the second is the model of actual neuroses as distinct from psychoneuroses. The appropriation of either of these models for the purposes of psychosomatic research always involves a reduction, either in the direction of a 'hermeneutics' or in the direction of an 'energetics'. In the case of the first model, the reduction produces interpretations of the bodily symptom that both address and ignore the body in its objectivity, meaning that psychodynamic 'causality' is simply substituted for physical causality. In the second model, the reduction moves in the opposite direction: the objectivity of the body is not ignored, but no room is left for the interpretation of the bodily sign in terms of its specific meaning, value, or end. This second reduction shows why the interpretive grid that I here propose, despite being derived from psychoanalysis, applies to many instances of psychosomatic research that are very distant from psychoanalysis itself. The alternatives made available by psychoanalysis (or rather, by its appropriation) already implicitly contain the structure of some possibilities activated elsewhere. What these alternatives hold in common is the focus on the disease itself as what requires explanation or interpretation.

I shall approach the 'minoritarian' tendency gradually, from the discussion started in this chapter, and to its full extent in the next one. As of now I may anticipate how this minoritarian tendency differs broadly from the other one. It differs by attempting to avoid both forms of the reduction, which implies displacing the focus of attention from the disease itself to a different level. It acknowledges that the somatic symptom is not interpretable in a symbolic sense, just as Freud thought, and that physical causality cannot be denied. But it goes further in claiming that this very fact, the lack of any symbolic significance of the physical symptom, calls for an interpretation. What is the meaning of this lack of meaning? What is the psychological significance of this absence of the psychological? In asking these questions, psychosomatics shifts to a higher level of abstraction. It no longer addresses the disease as such, but rather the subjective conditions of possibility for one form of pathology to develop instead of another. The meaninglessness of physical disease is contemplated from within a wider context that re-signifies it.

The body as a symbolic text

We thus have two points of departure for the task of describing what I have called the 'majoritarian' tendency of psychosomatics: the paradigm of hysterical conversion, and the distinction between actual and psychoneuroses. The earliest proponents of an application of psychoanalysis to the problem of organic illness violated the Freudian prohibition in the sense of extending the logic of interpretation, originally devised to decode the problem of symbolic conversion in hysteria, potentially to the sphere of somatic disease *tout court*. In doing so, they ignored the distinction between actual and psychoneuroses and Freud's conviction that conversion did not occur prior to the Oedipus complex (Taylor 1987). They attributed symbolic significance to all types of symptoms, which would figure as compromise formations for pregenital conflicts in the unconscious. The somatic sign simply replaced the psychopathological symptom and similarly constituted, for these authors, evidence of a psychic process of symbolic elaboration. It was a direct and unmediated way of regarding bodily processes from the perspective of subjectivity, seeking no compromise with the body described in its objectivity. Authors cited as classics in this type of orientation are Georg Groddeck and Felix Deutsch, although similar positions were suggested by Karl Abraham (1927) and Sándor Ferenczi (1955), and maintained by Angel Garma (1953, 1958) and Melitta Sperling (1960, 1973).

In most historical overviews of psychosomatics Groddeck and Deutsch have attained the status of pioneers and precursors, but also of icons for all that is excessive with respect to the requirements of scientific reasoning. Of the two, however, Deutsch only can be regarded as having offered a systematic theory based on the model of conversion. Remarkably few authors clearly acknowledge that Deutsch himself did not accept this model as the sole explanation for the 'choice' of somatic disease (Taylor 1987). In this context I address his work as representative of conversion theories despite this acknowledgement, for the purpose of reconstructing a discursive position rather than the position of an author. Deutsch proposed that Freud's concept of conversion 'may be carried beyond its original meaning' (Deutsch 1959 [1924]: 59), by assuming that 'a continuous conversion process, necessary for the maintenance of health and well-being, takes place in every normal individual' (ibid.: 65). The theoretical precondition for the conversion process itself lay in the body's capacity for symbolization, which occurs as a reaction to primary experiences of object–loss. Deutsch proposed that the objects could be retrieved, or 'reunited with the body by way of symbolization', through a process he named 'retrojection' (Deutsch 1959: 76). Different body parts or organs would thus be psychically cathected, they would become memory symbols deposited in the body. On account of the process of symbolization, the physiological functions of these body parts could be modified when the ego failed to maintain energetic-libidinal homeostasis through the defences that are proper to it. The organic symptom, accordingly, is 'the protective device against an impending loss of the object which has been retrieved through retrojection and which rests symbolized in the body, where it maintains the body's unity' (ibid.: 77). Since every part of the body possesses the potential for the symbolic expression of loss and separation which evoke anxiety, the ego avoids separation anxiety by turning 'to different parts of the body which are adequately symbolized and may serve as substitutes for the loss . . . there is an interchangeability of organs as far as their symbolic value is concerned' (ibid.: 79; see also Deutsch 1922).

Conversions, Deutsch writes, are forms of psychic expression that have become necessary in order to:

> adjust the individual's instinctual drives to the demands of the culture in which he lives . . . . *One might say that human beings would be most unhappy or would take far more flight into neurosis if they could not fall sick from time to time.* For it is during periods of sickness that the conversion process finds an inconspicuous outlet, which is barred at other times.
>
> (Deutsch 1959 [1924]: 66)

We have here the rough elements of what later would become, with a different theoretical status, the fundamental structure underlying the possibility of different types of illness: the outline of a capacity to exploit the alternative between psychic and somatic suffering. As Deutsch points out, this capacity is linked to the possibility of an inconspicuous expression of the self in the context of specific cultural demands. Because of these implications, whose 'revolutionary' character appears all too evident, it might seem strange to include these early instances of psychosomatic discourse in the majoritarian tendency of psychosomatics. If this attribution is appropriate, however, it is because Deutsch offers symbolic interpretation as an explanation for the specific somatic sign, in a form that competes directly with the propositions of physical causality. I suggest that Deutsch respected one type of plausibility at the expense of another. The institutional plausibility of addressing the aetiology of a specific bodily ailment was immediately preserved, at the price of the epistemological implausibility of denying the relative autonomy of organic functioning. As Deutsch himself remarked, the notion of conversion could only begin to suggest how the psychic and the organic are aetiologically related:

> Although the clinical observations . . . suffice to make the conversion process appear somewhat less mysterious, one must admit that they do not reveal the roots of the transition of the psychic into the organic.
>
> (Deutsch 1959 [1924]: 66)

The question of transition from one type of content (the psychic) to another type (the somatic) was only nominally resolved by the proposition that 'the temporal coincidence of psychic and physical manifestations develops from the *identity* of these processes' (ibid.: 69). This is a highly speculative basis on which to regard the fullness of a physical symptom as perfectly coincident with a fullness of psychic meaning. Deutsch's endeavour to extend psychoanalytic discourse to organic disease thus remains coherent with psychoanalytic theory in its reference to the process of symbolization as the necessary point of access to the psychic domain. But it breaks with psychoanalysis by ignoring its conditional norms of usage, which Freud had made explicit through his prohibition. Deutsch preserves the hermeneutic aspect of psychoanalysis, but relinquishes what makes it both necessary and possible: namely, the difference between what is somatically 'true' and what is somatically 'false'. Ultimately, he could not defend the legitimacy of interpretation for organic disease theoretically, but only on account of the evidence of therapeutic results based on analytical practice (ibid.: 62). Therapeutic results as such were acknowledged also by Freud, who evidently did not see in this a reason to lift his theoretical ban on engaging psychoanalytically with organic disease (see Freud 1950: 125).

These general considerations offer the grounds for distinguishing carefully between the figures of Felix Deutsch and Georg Groddeck. Groddeck's writings and practice have similarly been described as an imperialistic extension of psychoanalytic insights to the domain of pathology as a whole (Taylor 1987; Todarello and Porcelli 1992). However, there is an important difference between these two figures and it lies in their respective modes of enunciation, or claims to 'seriousness'. Groddeck explicitly renounced the status of scientificity for his propositions by maintaining that their value lay beyond the question of whether what he said was true or false and should be sought instead in the effectiveness of his statements as therapeutic devices. Between 1916 and 1919, Groddeck expressed his thoughts weekly in a series of 115 psychoanalytic lectures. The lectures were considered part of the treatment to be received by patients of his Baden-Baden 'Satanarium'. Groddeck is explicit on the status of his pronouncements in the fourteenth lecture, where we read:

> These lectures are not being delivered for reasons of education or culture. They are part of my treatment, which is why it is necessary for listeners to believe them . . . . You must make an effort to believe, you must try to silence all doubts in yourselves. It makes no sense to refute what I say through reasonable arguments. It is easy to find this or that wrong, but this is not the point of the exercise. You have come here to be helped. What I deliver is a remedy, a medication.
>
> (Groddeck 1978a: 134)

Regardless of their content, the administration of lectures as a form of therapy is certainly not in line with a psychoanalytic standpoint. Groddeck used psychoanalysis *in* (not as) a therapeutic practice more than he elaborated a psychoanalytic theory about organic disease. It is therefore incorrect to reconstruct his position from notions extrapolated from their very specific context of enunciation, and thereby misunderstood as theoretical and explanatory.

Not surprisingly, the issue of locating himself in relation to the broader scientific community seems to have been a constant preoccupation for Groddeck. Appearing for the first time before a congress of the Psychoanalytic Association at The Hague in 1920, Groddeck introduced himself as a 'wild analyst'. The reception of his work among psychoanalysts has frequently employed the terms of this self-definition to produce a tame, codifiable trace of his endeavour. Fédida, for example, writes that 'only a true psychoanalyst can proclaim himself through the liminal proposition: I am a wild analyst' (Fédida 1969: 926). It thus appears easy for psychoanalysis to reappropriate Groddeck's work. It is not equally easy, however, to accommodate it in the contentious discourse of psychosomatics. In the ongoing struggle to define legitimate boundaries for this field of knowledge places have been assigned, roles ascribed, choices prospected. Groddeck's name is unanimously invoked, with those of Deutsch, Jelliffe and others, as that of a man full of wise but imprecise intuitions. His 'psychoanalytic' propositions on organic disease have been treated as a theoretical position beside others, whose validity and consistency are similarly open to scrutiny from a methodological and epistemological viewpoint. Accordingly Groddeck – who 'did not differentiate between organic and psychological disorders, nor between health and illness' (Taylor 1987: 28) – has more than anyone else come to represent the paradigmatic instance of the excesses of psychosomatics as a pseudo-scientific enterprise. Freud anticipated this in his reply to the first letter Groddeck addressed to him (Groddeck 1977a [1917], letter 5 June 1917). He warned that the omnipotence and omnipresence Groddeck ascribed to the unconscious, obliterating the difference between the psychic and the somatic, would seal his enterprise as belonging to the realm of mysticism and philosophy, as indeed has happened. More than one commentator has remarked how the reception of his written works was tainted by ambiguity since the very beginning. The early translations of his books into English were carefully labelled with editorial warnings and solemn introductory notes sounding almost as apologies for introducing Groddeck to the US public. A passage from an editorial preface to one of Groddeck's books written in 1932 may serve as an illustration of this general attitude: 'It cannot be denied', wrote the editor,

> that there are many psychoanalysts who believe that Dr Groddeck . . . opened new and productive fields for psychoanalysis with his fearless interpretations and fantastic connections – but he overemphasized the importance of the Unconscious in regard to the organically sick. He endangered the carefully earned esteem of psychoanalysts with his carefree behaviour, and often even enjoyed provocating. Such considerations, however, . . . are not a reason to deny publication to an author who so often has the most surprising things to say and who is so stimulating. The psychoanalytic movement does not constitute a sect in which each member is liable for every other member.
>
> (Storfer, in Tytell 1980: 93)

For most contemporary writers in psychosomatics the interest in reading Groddeck is therefore essentially historical, in order to reconstitute a past from which to take distance, or even, in a sense, pre-historical, belonging to the order of myth. Groddeck is the figure of an impossibly innocent psychosomatics, of psychosomatics prior to encountering the rigours of scientificity and happily oblivious to them. Reading and re-reading Groddeck has been recommended as an antidote to intellectualism, rationalism, sterile verbalization and shallowness, to be safely indulged once psychoanalysis has finally grown out of the danger of mysticism.

If Groddeck's writings can be valued as anything other than a bizarre relic from the early history of psychosomatics, it is only through the rare acknowledgement that he should not be read as the initiator of a new theory. In other words, we should not start reading from the assumption that Groddeck's propositions are valid or invalid in the same sense as scientific ones are; Groddeck spoke neither as a physician, nor as a psychiatrist, nor as a psychoanalyst, but first and foremost as a 'healer' (Dejours 1980: 52; see also Pontalis 1977). More than as the precursor of contemporary psychosomatic theories, it is probably less erroneous to regard Groddeck as the precursor of what has been termed *psychanalittérature* (Tytell 1980). This term refers to a way of writing psychoanalytical works in the form of fiction; a mode that seeks effectiveness through textuality more than through theory-building, which was developed in France in the wake of the 'return to Freud' promoted by Jacques Lacan. 'Effectiveness' is the key word here. Thus, it is possible to retrieve the value of what Groddeck was doing from the strictures of science-historical narrative, and therefore to reappraise his efforts to establish a 'wild' space from which to speak to the scientific community. Groddeck's many propositions on the intentional and symbolic character of illness – on illness as an expiation for the thought of being a criminal, as a form of protection, as a hiding place, as a form of creativity – should be read as forms of provocation. Literally, they are means deployed to produce an effect, in the patient over and above anywhere else. If we reconsider his writings as functions of a therapeutic practice, rather than as theoretical efforts, they acquire a completely different relevance. This relevance, however, will become fully apparent only once we have come full circle in the description of psychosomatics as a system of dispersion.

It is time to conclude this outline of the discursive position which draws on an extension of the hysterical model of conversion. Its importance lies not in what it offers as a solution to the question of psychosomatics, but in how it contributes, as a logical precedent, to the structuring of problems. The second 'paradigmatic' option in the majoritarian tendency of psychosomatics starts precisely by rejecting the assimilation of physical illness to the model of hysteria, drawing instead on the distinction between actual and psychoneuroses as a theoretical tool. As we have seen, underlying both options is a question of determining whether and to what extent illness can be interpreted in a symbolic sense for the purpose of establishing its aetiology. The attribution of a fullness of psychic content to all types of symptoms was an overt violation of the clear limits set by Freud. Accordingly, 'conversion' theories are described by those who do not endorse them as instances of psychogenetic reductionism (Levin and Solomon 1990; Lipowski 1986; Todarello and Porcelli 1992), or at best as yielding meta-biological speculations (Brede 1972). The immediate alternative to this predicament lies in taking actual neuroses, as opposed to hysteria (the classic 'psychoneurosis'), as the 'psychoanalytic' model to acknowledge the body in its objectivity.

The opening towards psychophysiology

It is almost a literary convention to attribute to Franz Alexander the foundation of psychosomatic medicine as a systematic field of inquiry. In one way this attribution is appropriate, if we consider that his hypotheses represent the first adaptation of psychoanalytic approaches to physical illness to the criteria of dominant therapeutic institutions. A German emigré to the USA, Alexander founded the Chicago Institute for Psychoanalysis in 1932; it was the first institute to be devoted to psychosomatic research in America. A standard story seems to have crystallized around the figures of Alexander and Flanders Dunbar in the same way as it has crystallized around Groddeck and Deutsch. Dunbar also initiated a large-scale project of psychosomatic investigation in 1932 at the Columbia–Presbyterian Hospital in New York, and continued to work on the correlation between organic disease and personality types until the late 1940s (Dunbar 1935, 1947, 1959). Dunbar and Alexander are equally credited with having offered the first 'specificity theories' of psychosomatic illness, linking personological or personality types to specific diseases. But Alexander's work allegedly supplanted Dunbar's by replacing her superficial analyses – which focused on the observable aspects of behaviour and conscious memory of the past – with aetiological accounts that were able to explain the psychodynamic origin of the personality traits Dunbar had merely described (Grinker and Robbins 1953; Weiner 1977, 1982a, 1982b). This standard story has been recently contested by historian Robert Powell, who shows that the retrospective reading of Dunbar through Alexander, whose work found a more fertile terrain, obscures the extent to which Dunbar's correlational hypotheses do not amount to a 'specificity theory', and were never intended to be aetiological (Powell 1977; also Taylor 1987). Powell is probably right in maintaining that Dunbar's work is currently misrepresented and that it should be reappraised in the context of a little known form of US psychoanalysis. Yet, it is significant that Alexander's did find a more fertile terrain, such as to make him the best-known psychosomatic theoretician of the 1930s and 1940s.

With respect both to Dunbar's approach and to the model of hysterical conversion, Alexander's position appears like an ingenious way of retrieving the possibility of a psychoanalytic explanation 'in-depth', without incurring the danger of suspending or ignoring the physiological laws that govern the body in its materiality. Following how Freud had distinguished the actual neuroses from psychoneuroses, Alexander assimilated psychosomatic illnesses to actual neuroses under the label 'vegetative neuroses' (Alexander 1943, 1950). He regarded these conditions as a non-symbolic consequence of 'chronic emotional states'. Accordingly, he proposed that a 'psychological microscope' be added to the optical microscope of physiology, to consider underlying psychological conflicts as discrete pathogenic agents that interfere with physiological processes (Alexander 1950: 37; see also Todarello and Porcelli 1992; Brede 1972). Increased blood pressure or sugar levels do not retrieve economic balance psychodynamically – in the sense that they do not appear *in the place of* affect. Rather, they constitute the physiological components of the global phenomenon we call anger. The chronicity of any specific emotional pattern is what renders the condition pathological even to the point of generating a lesion, as when stomach hyperacidity culminates in an ulcer. Vegetative neuroses should therefore be considered as the physiological reaction on the part of vegetative organs to affect understood as pure force, affect prior to undergoing its properly psychical 'vicissitudes' of meaning. As for the meaning of the term 'psychic' itself, this is effectively reduced to stable specific complexes that give rise to behavioural solutions typical of each. 'Psychic' here refers to the emotional concomitants implied by those behavioural solutions. For instance, the conflict between an infantile dependency need and the super-egoic protest to it gives rise to the perpetual containment of aggressive and self-assertive impulses, which in turn will cause hypertension. Alexander's 'conflict specificity' hypotheses correlated a number of more specific psychic conflicts with the fact of being chronically subject to specific emotional patterns, and therefore predisposed towards specific diseases. Extensive tests argued for the diagnostic validity of these hypotheses, showing that the presence of a given condition could be predicted in a large number of cases on the basis of psychological data alone (Alexander *et al.* 1968).

Two general points are worth making in relation to the implications of Alexander's work. The first concerns the fact that the norms of health and pathology in his account remain fixed by physiology. Unlike the hysterical conversion model, where the illness itself represents a solution the patient has found and therefore represents a value, Alexander's model maintains a linear correlation between psychic and somatic suffering, both envisaged as simply and equally negative. The 'choice' of illness here does not refer to the possibility of alternating between psychic or somatic suffering, a possibility that entails a form of critical reflection on the social context that makes such a choice possible in principle. On the contrary, the 'choice' of illness for Alexander refers merely to the specific organ that is automatically (vegetatively) linked to a specific emotional pattern. The second point concerns the long-term consequences of the apparent shortcut Alexander provided with respect to the possibility of correlating 'psychoanalytic' explanations to the workings of physiology. If Alexander is invoked as the sole most prominent psychosomatic theoretician of the 1930s and 1940s, it is perhaps because he opened the project of psychosomatics to correction on the part of psychophysiologists. He thus initiated a form of dialogue that was only a pseudo-dialogue, to the extent that his 'psychoanalytic' hypotheses were only pseudo-psychoanalytic. Let us see how.

The notion of 'multifactoral aetiology' is often invoked to disclaim psychogenetic hypotheses, and thereby the contention that psychosomatic illnesses constitute an aetiologically specific subgroup of pathology. On this basis it is not unusual for Alexander to be dismissed as the representative of a psychogenetic orientation, since he proposed a theory of conflict-specificity applicable to a subset of medical conditions (e.g. Lipowski 1986). It is not often acknowledged that Alexander believed in a multifactoral model of disease – not a psychogenetic one – and considered the specific conflicts he had identified as only an element in the global development of certain pathologies (Taylor 1987). In Alexander's model the notion of multifactoral aetiology is not incompatible with the idea that 'psychosomatic disorders' exist as a distinct pathological subgroup. On the contrary, this model supposes that specific psychological factors can be identified as necessary and not sufficient causes in the development of certain diseases, but presumably not of others. In other words, Alexander was explicitly concerned to acknowledge a multifactoral aetiology for the subgroup of conditions he had studied, but not equally to suggest the application of a psychosomatic viewpoint to the field of pathology as a whole. This position can be regarded as a specific epistemological effect of how Alexander transposed concepts from psychoanalysis to general medicine. Within Freudian doctrine, as we have seen, actual neuroses figure indeed as a specific subgroup: they are specific, however, only in relation to the domain of psychopathology. They are specific precisely on account of the fact that despite their psychic appearance they belong aetiologically to the sphere of somatic medicine, or psychophysiology. As far as Freud's model is concerned, actual neuroses are entirely theoretically aspecific from the viewpoint of somatic pathology. Using the model of actual neuroses as the missing link between the psychic and the somatic, Alexander applied it to organic conditions of unknown aetiology with a reversal of emphasis. Psychosomatic disorders were in his view a specific subgroup with respect to somatic pathology, but now on account of the fact that despite their somatic appearance they belonged aetiologically to psychoanalysis, due to the necessary (albeit insufficient) presence of a psychic causal factor. What is most often overlooked, in this passage from psychoanalysis to general medicine, is precisely this reversal of emphasis. What figures as 'psychic' in Alexander's model is exactly what Freud had identified as 'somatic'.

When Alexander used the term 'specificity' in his work, this term referred to the distinctiveness of conflicts he believed to underlie specific pathological conditions, within the restricted group of diseases he deemed pertinent to the attention of psychoanalysis. Yet, from a Freudian viewpoint, both their ascription to the domain of psychoanalysis and their specificity with respect to somatic pathology appear unjustified. Alexander therefore left a double legacy through his use of the notion of specificity. On the one hand, he advocated psychoanalysis on the basis of regarding it especially relevant to a specific subgroup of organic conditions, in overt contradiction of Freud's views on the matter. On the other hand, he articulated 'psychoanalytic' explanations on the basis of evidence of a specific link between certain conflicts (associated with definite emotions) and certain diseases: a specific link that was open to scrutiny and correction on the part of psychophysiology. We can see how this configuration, while superficially initiating unprecedented opportunities for dialogue between general medicine and psychoanalysis, would eventually backfire on psychoanalysis itself. Alexander had grossly reduced the concept of the 'psychic' in a way that amounted to a despecification of the term with respect to Freud's use. But, viewed from the perspective of general medicine, this constituted a *bona fide* application of psychodynamic hypotheses to the domain of physiology. Even better, these 'psychodynamic' hypotheses were testable on the part of rapidly growing research on the concept of stress, which was then fast developing in the wake of Hans Selye's work. The refutation of Alexander's specificity theory appeared as a refutation of the specific pertinence of psychoanalysis to psychosomatics. This predicament was reinforced by the persisting allegation, also promoted by Alexander's work, that psychoanalysis invites a restrictive application of the term 'psychosomatic' to a subgroup of aetiologically uncertain conditions, suggesting a dichotomy of psychosomatic versus non-psychosomatic diseases (see e.g. Levin and Solomon 1990; Lipowski 1986). Although psychoanalysis would still continue to be used in connection with psychosomatics in the USA, this would only be in a more limited sense: as one among many different psycho-sociological tools used to identify concomitant factors leading to physical illness; and as a therapeutic option when others prove to be ineffective (Lipowski 1986).

There is therefore a certain continuity between Alexander's 'psychoanalytic' propositions and the development of psychosomatics in the direction of investigating life-events and other stressful factors that allegedly predispose people towards physical disease in general. The posited link between chronic emotional states and a predisposition towards certain diseases could easily bypass a psychoanalytic explanation and be described instead as the function of individually specific styles of response to stress, determined by heredity or otherwise (e.g. Lacey *et al*. 1953; Kaplan and Kaplan 1967; Wolff 1950). Such descriptions might include individuals' conscious attitudes (or cognitive styles) in relation to external events (e.g. Grace and Graham 1952). In connection with events perceived as stressful, individuals would be said to respond characteristically with a 'gastric' or a 'muscular' or a 'cardiovascular' reaction that could respectively develop into an ulcer, a migraine or palpitations. This implies regarding the specific symptom as entirely devoid of any psychic content or motivational value, figuring instead as an automatic byproduct of cognitive or behavioural style. These propositions, developed independently of any reference to psychoanalysis, remain congruent with Alexander's emphasis on the non-symbolic, non-interpretable character of the symptom, which had in fact rendered his own hypotheses quite remote from psychoanalysis itself. In this manner, the question of interpretation was expunged from the problematic of psychosomatics in favour of ascertaining pathogenic factors in the form of stressful events coupled with responses to them. This approach also had the clear advantage of being liable to large-scale epidemiological investigations (Todarello and Porcelli 1992).

It is at this point, however, that the tension structuring the field of psychosomatics makes itself felt again and becomes productive. Epidemiological studies investigating the correlation between stressful life events and disease, as in the various applications of the 'Social Readjustment Rating Scale' (Holmes and Rahe 1967), were soon criticized for disregarding the fact that the relation between life events and illness is not a simple linear one, as Hinkle had already noted at an early stage (Hinkle 1961; see also Cohen 1983; Holroyd and Lazarus 1982; Rabkin and Struening 1976). The epidemiological method found its limit in discovering that psychosocial events are not equally 'stressful' for everyone in the same way, and it is impossible to reliably predict, for the vast majority of them, how they would be interpreted by any one individual. The question of interpretation, expunged from one end of the psychosomatic spectrum, reproposed itself at the other end. How else to define the stressful quality of experience but as a function of the subject who interprets that experience? The focus on an individual function of interpretation as a pathogenic variable constitutes at once a displacement and a reinstatement of the role of symbolic elaboration. Whether or not the somatic symptom can be regarded as symbolically significant becomes a secondary question. The primary question is whether and how 'symbolic elaboration' enters the more general economy of interpretation that informs different subjective responses. In this way, the non-interpretability of the somatic symptom is restored to a form of ambiguity, an opaqueness that does not, in and of itself, exhaust the meaning of illness. This opaqueness calls again for interpretation at a different level of abstraction. The problem is not how to identify a positive psychic content of the symptom, but rather to understand whether the very lack of such a psychic content may be itself significant, a signifier in its own right.

The role of a subject who interprets

In their studies on the particular type of stress represented by events of loss, evidencing strong correlations between these and the onset of illness, a group of psychoanalytically trained internists based in Rochester hypothesized a concomitant psychobiological state which they named 'giving-up/given-up complex' (Engel 1968; Engel and Schmale 1967; for a review, see Taylor 1987). This complex describes a psychological adaptive failure corresponding to a transitional state of the self, during which adequate defensive strategies to face the loss of an object are not available or not yet developed. Subsequent studies provided elements to suggest that a reciprocal relationship may exist between the effectiveness of ego-defences and the level of activation of hormonal systems connected with stress as well as with immunological functions (see Taylor 1987). Engel and Schmale's work can be read as a 'hinge' between the 'majoritarian' and the 'minoritarian' tendencies of psychosomatics. Their earliest studies evidenced that the fact of perceiving an event as a loss was more important than whether or not the loss had actually occurred. Real losses such as divorce or death, in other words, were not more liable to predispose an individual towards physical illness than were possible losses (e.g. a negative change in the behaviour of a significant other) or symbolic ones (e.g. menstruation, poor academic results, or a friend forgetting a significant date) (Schmale 1958). The fact that Engel and Schmale's concept of object-loss is falsely simple, as Taylor notes (1987), may be read as an effect of the broader context within which they worked. This context was preoccupied chiefly with establishing positive correlations between psychic and somatic states. Engel and Schmale's work made room for the idea that a subjective function of interpretation is at work in producing susceptibility towards illness. But this aspect remained outside the focus of attention and served merely to reinforce the notion that loss, even the loss of a symbolic object, has an impact in the pathogenetic process. Accordingly, Engel and Schmale treated 'objects' as discrete entities, regardless of whether they are symbolic or real. Objects themselves appeared to constitute the significant variable in terms of their presence or absence. They did not elaborate much further on how objects themselves acquire their status as significant objects for a subject.

These developments highlight the point at which the pendulum starts to swing back, from an 'energetics' that regards disease under the aspect of relations of force (the impact of stressful factors and events on the individual), to a 'hermeneutics' that regards disease under the aspect of relations of meaning. What charges the loss of an object with its force, the source for its capacity to have an impact on the individual, is not its objectively quantifiable quality of presence. On the contrary, it is the meaning which constitutes it as an object for a subject in the first place. This does not mean that the symbolic significance of objects or events therefore constitutes the more fundamental variable, leading to an indifference as to whether the loss refers to a 'real' object or to a 'symbolic' one. What it means, more precisely, is something else. If different types of object can function as vectors of significance, there are different ways in which the 'real' is real for different individuals. There are different ways of establishing relationships of interdependence with the environment, such that different things are capable of producing a real effect, a reality-effect, on different individuals.

Psychiatrist Graeme Taylor has proposed that the necessary role of psychoanalysis to the problematic of psychosomatics can once again be appreciated in the light of concepts developed in the context of systems-theory. Systems-theoretical perspectives on the question of homeostatic regulation have expanded on the early propositions of Claude Bernard (1878) and Walter Cannon (1932). On this basis they have argued that the composition of what Bernard called *milieu intérieur* is partly determined by processes of regulation at the level of cells and cell subsystems, but also that the social matrix of an individual can have a role in the maintenance of physiological homeostasis (Taylor 1987; see Schwartz 1979, 1981). What this suggests is that the distinction between the *milieu intérieur* and the *milieu extérieur* is not as clear-cut as was previously supposed. One aspect of this idea is particularly relevant in Taylor's view. This is the notion that the homeostatic regulation of the newborn infant is partly delegated to processes that occur in the interactive relationship between the infant and its mother, as argued by Hofer (1983) among others. Taylor proposes that this has opened the way for thinking of all object relations as exchanges of interpersonal regulatory processes that complete the self-regulatory processes of the individual. However, the mother–infant relationship remains crucial, for defining the initial possibility of a gradual passage from regulatory processes that are entirely interactive to the acquisition of a self-regulatory capacity that is primarily 'psychological' (Taylor 1987; see Hofer 1978; Peters 1971). The term 'psychological' here is restored to the complexity of a psychoanalytic meaning. It refers to the notion that self-regulatory processes depend on the development of a mental organization capable of symbolization. Thanks to the ability to form symbols, internal representations may perform regulatory functions previously delegated to an external agent. Such functions, in turn, account for a greater, albeit never complete, autonomy of the individual from environmental factors (including social relationships and environmental feedback).

The distinction between interactive regulatory processes and greater autonomy, or self-regulatory processes, is therefore parallel to the distinction between actual and symbolic forms of dependence. Symbolic forms of dependence afford greater flexibility and therefore greater autonomy. This is because the 'symbol' always retains a certain amount of ambiguity, which prevents it from ever being entirely assimilated or confused with what it appears (Dejours 1986). From a systems-theoretical perspective, the greater susceptibility towards disease in general is traced to deficits in the capacity for self-regulation. Certain individuals are said not to have reached an appropriate level of self-regulation and continue to rely 'excessively' on other persons (or other objects) in order to maintain their psychobiological balance (Hofer 1984; Weiner 1982a, 1982b). Psychoanalysis again appears relevant to the problem of psychosomatics to the extent that it attempts to qualify the sense in which certain forms of dependence are 'excessive'. It does so by addressing the role performed by a 'function of symbolization' in defining the quality of relations between self and others. As a preliminary and somewhat simplified illustration of this point, we may return to the example of object loss. In Engel and Schmale's approach, as I have described it, the characterization of 'real' or 'symbolic' applies to objects themselves, as categories of the observer. These terms do not refer to the mode of relation the subject establishes with objects, and therefore to the function objects are called upon to perform, regardless of whether they are symbolic or real from the observer's point of view. From a systems-theoretical perspective, the relation between subject and object appears primary with respect to the terms it relates. From this perspective, it is possible to imagine how an actual (or 'literal') dependence on a symbolic object may render the subject more vulnerable to its loss than the symbolic dependence on an actual object. The role of symbolization is thus contextualized in a more complex framework. It is not simply a question of acknowledging that relevant objects are not identifiable as such from the outside, because this relevance could stem from their 'symbolic' value for the subject, which the observer cannot objectively predict. The difference between the subject's point of view and the observer's exists indeed; but it cannot be conceived as completely incommensurable, or it would be impossible, at any one point in the research process, to define concepts like 'vulnerability' or even 'disease' itself. If these concepts are defined and used, then the 'symbolic' character of the object must have a meaning in the context of the observer as well. What is this meaning? The 'excessive', or pathological significance of a symbolic object signifies something quite different from an activity of symbolization. On the contrary, it signifies a deficit in such an activity. A deficit whereby the individual, understood as a complex psychobiological system, is unable to acknowledge symbols as such and instead relates to them in a mode that is of the order of the literal or the actual. From this perspective, there is room to account for the reason why 'not all people manifest a giving up/given up complex in response to object loss' (Taylor 1987: 62), or why some individuals 'can be traumatized by a yes or a no, while others can defend themselves with an effectiveness that is worthy of admiration' (Dejours 1986: 58).

Conclusion: a reversal

The propositions I have just reviewed recast the problematic of psychosomatics with respect to the majoritarian tendency with which we began. 'Majoritarian' statements attempt to address, in various ways, the 'mysterious leap from the mind to the body' (Deutsch 1959). In this attempt they simultaneously find their purpose and their limit. In what I call the 'minoritarian' tendency of psychosomatics, the focus of attention appears inverted. What is addressed is 'an equally mysterious leap in the reverse direction' (Taylor 1987: 117). The question is how to account for the fact that 'stressful events' can be experienced in the order of the mental or of the somatic, giving rise to different forms of coping which may be differently successful. The fundamental assumption regards an initial stage of somatopsychic undifferentiation, out of which different qualities of mental functioning, and thereby of relation between 'body' and 'mind', may develop. Thus the terms 'body' and 'mind' are no longer at the start of psychosomatic inquiry, but constitute rather what needs to be explained, explored, redefined. Winnicott's words exemplify this reversal:

> How easy it is to take for granted the lodgement of the psyche in the body and to forget that this again is an achievement. It is an achievement which by no means falls to the lot of all.
>
> (Winnicott 1988: 122)

And similarly,

> [I]n psycho-somatics one cannot assume a close association between the psyche and the soma; psycho-somatics must take into account the

> states both common and important in which the relationship between psyche and soma is loosened or lost.
>
> (ibid.: 27)

'Body' and 'mind' had previously described sources, or stable points of origin. They were the source of different perspectives of knowledge, or the source of different kinds of symptoms. In the 'minoritarian' tendency of psychosomatics, 'body' and 'mind' describe not origins but points of arrival, 'achievements'. There are many possible ways of achieving a 'body', which equally involve many ways of achieving a 'mind'. As the referents for these terms multiply, the question becomes how to identify typical forms of pairing between them: What forms of the 'body' can be related to what forms of the 'mind'? From this perspective, explaining the choice of a specific somatic disease is no longer a theoretical priority. The difference between forms of somatic pathology appears secondary with respect to the fact that they are all 'somatic', that they all call into action the same order of bodily experience. As such, it is argued that they are rooted in a single general structure of mental functioning, a single way of establishing one's mode of existence in the inter-subjective environment. The next chapter explores these themes in greater detail. It will begin to show how the relations of kinship between the concepts of illness and madness, discussed earlier in this book, come to resurface in a discourse relating to embodied subjectivity.

7

INTERPRETING THE SIGNS OF EMBODIMENT

In psychoanalysis, independently of psychosomatics, the need to develop a theory about primitive mental functioning and about the earliest mechanisms giving rise to a sense of self arose from the engagement with schizophrenic patients and patients suffering from 'narcissistic' and 'borderline' disorders. Psychoanalytic treatment had been traditionally considered inadequate for these patients due to the fact that they appeared unable to establish a classical transference neurosis. Thus psychotic patients resembled 'psychosomatic' ones, to the extent that somatic symptoms were also acknowledged as not amenable to analytic interpretation. For this reason, research developed in relation to psychosis appeared particularly significant in relation to psychosomatics (Taylor 1987; Todarello and Porcelli 1992). This research had supposed that a 'psychic deficit' could be related to the predisposition of certain individuals towards psychosis. Tracing such a psychic deficit involved a shift of attention to phases prior to those of psychosexual development described in detail by Freud. As Mahler, Pine and Bergman wrote in 1975, drawing from their research on symbiotic child psychosis,

> The biological birth of the human infant and the psychological birth of the individual are not coincident in time . . . . We refer to the psychological birth of the individual as the *separation–individuation process*: the establishment of a sense of separateness from, and relation to, a world of reality, particularly with regard to the experience of *one's own body* and to the principal representative of the world as the infant experiences it, the *primary love object* . . . . Like any intrapsychic process, this one reverberates throughout the life cycle. It is never finished; it remains always active . . . . But the principal psychological achievements of this process take place in the period from the fourth or fifth month to the thirtieth or thirty-sixth month, a period we refer to as the *separation–individuation phase*.
>
> (Mahler, Pine and Bergman 1975: 3)

Mahler, Pine and Bergman highlight that the Freudian notion of what makes the psychological 'properly' psychological – the evidence of a process of symbolic elaboration – is only one among several different possible outcomes of a more fundamental process of development of mental functions. Such a process, in their view, may or may not yield the normal capacity for symbolization that Freud identified as 'psychic life'. In some instances of psychosomatics, the acquisition of such a capacity is believed to determine the possibility for 'a firm sense of identity' as well as 'the capacity for developing intimate nonsymbiotic object relationships' (Taylor 1987: 232). These, in turn, are supposed to affect the organismic capacity for self-regulation.

In what follows I survey only the broadest lines of this argument; I shall draw on the work of some of its best known representatives, disregarding more specific terminological and conceptual differences between them. My overall purpose is to illustrate how the question of psychosomatics shifts from the 'truth' of the bodily symptom to a 'truth' concerning the modes of subjective embodiment. This will lead me to discuss in greater detail the work of Christophe Dejours. In a recent book, Dejours has argued with unusual subtlety and precision for the complementarity of psychoanalysis and contemporary biology. He also argues, however, that the Freudian framework is inadequate to make this complementarity explicit, and therefore proposes what he calls a 'third topography' to account for somatic illness in psychoanalytic terms. Dejours' topography maps three different forms of embodied subjectivity, and describes their relations of mutual implication and exclusion. It is a blueprint that connects all the different terms of psychosomatics as a form of problematization. It will enable us to come full circle in the description of this problematic, in order to examine what this discourse produces as the 'truth' of the subject who falls somatically ill.

The ontogenesis of distinctions

An important relation is therefore posited between the formation of a 'sense of identity' and the conditions leading to a greater autonomy from the perspective of 'psychobiological regulation'. The two expressions between inverted commas already point to what we recognize as 'mind' and 'body'. But in order to see how they may be related, it is suggested that we must turn to a phase in human life before that distinction is made and is operative. We must turn, in other words, to 'the observable and inferred beginnings of the infant's primitive cognitive-affective state' (Mahler, Pine and Bergman 1975: 4). In the newborn infant these beginnings allegedly correspond to an original 'fusional' phase characterized by unawareness of self–other differentiation and by somatopsychic undifferentiation. The infant lives through a symbiotic relationship with the agent of maternal care, most often simply and controversially referred to as 'the mother' (see Chodorow 1978, 1989; King 1994; Parker 1994). This relationship constitutes the two as a single system (Mahler 1968). The infant is non-distinct from the mother both from a 'psychological' and from a 'biological' point of view. It is even improper to employ such terms, since the two perspectives only arise from that initial relationship and do not exist as such beforehand. To begin with, there is only a total 'Me', a being that perceives the whole of reality as itself and itself as the whole of reality, a being unable to distinguish between inside and outside, or between physical sensations and mental representations (Winnicott 1988).This being inhabits a world of bodily experiences, where the 'mental' (or the protomental) is the direct expression of the somatic and especially of somatic anxiety about bodily fragmentation. Eugenio Gaddini (1982) illustrates this point through the conceptual distinction between fantasies in the body and fantasies on the body. Fantasies 'on the body' imply that a separation has already occurred between the psychic sphere (as the subject producing and elaborating fantasies) and the somatic sphere (as the object of fantasies). To illustrate the point we may consider the psychic mechanisms of 'introjection' and 'projection'. At the stage of 'fantasies in the body', introjection and projection coincide perfectly with physiological processes of incorporation and excretion. In the course of development these mechanisms acquire an increasingly 'mental' character, initially paralleling somatic experiences, but normally coming gradually to operate in ways that are autonomous from these (Todarello and Porcelli 1992).

Bion (1962) proposed that in the original fusional phase the mother functions as the 'thinking apparatus of the infant'. The child 'delivers' primitive sensations and senseless perceptions which generate tension – what Bion called *beta* elements – to the mother. Through her own mental (or *alpha*) functions, she receives and transforms these elements ('alpha-betizes' them) into material that can be mentally elaborated further (Grotstein 1980: 503). The response the infant receives from the agent of care is therefore a mentally mediated response, a response that contains and transmits the codification of experiences into 'internal' and 'external', 'safe' or 'dangerous', 'relevant' or 'irrelevant' (Grotstein 1980). Through the constant interaction with its mother and identification with her, the infant gradually acquires its own mental functions, or what we call 'mind'. Thanks to these, it can autonomously deal with unpleasant bodily sensations, by recreating the absent soothing object into a present, albeit imaginary one. The process of separation–individuation of the infant from its mother entails therefore a passage from a fusional self–object unity to 'self' and 'object' as discrete terms of a relation. This, on the one hand, is described as the condition of possibility for a stable sense of individual identity. On the other hand, it is described as the condition of possibility for the differentiation of the psychic from the somatic. An autonomous 'self' proceeds from the successful mentalization of bodily experiences. An autonomous 'self', in turn, has the capacity to process experience mentally and therefore to deflect this process to a large extent from physiology (Todarello and Porcelli 1992). The 'psychic' and the 'somatic' thus understood are *both* involved in the management of bodily existence.

The gradual process of differentiation is described as 'healthy' if it results in a progressive integration of the functions of psyche and soma, where each side is able to take charge of the aspects it is most suited to deal with. The 'correct' physiological functions are stabilized through the 'correct' development of mental functions, a development that enables the two to work independently and not to interfere with each other. Conversely, the process is described as 'pathological' if it results in a poor form of integration and the mental works out of synchrony, excessively or insufficiently, with respect to the somatic (Winnicott 1965, 1988). In producing more or less healthy outcomes, the quality of mental functions that the infant first meets with, and through which his or her experience is codified and differentiated, are logically crucial. Winnicott is most well known for having underlined the importance of the quality of maternal care in producing the success of the separation–individuation process, and therefore a type of mental functioning capable of ensuring a good level of integration (Winnicott 1965). A 'good enough' mother (as opposed to the perfect mother represented by the womb) is physically and emotionally available, but not only. She must also herself be autonomous enough to generate and tolerate episodes of frustration of the child's needs, episodes that facilitate attention on the separateness of the 'self' from the 'object'. The environment created by the mother is healthy, for Winnicott, to the extent that it allows for the development of the child's imagination and of its identification with her feelings, both of which are necessary to promote mental activity and functions of symbolization. Thanks to these functions, her physical absence (the 'actual' frustration of needs) can be compensated by an interiorized mental presence. This also means that the infant becomes capable of delegating to psychological functions certain aspects of biological regulation.

On account of this reciprocity, any deficits in the formation of the boundaries of the 'self' are also deficits in the capacity to manage crises mentally, as opposed to somatically. In a general sense, this is reminiscent of the discussion of 'somatization' undertaken in chapter three, through the work of Georges Canguilhem (1989). Canguilhem's thought also enables us to imagine how a deficit in the ability to distinguish between self and other (or between the vital and the social, in that case) may produce the possibility for a 'subversion' of the logic of the living organism. In the absence of such boundaries, so to speak, the living subject cannot distinguish its own teleology from the teleology of what is other with respect to itself. It cannot distinguish between activities that ultimately promote its life and those that may ultimately destroy it. We can return to Mahler, Pine and Bergman to restate this point in this different context:

> From the beginning the child molds and unfolds in the matrix of the mother–infant dual unit. Whatever adaptations the mother may make to the child, and whether she is sensitive and empathic or not, it

> is our strong conviction that the child's fresh and pliable adaptive capacity, and his need for adaptation (in order to gain satisfaction), is far greater than that of the mother, whose personality, with all its patterns of character and defense, is firmly and often rigidly set (Mahler 1963). The infant takes shape in harmony and counterpoint to the mother's ways and style – *whether she herself provides a healthy or a pathological object for such adaptation*.
>
> (Mahler, Pine and Bergman 1975: 5, added emphasis)

If the mother is not a 'healthy' referent for adaptation, one possible outcome is that the progressive mentalization of bodily experiences is perturbed, and with it also the possibility on the part of the child to retain a clear sense of self in the absence of the mother. As a consequence, the possibility of an economy that is 'inverted' with respect to the developmental pattern may be set in place. In such an inverted economy, the soma may take over functions of identity-formation and maintenance that would normally be delegated to mental functions, functions which develop later with respect to somatic ones. Somatic illness may thus occur in the place of the mechanisms through which the process of separation–individuation should occur. This substitution has been variously described by different authors, and usefully reviewed by Todarello and Porcelli (1992). For Gaddini (1980) illness may, for instance, take the place of a 'transitional object':

> the physical care of illness fills the space between mother and child: the symptom is an operation of massive denial of separation as a defence from primary disintegration anxiety.
>
> (Todarello and Porcelli 1992: 118)

In this case, illness and the transitional object perform the same function of rendering the mother present, but with a crucial difference. The transitional object does so through fantasy, by resting on a function of symbolization. Illness instead does so in the order of the real or the actual, since the function of symbolization is absent or defective. In another account (Ammon 1974), the lack of empathic responses on the part of the mother (which may originate in a problem related to her own sense of identity) is said to generate forms of hyper-accommodation to the demands of external reality on the part of the infant, which may persist into adult life. The individual then adapts to these demands even when they do not reflect or satisfy his or her own needs. This pathological adjustment reproduces, in the adult, the infant's fusional identification with the (unempathic) maternal object. The somatic symptom in this case is an integral part of the patient's identity:

> The question 'Who am I?', which is linked in the patient to an existential anxiety, is replaced by another question: 'What have I got?',

> for which an answer is incessantly sought. The quest for identity, in other words, is replaced by the quest for a symptom that functions as a surrogate of identity.
>
> (Ammon 1974: 96, in Todarello and Porcelli 1992: 121)

In yet another account (Sami-Ali 1987), the mother who is not in tune with the affective and bodily messages of the infant may impose stereotypical behavioural patterns that she derives from her sociocultural environment. Instead of considering the wish and need of the child, such a mother treats his or her body in accordance with 'what ought to be done'; in this way, what is interiorized by the child is not an empathic relation reflecting its own singularity, but rather the maternal super-ego, which 'takes root in the behavioural patterns of the [child's own] body, determining an attitude of wholesale repression of the subjective and of the imaginary' (Todarello and Porcelli 1992: 119). Illness, in this case, occurs in the place of the imaginary and of the subjective. In Canguilhem's terms, this may be described as a situation whereby 'social norms' are apprehended as, and confused with, 'vital norms'. Instead of being simple constraints, social norms come to function as determinisms: in what it calls for and what it follows, the organism does not behave as a being with a trajectory of its own. Instead, it automatically adjusts to the demands of external reality without internal negotiation or conflict. When this adjustment contradicts vital needs, the subjectivity of the organism becomes apparent as illness.

What is common to all these formulations is the shifting backwards, to a higher level of abstraction, of the problematic of psychosomatics. The pathological evidence presented in the body is ignored, but not in the sense that physical causality is denied its relevance in the specific event of disease. Such evidence is ignored because the problem of disease is addressed at a different level of generality. What is interrogated are the different possible structures of embodiment that may result from the original state of psychosomatic indistinction. Different structures of embodiment imply different capacities for apprehending, envisaging, and encountering 'reality' as what is other, what is different, or what is external to the subject. And these different ways of encountering the real are supposed to produce 'preferential' coping mechanisms that produce one type of illness instead of another. The alternatives in question, at this level of generality, are not between given forms of somatic pathology, but rather between the 'somatic' as opposed to the 'psychic', and more specifically, as I will discuss below, as opposed to the 'neurotic'. The structures of embodied subjectivity thus represent, in the discourse of psychosomatics, the fundamental contexts that relate more local and circumscribed theoretical possibilities. Examples of such possibilities are the symbolic interpretability of the symptom, at one end of the spectrum; at the opposite end, we have the psychophysiology of 'stress', as researched experimentally on laboratory animals. Both of these are valid constructs within narrowly defined conditions of applicability. The first is limited by the objectivity of the body; the second, by the subjectivity of 'stress' in ordinary contexts of human interaction. When and how can the bodily symptom be interpreted symbolically? When and how do certain situations qualify as 'stressful'? These apparently very distant questions find a common ground in the posited difference between structures of embodied subjectivity. This common ground substitutes the generic 'when' and 'how' with another question: 'for whom?'. The example of 'stress' serves as a useful introduction to this level of the problematic.

Stress in the human context: defining the subjective variable

Dejours (1986) explains that the traumatic character of an encounter with the environment is a discontinuous function with a quantitative (or economic) and a qualitative (or dynamic) variable. 'Trauma' denotes excitation or stress that is excessive, but *strictly in relation to the binding capacities of the subject's psychic apparatus* (Dejours 1986: 57). Let us consider the partitioning of these variables, the quantitative and the qualitative, in more detail. From a biological point of view, the constitution of the psychic apparatus, as Freud described it, corresponds to a functional integration of the central nervous system (at the levels of the diencephalon, of the limbic system and of the cortex). In its turn, the central nervous system taken as a whole is responsible for the regulation of organic behaviour. The Freudian 'psyche' and the 'soma' are both aspects of biological functioning, linked to different 'functional regimes' of integration between subsystems of the central nervous system itself (see also Grosz 1994). The psyche and the soma, however, are also both aspects of mental functioning, whose qualities are similarly linked to the 'functional regime' or mode of central nervous integration they represent:

> Mental functioning is *associated* to functional regimes of the central nervous system, and not to organs of that system. There is no localization of psychic functioning, but only variations within this functioning that evolve with the functional regimes of this pyramid of integration.
>
> (Dejours 1986: 106)

The forms of mental functioning described by Freud therefore appear as a subset of possibilities within a more general connotation of 'mental functioning' as such. This implies that the soma to be contrasted with the psyche is not the totality of biological determinations. Rather, only the mode of organic behaviour that corresponds to the first level of integration (the hypothalamic-pituitary level) should rightfully be contrasted with the psyche. This level of central nervous integration is the level that is responsible for the activation of archaic and automatic behaviours conveyed by hereditary sequences. Again, this mode of organic behaviour does not denote the absence of mental functioning, but rather a specific modality of it, different from what Freud had described in particular. This specific modality, like all others, represents a certain regime of management of the constant competition between the activation of automatic behaviours and their taming on the part of higher, ontogenetically acquired, forms of regulation:

> The fundamental point . . . is precisely this permanent competition, that never ceases throughout the course of one's entire existence, between the activation of archaic hypothalamo-limbic behaviours and their taming on the part of limbo-cortical regulations. This competition must be able to be deciphered at the level of psychic functioning. Psychic functioning, let us say it once more, is not the homologue of tele-encephalic functioning, but the homologue of the whole series of central integrations. If the Soma stands opposed to the Psyche, it remains to be specified what the Soma actually accounts for: is it the entirety of biological functioning? The conceptual opposition in fact only makes sense *in the order of behaviour*.
>
> (Dejours 1986: 149)

Under extreme conditions anyone is liable to experience trauma and to respond with stereotyped archaic reactions, such as the ones described by Selye in his work on the General Adaptation Syndrome (1946, 1950). Such reactions constitute an autonomization of the hypothalamic brain and of its visceral efferents and imply a movement of dehierarchization of the central nervous system. In this movement the structures developed in the course of ontogenesis to control the diencephalon (the limbic system and the cortex) are bypassed and rendered powerless with respect to the task of ensuring regulation. Under such conditions, the organism automatically responds to external events without the mediation of a reference to its past experience. As Dejours puts it, 'the rule of the economic expels the order of the dynamic' (ibid.: 57).

Selye's concept of stress was developed on the basis of animal experiments that reproduced such limit-situations, situations which would resemble torture in a human context. In such situations, the catastrophic reactions of the organism are in fact stereotyped, aspecific, and similar in all individuals. But as soon as different situations are examined that are less extreme with respect to posing a direct threat to physical survival, the concept of stress loses any objective value, to the extent that it is no longer clear what should be qualified as such. In less extreme situations of this kind, which comprise the vast majority of those encountered by human beings in day to day life, the dynamic variable becomes paramount in defining whether or not a certain encounter with reality is traumatic. The dynamic variable describes the functional regime ordinarily privileged by any one individual as a result of ontogenetic development. What does this mean in practice? Automatic anxiety and its somatic manifestations (in which we recognize what Freud grouped under the label of 'actual neuroses') may be activated at any time, for any individual, when extreme conditions are met. Alternatively, under ordinary conditions, they can be activated due to a structural deficit that signifies also a certain quality of the subject's mental functioning. On this basis, Dejours concludes that what Freud referred to as 'anxiety neurosis' (one of the actual neuroses) denotes, rather than a specific neurotic structure, an acute form of decompensation to which anyone is theoretically vulnerable. In practice, however, it is most frequently experienced by individuals who are characterized by a functional regime, or structure of mental functioning, that is deficient with respect to the mechanisms Freud identified as properly 'psychic'. To this structure of mental functioning Dejours assigns the name of *caractéropathe* (Dejours 1986: 60–2).

The structure of the *caractéropathe*, as I shall discuss at greater length below, is distinguished from the structure of mental functioning of neurotics, on the one hand, and of psychotics on the other. It is distinguished by its greater liability to respond somatically, with automatic anxiety, to encounters with the interpersonal environment that are perceived as destabilizing at a conscious or an unconscious level. It is also distinguished by a lessened capacity to restore a compensated balance in the aftermath of such an encounter. If somatic anxiety constitutes an acute crisis to which anyone is theoretically vulnerable, from a clinical point of view there are two possible outcomes of it: either the return to a state of balance, or the passage to a chronic pathological state marked by a phase of 'depression', a chronic state devoid of anxiety but corresponding to a general lowering of vital tonus (a 'lower order of human existence', we might say).

Such chronic states were first described by Pierre Marty under the label of 'essential depression'; they must be distinguished from mental (psychotic or neurotic) depression on account of the absence of the typical psychopathological symptoms (guilt feelings, self-reproach, etc.) (Marty 1968, 1980). This passage into a chronic state, to which 'characteropathic' individuals are particularly prone on account of the quality of their mental functioning, is what opens the way for somatization proper. That is, for the slow aspect of somatization that inaugurates the destruction of a tissue, involving immunopathological processes (Dejours 1986: 107–13). Thus 'chronic emotional states' figure in this model as predisposing factors just as they did in that of Alexander, which was ultimately reductive on the side of physiology. In Dejours' work, however, the conditions of possibility of such states are posited at a level that is logically prior to, and more fundamental than the development of a psychic conflict. For the ontogenesis of the *caractéropathe* as a structure of mental functioning Dejours explicitly refers to the quality of mother–infant relationships and to its role in facilitating the development of a capacity for symbolization (Dejours 1986: 188–9).

In the context of analysis proposed by Dejours, the difference between forms of somatic pathology appears secondary with respect to their belonging to a single type of functional regime. Somatic illness is a mode of reaction that is associated with a type of mental functioning routinely 'preferred' over others by certain individuals. Such a mode of reaction differs most significantly from two other modes: the psychotic, and the neurotic. The words of Luis Chiozza illustrate this context of analysis very clearly:

> We differentiate between neuroses and psychoses not only on account of their different psychic manifestations, but also and especially because, from a psychoanalytic point of view, they appear as different and specific manners of falling ill. In the same way, it is necessary for us to ask ourselves, as psychoanalysts and starting from our own field of research, what somatic illness signifies, *any* somatic illness.
>
> (Chiozza 1981: 208)

Despite their differences, most contemporary authors in the psychoanalytic branch of psychosomatics share the conviction that 'truly' somatic illness (illness devoid of any primary symbolic significance) does not imply that the symbolic dimension is irrelevant in the pathogenesis. It is relevant by not being there, once this is regarded as evidence of a deficit in a regulatory function of symbolization. The psychic and the symbol appear again significant by default, having come full circle in the dialectic between the 'hermeneutics' and the 'energetics' of disease. Dejours calls this an 'epistemological reversal' (Dejours 1989: 31). In the early extensions of the conversion model to cover all somatic manifestations, the assumption was that any somatic symptom was interpretable as to its hidden symbolic sense. Alexander's work, conversely, set out from the distinction between psychoneuroses and actual neuroses to state, in agreement with Freud, that the 'actual' symptom was not interpretable as a symbolic formation. In this further context, it is precisely this lack of sense or absence of the psychic that becomes the object of interpretation. A lack of symbolic sense is not equivalent, in these propositions, to a non-sense; a lack of sense denotes a sense that is missing from where it should be, moved elsewhere to become unintelligible. The sense of the (psycho)somatic symptom is to be found in its being the negative of a psychic one.

Action or symbolization

Authors differ in the explanatory frameworks they adopt to provide a dynamic account of how a deficit in symbolization results in a predisposition towards somatic pathology, and therefore how the differences between nosographical groups are to be articulated. For Pierre Marty and the École Psychosomatique de Paris, for instance, a neurotic type of mental organization constitutes a solid defence system with respect to the possibility of a more profound disorganization. The structure of the neurotic corresponds to the Oedipal organization of the genital phase described by Freud. This structure has the possibility of regressing and fixating onto prior stages of psychosexual development in the event of an excess of excitation provoked by an encounter with the real. In this sense, the psychic apparatus manages the upsurge of anxiety and affect within itself, without overspilling into the somatic, thus preserving and guaranteeing what is essential for physical survival. This way of managing traumatic encounters with the real generates symptoms in the Freudian connotation of the term: personalized compromises with a phobic, hysterical, or obsessive character. The classical neurotics described by Freud are 'well mentalized' in the sense that they permanently have at their disposal a great quantity of psychic representations associatively linked together and rich in symbolic and affective value. It is through these representations that the subject may elaborate or 'translate' his or her encounter with reality into a personalized compromise which safeguards the integrity of psychic organization and the vital economy of the individual. But if psychic and symbolic representations are not sufficiently available, or if they are inaccessible, this type of mental regression and fixation is not possible. In such a case, the subject has no other recourse but to action in the real in order to respond to the endogenous and exogenous excitations life meets him or her with (Marty 1991). Such action in the real can take the form of overt behaviour in the external world, but only if there is the opportunity for it. Alternatively, the 'real' in question is the internal reality of the soma.

Thus, the 'actual' stands opposed to the 'psychic' in the same way as 'action' is opposed to 'symbolization', and the 'true' real of the body and of intersubjective reality is opposed to the 'false' real of fantasy and the symbol. The substitution of action for symbolization is evident both in the style of thought and in the style of pathology manifested by patients that Marty calls *névrosés de caractère* and *névrosés de comportement*. As for their style of pathology, their illnesses are *actual* in the sense that they are real, they are alterations of the somatic body. As for their style of thinking and of verbal expression, Marty and de M'Uzan have coined the term *pensée opératoire* (Marty and de M'Uzan 1963), translatable in English as 'operatory thinking'. This is a form of thought and even a form of 'life' (*vie opératoire*) characterized by the prevalence of rational features and by the poverty of fantasy and metaphorical content. It is a form of thought that constantly refers to the subject's own actions and experiences but without displaying any affective investment, as if the subject were a mere spectator rather than an actor of his or her existence:

> In vain one looks for any associations of ideas. Words indicate things that belong to the reality of the social order. There are no metaphors . . . . [D]reams have disappeared, or at least so has their typical quality . . . . [T]he problem of interpretation does not pose itself.
>
> (Marty 1980: 19–20)

And similarly,

> The actual and the factual dominate the picture. All character manifestations appear devoid of individual value. The pursuit of artistic activities only produces works without any quality. Behaviours . . . are reduced to a mechanical, 'functional' aspect . . . . Since desires have left their place to needs, . . . the individual, as we said, appears reduced . . . to an assemblage of instruments without soul.
>
> (ibid.: 101–2)

This mode of thinking also corresponds to a form of therapeutic interaction marked by a conformist and mechanical adherence to the requirements of external reality. The patient answers questions when they are posed without digressions, and approaches the analyst as someone to be put in charge of symptoms and who should deliver their resolution, in a strictly technical manner. The mechanisms of transference and counter-transference cannot be set in place, and the type of therapeutic relationship that is established is described as a *relation blanche* (Marty and de M'Uzan 1963: 346). In Todarello and Porcelli's words, it is a form of 'hyperinvestment of the factual and the contingent', where there is no trace of repression or of a 'return of the repressed' which is also signalled, as Marty points out, by the lack of dreams or by their equally banal, 'objective' quality (Todarello and Porcelli 1992: 123). For Marty, this style of thought and expression originates in a 'bypass' of the psychic, or in the fact that 'the psychic apparatus is unavailable to elaborate the excitations, excitations that do not fail to produce themselves and to accumulate (the unconscious receives but no longer sends anything out)' (Marty 1991: 26).

How is this unavailability of the psychic linked to the outcome of action in the real, that is, to the involvement and the eventual destruction of the actual body? To account for this passage, Marty proposes the notion of 'progressive disorganization', which he describes as 'the very type of a durable counter-evolutionary movement' (Marty 1980: 9). Such a movement follows the permanent or repeated excess, and ultimately the accumulation, of psycho-affective excitations that are not subject to mental elaboration, and whose discharge through behaviour is reduced or precluded. Progressive disorganization consists in an infinite regression that does not meet any point of (psychic) fixation as a buffer or as a point of arrest. This movement implies a gradual dehierarchization and anarchization of functional organizations – starting from the psychic – in a counter-evolutionary pattern that may eventually reach the levels of biochemical, endocrine and immune functioning. Thus, there is a difference between regression in the 'well mentalized' neurotic and progressive disorganization in the *névrosés de caractère* or *de comportement*, both of whom are 'badly mentalized'. This difference lies in the fact that the first type of regression, by being fixed and arrested onto mental representations, allows for reorganization and reversibility of the symptoms, even when these are somatic. Conversely, the infinite regression represented by progressive disorganization gives rise to degenerative diseases which threaten the life prognostic of the individual. The progressive character of disorganizations, Marty maintains, implies that they theoretically lead to death.

For Marty and the École Psychosomatique de Paris the major clinical forms of mentalization can be broadly grouped into 'well mentalized neuroses', 'badly mentalized ones' and neuroses whose mentalization is 'uncertain', manifesting striking variations both in the quantity and quality of mental representations. The group of 'uncertain' neuroses, according to Marty, comprises the vast majority of individuals in our civilization, individuals who ordinarily display all the characteristics of 'normality' (Marty 1980: 12–13). On the basis of the susceptibility of such individuals to progressive disorganizations and therefore serious physical illness, Marty suggests that there is a health-preserving value in mental illness:

> It seems . . . that only the regular organization of an active *mental* pathology (this notion extends also to the psychoses) can be considered as a guarantee against the risks of progressive disorganization.
> (Marty 1980: 14)

This type of explanation (resting on the notions of regression and disorganization) and of terminology ('well' or 'badly mentalized neuroses') are specific to the school of Marty. This school has been criticized for failing to transcend the Freudian representation of the psychic apparatus, and therefore for preserving the 'neurotic' label for conditions that are more than the mere negative of a neurosis. However, several of the points reviewed above constitute a theme that is common to virtually all authors in the minoritarian context of psychosomatics. The most central of these themes is the notion that the possibilities of organic and mental pathology constitute alternatives, opposites that cannot be embraced at the same time, but between which it is possible to move. This echoes the description of the *Gestaltkreis* discussed in chapter five, where similarly it was impossible to be in two places at the same time, and where the 'travelling' implied the constant alternation of perspectives, from the physical to the mental and vice versa. Accordingly, if the discourse of psychosomatics in this orientation speaks of 'mental' and 'physical' pathology, it is in the full awareness that these categories define and exclude each other in knowledge, as much as they imply each other in the organism. Bodily and mental refer to symptoms, but not to the 'truth' of the illness:

> the activity of thinking does not take place in the brain alone, but passes through the whole body. It implies as a correlate that there are no grounds to maintain an opposition between diseases of the mind

> and diseases of the body, or between *mental* and *somatic* illnesses. Mental illnesses will always also be diseases of the body, and diseases of the body will always also be mental illnesses . . . . In this perspective, *psychosomatic illnesses do not exist*. There is no distinction to be made between certain diseases of the body that are allegedly more psychological than others, and others, equally of the body, that are allegedly less so . . . . What is psychosomatic is not the disease, but *the clinical and theoretical approach*.
>
> (Dejours 1989: 116)

Alternation, inversion, and mutual implication. These forms of relation between the mental and the somatic in the symptom are mirrored in the substitution of the symbolic for the actual, and of the actual for the symbolic. This theme runs through several levels of description: from the level of cognitive and communication styles (in the absence of overt pathology) to the style of pathology itself. The possibility of somatic illness as an alternative to psychic suffering was also addressed, as we have seen, by the earliest proponents of the conversion model, for whom physical illness represented a form of 'psychic saving'. They, however, considered this possibility only through a reference to the positivity of the symbolic process, rather than also to its negativity or absence in the 'actual'. In Dejours' and Marty's propositions what appears to be attained is the articulation of Von Weizsäcker's logic of mutual occultation, or 'principle of the revolving door'. According to this principle, the physical signs we can see are the psychic symptoms that we cannot see by definition.

Dejours' 'third topography'

Marty and his school infer the inverse correlation between mental and somatic pathology from their analysis of the failure of neurosis. Thus, they remain within the Freudian system of representation, stretching it to the very limits of what it can account for. Dejours is critical of this approach because it produces a model that does not allow for a specific analysis of the psychodynamics of somatic illness. He maintains that it is impossible to represent the structures of the *névrosés de caractère/comportement* and of the psychotic with reference to the Freudian first and second topographies. The metapsychology of these pathological forms can therefore only be described in terms of incompetence or default with respect to neurosis itself (Dejours 1986: 156). The very term 'neurosis', which Marty and his school preserve, is misleading according to Dejours. It obscures, in his view, that there is a structural difference in the mental functioning presented by these patients with respect to neurotics proper. Dejours accordingly proposes the label *caractérose* as a term to be added alongside those of neurosis and psychosis. He also proposes a revision of the Freudian representation of the psychic apparatus, a 'third topography' wherein the possibility of all these pathological forms, and the relations between them, can be accounted for. Dejours' proposal specifies how psychotic and somatic breakdowns represent symmetrical alternatives both in the order of the 'actual', and both structurally different from neurosis. This produces a significant and unexpected similarity between somatic illness and psychotic episodes, since they appear equivalent from a structural point of view. The 'third topography' is a map for the forms of embodied subjectivity, or for the modes of subjective interpretation that mediate the individual's encounter with the real. Let us begin to approach it by returning to Dejours' description of the competition between phylogenetic and ontogenetic structures in the individual.

As we have seen, the example of automatic anxiety, the possibility of its upsurge in any individual under extreme circumstances, testifies to an ever-present possibility of reactivation of archaic behavioural sequences that are conveyed by phylogenetically inherited programmes. These archaic behavioural sequences possess a stereotypical, automatic, and compulsive quality. They are aspecific and similar in all individuals, as a response that takes the individual's past experience into no account. They present an incoercible thrust that can only be exhausted by an actual discharge (behavioural or somatic). Ultimately, therefore, they possess a quality of violence. The possibility of psychic regulation and taming of such behaviours appears as an evolutionary product thanks to which human beings, through language, have access to an 'economy of desire' as opposed to an 'economy of need'. Psychic life constitutes itself in opposition to the activation of self-preservation in a biological sense. It does so, according to Dejours, by 'subverting' the energy of genetic programmes to its own advantage:

> It may be that the very existence of a *psychic programme*, which cannot develop except by subtracting part of the biological energy of the body, radically transforms the animal economy of man. And it may be that this operation of subversion, that of course gives man access to intersubjectivity, on the other hand confers upon him a certain fragility with respect to his animal heritage. A fragility that, short of the success of the subversion itself, condemns him to being a victim of his own vital energies that then tragically turn against him. Man is in some ways condemned to being more than an animal, or he will not cease to contend with his animality, at the price of incommensurable suffering.
>
> (Dejours 1989: 131–2)

It is therefore due to this peculiarity of the human species with respect to other animals that the notion of self-preservation acquires, for humans, a certain ambivalence. The programmes (or instincts) geared towards the self-preservation of biological life in animals retain this function for humans only in a phylogenetic sense. Their activation, and their violence, represent a threat to the survival of the individual facing the concrete problems of interaction posed by day to day reality, in a social context the existence and character of which is itself owed to language. Two senses of 'preservation' must therefore be carefully distinguished: the preservation of biological life in a strict sense, which relies on innate behavioural sequences; and the preservation of the psychic apparatus, whose role is precisely to protect the individual from the activation of such instinctual behaviours and their violence. These two senses of 'preservation' imply the possibility of a contradiction between them.

In principle the constitution of the psychic apparatus also works for the preservation of biological life. It does so to the extent that it is capable of metabolizing excitation provoked by an encounter with reality into a psychic product, through the process Dejours names 'subversion' that I shall review in more detail below. This process represents a 'capitalization' of the subject's experience of the present into a personalized history. Thanks to this meaningful history, the individual is protected from analogous stimuli on the part of reality in the future. Such stimuli will be liable to being directly perceived and managed as mental events and will not pose a threat to the physical survival of the individual. Conversely, if there are obstacles or structural deficits in the way of this metabolization, then individuals will reproduce the violence of their innate reactions to the threats posed by the environment again and again. In that position, and through passages that I will discuss, they will be faced with the alternative of preserving their psychic integrity *or* their biological integrity. Thus, generally speaking, the differentiation between mental structures is given by the strategy privileged by each of them in confronting the ever-possible upsurge of instinctual behaviour and violence. The conditions for one strategy to be privileged over another lie in the ontogenetic development of the psychic apparatus itself, and in whether this has led to a 'healthy' integration through the mediation of an active symbolic function. Let us now look at these alternatives in more detail.

The first step in the definition of the third topography for Dejours lies, as we have seen, in acknowledging the fact that humans maintain, throughout life, a series of innate behavioural programmes that coexist with an ontogenetically acquired psychic structure. The innate behavioural programmes cannot be directly modified or transformed by the psychic apparatus. They constitute, for Dejours, a primitive or primary form of unconscious, 'primary' in the sense that it consists of the instinctual forces derived from phylogenesis which were never repressed. If this then is the Primary Unconscious, the Secondary Unconscious corresponds to the system *Ucs.* in the first Freudian topography. The Secondary Unconscious is what we know through the 'return of the repressed' and through the classic symptoms of neurosis. By definition, the Secondary Unconscious consists of representations and makes itself known through these in the system *Pcs.*, whereas the Primary Unconscious is not represented and therefore, from a Freudian point of view, remains unknowable. Dejours suggests that its existence can nonetheless be inferred from the manifestations of non-neurotic patients, such as different forms of violence, of *passage à l'acte*, of perversions and somatizations. These derivatives of the Primary Unconscious have in common the fact of not being 'mentalized' or represented, and constitute the set of symptoms recognized as non-neurotic, or pertaining to psychiatric pathology (Dejours 1986: 158–9).

The point of the third topography is to account for non-neurotic forms of pathology as originating structurally in the failure, on the part of the psychic apparatus, to metabolize the violence stimulated in the Primary Unconscious by an encounter with reality. In order to understand these pathological processes we should first follow the sequence which leads to the non-pathological and constructive outcome of such an encounter. First of all we should ask: What is an 'encounter with the real' in Dejours' use of these terms? An encounter with the real is an event whose quality or intensity involves a breakdown of the mechanism of disavowal (*Verleugnung*) and is therefore a potential threat to the stability of the system. In other words, we have an encounter with the real whenever the subject is compelled to confront reality as it is, as something other than what is included in the subjective construction that makes reality appear stable, predictable, reliable. Such an event stimulates the Unconscious in the broad connotation of the term, that is the Primary and the Secondary Unconscious taken together, and generates what Dejours calls a sensation. There are different possible destinies of such a sensation: if the breakdown of disavowal and the excitation are not quantitatively too great, the individual can afford to maintain the sensation in a state of latency, standing-by in the form of a perception while it awaits elaboration. A fundamental precondition for this process, beside the quantitative compatibility of the excitation, is the participation of the system *Pcs.* and therefore its functional availability. A perception, as opposed to a sensation, presupposes a comparison with preexisting mnemonic traces. Thanks to such a comparison the subject may establish that it is not urgent to discharge the excitation. A 'perception' here is therefore not to be understood in its psychopharmacological connotation but in its psychoanalytic one, as a *Gestalt* that gives rise to associations by analogy with representations that form part of the psychic history of the individual. Through the deviation of the initial perception towards other representations in the mode of thought that is characteristically preconscious, the event of encounter may give rise to an affect feared by the subject. In this case the subject maintains the chain of associations itself into a state of latency through the system *Pcs*. The passage from sensation to perception, and thereafter to chains of associations left in a state of latency, are the preconditions for the subsequent elaboration of this material by the *dream*. Through the dream the original sensation may be properly repressed into the Secondary Unconscious, where it acquires the status of a mental representation.[1] This process taken as a whole makes possible the subversion of the energy of innate instinctual programmes towards mature psychic functioning, for use within psychoaffective and psychosexual relationships.

One way of describing what happens in this process is to say that an activation of the Primary Unconscious, and therefore of non-represented instinctual sequences, is translated into a new psychic form that goes to enrich the Secondary Unconscious. The mediation provided by an encounter with the real (or with what is other) is crucial for this passage. A great value for the vital economy of the individual depends on its outcome. If the process is successful, the bodily state experienced in the encounter is stored in a represented form as repressed material that, as such, can be recalled. It is a 'colonization' of the Primary Unconscious on the part of the Secondary Unconscious. It is a 'mental capitalization' of experience thanks to which, in the event of a similar stimulation on the part of reality in the future, the new event will be met by a mnemonic trace allowing for the activation of neurotic defences through preconscious dynamics. In other words, the activation of archaic responses and their compulsive, 'actual', and violent character is preempted and bypassed. We can see therefore the sense in which the structure of the neurotic represents a good form of integration between psyche and soma, and constitutes a solid protection allowing for the coincidence of both aspects of self-preservation.

The major obstacle to the fulfilment of this process of integration, short of the sheer excessiveness of the stimulus which would lead to trauma and automatic anxiety also in the neurotic, is constituted by the relative poverty of the Secondary Unconscious within certain individuals. If the Secondary Unconscious is poor of images, the functioning of the system *Pcs.* is necessarily weak. In their states of balance, such individuals differ from neurotics by a modality of behavioural and cognitive adequation to reality where it is hardly possible to detect any 'return of the repressed'. This form of adequation is efficient and realistic, signalling the prominence of logical conscious processes. Logical conscious processes give rise to associations that may differ as to their abstractness or concreteness, but that share the feature of being impersonal, lacking in links with the Unconscious, and derived from shared learning and from cognitive development. Here Dejours' description parallels the description of *pensée opératoire* given by Marty in relation to psychosomatic patients. But Dejours also points to a parallel with descriptions of hyper-rational and paranoid thought in psychotics. Such individuals, he maintains, are also less protected with respect to neurotics in the event of an encounter with the real. This is because only their Conscious system is sufficiently solid to work as a dam against the inflow of excitation which follows a stimulation of the Primary Unconscious. The difference between the structures Dejours names 'caracteropathic', 'psychotic' and 'psychopathic' stems from the alternative destinies available for stimulations of the Primary Unconscious that cannot be taken charge of by the system *Pcs.* on account of its weakness, and of the poverty of contents in the Secondary Unconscious. What, then, are these alternatives?

A first indication is provided by considering what happens when the stimulus is simply excessive with respect to the binding capacities of the psychic apparatus, no matter how this is structured. In this case the sensation creates such a reactive disturbance in the Primary Unconscious that excitation must be immediately discharged. The urgent need of an immediate discharge gives rise to two general possible alternatives, the first being behavioural and the second being somatic. Unlike the process of subversion reviewed above, these alternatives are actual both in a temporal sense (as Freud originally used the term), and in that they represent an actualization into material reality (external or internal) of the consequences of the sensation. The behavioural alternative is an attempt to extinguish excitation in reality itself, either through a destructive act whereby the subject violently attacks the source of excitation (*passage à l'acte*), or through the attempt to escape this source with flight. When this alternative is actively resisted by the subject a massive inhibition may occur, such as in prostration, stupor, or even an episode of catatonia or loss of consciousness: a veritable flight without a flight. The somatic alternative, which sets in instead of a motor discharge or inhibition, takes a different route. This route starts with the onset of trauma with its concomitant of automatic anxiety. While in the neurotic these alternatives are actualized only in the face of extreme circumstances, in what Dejours calls the psychopath they represent the only or most immediately available options to manage sensations that cannot be turned into perceptions. The alternation between violent outbursts in *passages à l'acte* and the development of automatic or actual anxiety is frequently seen clinically in such patients. A weaker but similar form of alternation, according to Dejours, is found in the patients Marty calls *névrosés de comportement*, who are described as frequently hyperactive and seeking discharge in motor activities (e.g. compulsive exercise) or other forms of externalized behaviour.

The destiny of excitation is different and more elaborate in the psychotic, who opposes a passionate recourse to rationality and logical thinking to the possibility of an irruption on the part of the Primary Unconscious and its violence. This investment in the logical process renders such patients, when they are in a state of balance, particularly adequate to the requirements of social and professional efficiency. They are not disturbed, as it were, by the constant return of personal and objectively 'irrational' preoccupations overspilling from the Secondary Unconscious through the system *Pcs*. When the encounter with reality breaches the dam provided by consciousness, however, the system *Pcs.* of the psychotic is not solid enough to offer an alternative buffer. The psychotic is unable to hold chains of associations in a state of latency, a state that is a precondition for their subsequent repression through the dream. The psychotic stops short of repression in the sequence of metabolization and, instead, repudiates or forecloses[2] the thoughts and associations arising from the perception itself. In other words, he or she expels them back into reality, from whence the thoughts return in the form of a persecutory idea, telepathy, or delusions. This return may also be in the form of a hallucination, if what is expelled is a more elementary form than an association of ideas: namely, the perception or even the sensation itself. Accordingly, anxiety in the psychotic is represented but not symbolized. The signifier – which is severed from the possibility of generating further associations in the Secondary Unconscious – does not preserve any trace of ambiguity in its meaning, which allows for its being entirely mistaken for what it appears. The capacity for symbolization in the neurotic allows for every psychic content to be referred to a different meaning; this possibility is foreclosed in the psychotic, giving rise to delusions (Dejours 1986: 53–5, 172–6).

The structure Dejours calls 'characterosis' coincides with the patients named by Marty as *névrosés de comportement* and *névrosés de caractère* who, according to Marty, comprise the majority of individuals in our civilization.The topography of characterosis is analogous to the topography of psychosis. The difference between them lies in the mechanism employed to deal with the sensation generated by an encounter with the real. Like psychotics, these individuals have a weak capacity for metabolizing excitation through oneiric activity and through the system *Pcs*. The *passage à l'acte* and hyperactivity remain available options for the *caractéropathe* as for all other non-neurotic structures here examined. When such options appear infeasible or insufficient, however, the *caractéropathe*, like the psychotic, has a more elaborate mechanism at his or her disposal that similarly stops short of latentization and repression. The psychotic, as we have seen, expels the sensation back into reality and thus externalizes the instinctual violence that is at the origin of the imbalance. The *caractéropathe* attempts instead to destroy the sensation itself. He or she does so by neutralizing, within him or herself, that which reacts to the situation. There is here a striking analogy with *passage à l'acte*, which is also an attempt to destroy the source of excitation; but there is also an inversion since, while psychopaths attack reality, 'characteropaths' respect reality and the external source of excitation. They choose, instead, to exhaust the violence within themselves. The sensation will be reduced to undifferentiated excitation that is discharged automatically through the classic forms of somatic anxiety. The mechanism involved in this process of reduction differs both from repression (*Verdrängung*) and from foreclosure (*Verwerfung*): it is rather a form of suppression (*Unterdrückung*), an abolition of affect that occurs before the development of a sensation into a perception. As such, the sensation eschews preconscious mental functioning altogether (Dejours 1986: 176–81). Anxiety in the *caractéropathe* is neither symbolized nor represented.

The similarity and difference between the psychotic and the *caractéropathe* can be detected also in the quality of their thought. The style of thinking known as *pensée opératoire* is structurally similar to a paranoid style of thinking, with a difference that can be described as one of intensity or tonus. In their states of balance psychotic and 'characteropathic' patients passionately appeal to logical and realistic thought in a manner that is almost identical. The difference appears during pathological episodes that are characteristic of each structure. The paranoid psychotic displays, then, a quality of thinking that is hypertonic, or very intense to the point of becoming paralogical. The 'characteropath' in an episode of what Marty has named *dépression essentielle* (the first sign of a disorganization) displays a hypotonic quality of the same style of thought. Dejours suggests that the reason for this difference is that hypertonic thinking in the psychotic is made such by the unmediated pressure exerted by the Primary Unconscious, or of instinctual violence. On the other hand, in the *caractéropathe* somatization opens a channel for the release of part of this pressure in the direction of the soma (Dejours 1986: 173, 177).

Conclusion: the invisible madness of the body

Christophe Dejours is, to my knowledge, the only author to have proposed a 'third topography' in the explicit attempt to provide a theory of psychic functioning that could be recognized not only by psychoanalysts, but also by scientists working in biology and the neurosciences. The topographical structures he describes do not represent a static typification of people, he claims, but rather the sketch of defence mechanisms that can be employed by all individuals, to a greater or lesser extent. Nonetheless, Dejours' account does contain the elements for a typification, through the idea that each subject tends to use one of these mechanisms preferentially, while the other mechanisms are resorted to only in an accessory or alternative way. What appears interesting in his formulation is the symmetrical analogy posited between psychosis and somatization, linking the two in such a way as to reduce the radical difference that is culturally assumed between so-called mental and physical illness, Dejours makes this analogy clear and explicit. But, as I have argued, it was always implicit in the conditions of possibility of psychosomatics as a modern discursive formation. Already in 1934, Meng spoke of psychosomatic illness in terms of 'organ psychosis'. More recently Chiozza, like Dejours, has proposed that we need to follow separately the destinies imposed on affect by neurosis, psychosis, and somatic illness. He claims that, in order to prevent the development of a feared affect, the neurotic destroys the coherent link of the affect with the idea (or representation) in relation to which the affect was initially activated: what is destroyed is the subjective meaning of a particular experience that belongs to the personal history of the subject. Psychosis, on the other hand, acts on external 'objective' reality via a destruction of the subject's cognitive relation with it, through the alteration of judgement we call 'madness'. In somatic illness, finally, what is destroyed is the coherence of the affect itself: the affect disappears and is dismembered into its different 'innervations'. Therefore, Chiozza suggests, somatic illness is a 'madness of the affect' by analogy with psychosis (Chiozza 1981). Psychosis is 'madness' from the perspective of the intersubjective environment, and as such it is visible to all. Somatic illness, on the other hand, is 'madness' from the perspective of the infra-subjective environment, undetected and undetectable as such in the outside world. Thus, all pathology involves a form of destruction, but psychosis and somatic illness share a mode that alters something that is actual and real: either in terms of the reality of socially shared experience, or in terms of the reality of the body. By contrast, the neurotic alters a phantasmatic construction that is unique to his or her own history, and that can be resignified and indeed recreated through symbolic elaboration. Joyce McDougall (1989) uses similar terms to illustrate what she calls 'neurotic versus psychosomatic solutions':

> In psychosomatic states the *body* appears to be behaving in a 'delusional' fashion, often *overfunctioning* excessively . . . to a degree that appears physiologically senseless. One is tempted to say that the body has gone mad . . . . On the basis of these reflections I came to propose a certain similarity between psychosis and psychosomatosis, insofar as both states serve an underlying reparative aim in the face of an overwhelming, though often unrecognized, sense of danger.
>
> (1989: 18, 29)

And, echoing Dejours' description of somatization as an archaic form of self-preservation:

> although many psychosomatic symptoms may rapidly lead to death (in contrast to hysterical symptoms, which are purely symbolic and rarely cause physiological damage), paradoxically, they too represent an *attempt to survive*.
>
> (ibid.: 30)

The most significant difference between somatic illness and psychosis is precisely that which is apparent even to the most casual observer in our social establishment. As Dejours explains, while the violence of an archaic reaction that bypasses psychic modulation is at the origin of both forms of pathology, the psychotic reveals this violence in manifest madness, while the somatic patient may not manifest it in any intelligible way:

> In other words, the psychotic who breaks down lets his primary unconscious explode . . . . The systems *Pcs.* and *Cs.* are in difficulty and the patient can no longer hide his madness. On the other hand, when the *caractéropathe* somatizes, he saves his face. The systems *Pcs.* and *Cs.* can survive the somatized instinctual thrust without great changes, so that the *caractéropathe* can break down without revealing his madness to the outside world, in his relation to Reality and to the object. This is true to the point that the *caractéropathe* in the middle of

> a crisis may well appear not only very 'normal', but even particularly peaceful, calm, or frankly nice, if one can allow here this sort of qualification.
>
> (Dejours 1986: 178)

As Dejours clearly indicates somatic illness, in the discourse of psychosomatics, comes to represent a form of 'madness in disguise', a sort of photographic negative of what we know as madness. There remains, however, a crucial difference between madness in disguise and madness without one: the madness of somatic patients is the organic madness of indiscriminate, and therefore *hyper*-adaptation to the demands of external reality. The somatic patient respects intersubjective reality; the quality and the extent of this respect frame the specificity of his or her way of falling ill. This is the point through which we may begin to bring the discussion back to a sociological terrain.

The notion of *pensée opératoire* describes a symptomatic manifestation of the respect the somatic patient bears to the canons of external reality. As we have seen, the term refers to a quality of thinking and a style of communication wherein fantasies and personal, imaginative, subjective elements are strikingly lacking, to the point of being described as a 'utilitarian' type of thinking. This clinical observation, initially proposed in France by Marty and his school, has been further researched on a much vaster scale through the concept of *alexithymia* (from the Greek *a* = lack, *lexis* = word, *thymos* = emotion, and therefore 'without words for emotions'). This term was independently developed by John Nemiah and Peter Sifneos in the USA from clinical observations that were strikingly similar to those of Marty (Sifneos 1972–3, 1973, 1975). Researchers, clinicians and theoreticians from all parts of the world have since described these clinical characteristics with noteworthy agreement (Noël and Rimé 1988; Pedinielli 1992; Taylor *et al.* 1991; Sifneos 1996). In the following and final chapter I shall explore the 'alexithymia construct' in some detail, in order to ask: Who is the subject of somatic pathology?, and what are the stakes in problematizing the respect that alexithymics bear towards external, intersubjective, social reality? The purpose of these questions is to illustrate the 'truth' about the self with which contemporary psychosomatics confronts modern individuals and society as a whole, and the options this truth substantiates in terms of technologies of the self.

8

WHO IS THE SUBJECT OF SOMATIC PATHOLOGY?

In this chapter, an analysis of the 'alexithymia construct' will take us back to the theme with which this book started, the theme of subjectivity in relation to the question of truth. In chapter one I argued that a certain understanding of the self, as the repository of a hidden truth, was part of the historical conditions of possibility that shaped the modern problem of psychosomatics. In this chapter, I discuss how psychosomatics modifies those initial conditions, what it introduces into the play of true and false that unsettles what could previously be taken for granted about the self, the social, and about disease. The example of alexithymia will enable us to survey these effects in quite specific terms. It will highlight a shift in the understanding of disease that concerns fundamentally the assumption of a 'primary passivity' of the body. Once this assumption is suspended, disease comes to represent an occasion for active reflection, on the part of each individual, about the self and about the self in the context of its social relations. This reflection is subordinate to the value of 'health' and implies a certain redefinition of that value. The construct of alexithymia illustrates how, in psychosomatics, medical knowledge comes to appeal directly to the consciousness of individuals, or we might even say to their conscience. This appeal to an active subject in the name of medical truth has profoundly unsettling implications in terms of a political consciousness of health. These implications are what this chapter begins to outline.

The alexithymia construct (including its French homologue of *pensée* and *vie opératoire*) has been described as a 'potential paradigm for psychosomatic medicine' (Taylor *et al*. 1991). And indeed, the construct appears to represent the single most important point of confluence and intersection between methodologically distinct approaches in psychosomatic research, ranging from psychoanalysis to neurophysiology. As Jean-Louis Pedinielli explains,

> Far from being a secondary clinical phenomenon only linked to any hypothetical psychosomatic conditions, alexithymia has a central place within a '*psychopathology of the somatic*' – a psychopathology of the

> relations to the body – whether it rests on a psychoanalytic, cognitive, or neuropsychological problematic.
>
> (Pedinielli 1992: 123)

The concept was initially developed as *pensée opératoire* in France in 1963 and as 'a problem in communication' by Nemiah and Sifneos in the USA in 1970. Significantly, it was developed in connection with the difficulty experienced by psychiatrists and psychoanalysts in attempting to treat patients suffering from 'classic' psychosomatic disorders psychotherapeutically. The apparent inability of such patients to verbalize feelings and to symbolically and imaginatively express emotion was described as early as 1948 by Ruesch, and reiterated shortly afterwards by MacLean (1949), Horney (1952), and Kelman (1952). Marty and de M'Uzan on one side of the Atlantic, and Nemiah and Sifneos on the other, made a critical turn on these initial observations that is well illustrated in a point made by the latter: 'psychiatrists' they wrote,

> have long been aware that such patients are often especially hard to work with psychotherapeutically, and using concepts borrowed from psychodynamic theory, they have attributed the characteristic emotional reticence of psychosomatic patients to the psychological defense of *denial*. They imply, in other words, that this group of patients do in fact have a rich inner life of feelings and fantasies, but that these are excluded from conscious awareness and expression by protective intrapsychic forces. Having thus labelled the phenomenon, they have generally been content to let the matter rest without further inquiry.
>
> (Nemiah and Sifneos 1970: 156)

The concepts of *pensée opératoire* and later of alexithymia were developed to problematize this assumption. They cast doubt on the idea that so-called psychosomatic patients did, in fact, have a 'rich inner life': an assumption that at least and especially in the wake of Freudianism had attained the status of an anthropological generalization. The outline of the historical constitution of Western forms of subjectivity and self-perception presented in chapter one has shown that this assumption has a long genealogy in Western history and, more importantly, that it need not be presumed to reflect a universal, necessary, and transcendental feature of human beings. I shall return later to how the 'rich inner life' of which Nemiah and Sifneos speak corresponds to what in chapter one I have called the 'hidden truth' or 'inner truth' that is such an important feature in the constitution and transformation of modern forms of subjectivity. For the time being, what should be highlighted is that the lack of an 'inner life' makes its appearance in psychosomatic discourse as a (pre-)pathological condition or, more precisely, as a condition liable to predisposing individuals towards somatic illness and disease (Lumley *et al.* 1996).

I can anticipate the general form of my argument in the following manner: in its earliest formulations that were derived from an extension of the conversion model of hysteria, psychosomatic discourse thematized the possibility that the physical symptom could express, in a socially inconspicuous form, a subjective meaning, a unique motivational truth that could be revealed by interpreting the symptom symbolically. In these formulations, disease as a form of expression directly provided at once the clue to the 'truth contained' within the individual, and to the truth of his or her relation to the self and to others. Like the hysterical symptom, the truly somatic one was the visible sign of a compromise solution the subject had found to his or her 'problems in living', and implied the subject's confrontation with these for its resolution. This linear and scientifically 'naive' hypothesis – which inaugurated the modern problematic of psychosomatics – corresponds to definite societal 'structures of demand' or conditions of possibility. Let us recall what these are: one is the cultural assumption that the self possesses a secret truth always awaiting to be revealed (as I argued in chapter one); another is the subject–object analytic that theoretically excludes the internal functioning of the body as a means of subjective expression (as I argued in chapter four); third, the fact that this analytic is normative in the sense that it plays a significant role in ensuring the functioning of institutions in their current form (as I argued in chapters two and three).

In its more recent forms, psychosomatic discourse has largely abandoned the model of hysterical conversion and the hypothesis of a symbolic significance of organic disease. However, a discourse relating to the inner truth of individuals is still present in an inverted form. Psychosomatics now seeks a meaning in the fact that organic illness is not interpretable symbolically. Thus the actual character of organic disease is regarded as the outcome of an individual adaptive strategy that rests on a 'bypass of the psychic'. The significance of the psychic is reinstated through its default (as I argued in chapters six and seven). Having followed to its extreme consequences the original task to decipher disease as the expression of a fullness of psychic content that is presumed to define the 'subjective' as such, psychosomatics thus yields a rather baffling conclusion: the truth about the self that bodily illness discloses when investigated psychosomatically is that there is no hidden truth to be found in such individuals. But here the statement that there is no hidden truth to be found does not stand as a critique of the cultural assumption: it stands rather as a problem to be confronted and solved by individuals and society to the extent that there is an aspiration to 'solve' the problem of illness itself. As we shall see, this apparent reversal constitutes a reinforcement of the cultural value attached to the notion of possessing a 'hidden truth' upon which the possibility for personhood and identity is predicated, by raising it to the status of an organic norm. At the same time, however, this reversal also modifies the terms in which the relation between self and truth is played out. If the capacity to relate to one's self and to others in terms of the reference to a hidden truth is presented as a life-preserving and sometimes life-saving asset, there is also an implicit recognition of the fact that this 'hidden truth' is not simply given but that it is a construction, albeit one that is deemed necessary for health.

To unravel these points, I shall begin by looking in some detail at how the figure of the alexithymic is construed in psychosomatic discourse. Alexithymia is the concrete example of a truth of knowledge that is stated about certain individuals in relation to their liability to falling somatically ill. It is a category for 'making up people' as Ian Hacking uses this phrase, namely, a new mode of description through which 'new possibilities for action come into being as a consequence' (Hacking 1986: 231), as well as new ways of thinking about what we are in contrast to what we might have been. It is a truth about the self which explicitly addresses the quality of relations between the self and its truth. It is a truth with which medical discourse confronts individuals in the name of the value of health. Lastly, it is a ubiquitous category in the sense that it applies – like physical illness itself – to a vast number of individuals who would be regarded as the prototype of the 'normal', socially well adapted person.

Inconspicuous anomalies

Alexithymic characteristics have been described in patients with 'classic' psychosomatic illnesses, but also in patients presenting somatoform symptoms, psychogenic pain, substance abuse and post-traumatic stress disorder, as well as in individuals displaying a variety of compulsive behaviours (such as binge eaters and compulsive excercisers) (Lumley *et al.* 1996; Sifneos 1996; Taylor 1987). Alexithymic individuals may not manifest any signs of psychopathology and may appear 'normal', but their capacity for regulating internal emotional states and physiological functioning is presumed to be rather limited. When faced with stressful situations such individuals, instead of developing classic neurotic symptoms, tend either to exceed in the consumption of food, alcohol or drugs, or to develop a vague physical malaise or, finally, to develop a proper physical disease with tissue alterations. As a minimal hypothesis the concept refers, rather than to an aetiological factor specific to certain conditions or even a diagnosis, to a 'personality trait' that constitutes a risk factor 'increasing general susceptibility to disease, which is specified by other variables' (Taylor *et al.* 1991: 157). Moreover, since the capacity for symbolic communication is so limited, alexithymia has been described as the single most important factor capable of diminishing the effectiveness of psychodynamic psychotherapy (Krystal 1982–3). However, alexithymia is not an all-or-nothing phenomenon, in that all individuals appear to have the capacity of resorting to a relatively asymbolic style of communication, especially in the face of overwhelming environmental stress. In this sense, alexithymia may be regarded as a temporary state as well as a more permanent trait depending on individuals and situations (Nemiah 1978; Pedinielli 1992). This point appears to corroborate Dejours' suggestion that individuals cannot be statically associated to one specific structure or strategy of defence, but can resort to all of them albeit in varying degrees and with a tendency to privilege one specific mode (Dejours 1986).

The explanation of alexithymic characteristics in themselves – that is prior to, or independently of, their connection to the pathogenesis of physical illness – has been suggested from a neurobiological perspective in different ways. One of the first explanatory models to be proposed was MacLean's 'triune brain' model, which hypothesized discontinuities in brain function along a horizontal axis (MacLean 1949). Others have suggested explanations based on studies of the emispheric specialization of brain functions, and have postulated a 'functional commissurotomy' as the basic mechanism underlying alexithymia (Hoppe 1977; Hoppe and Bogen 1977). More recently attention has turned to the neural pathways that mediate the properties of emotions (see Sifneos 1996). Adopting Graham's concept of 'linguistic parallelism', Taylor suggests that there is no reason to exclude the brain (and therefore cerebral disorders) from being considered a potential 'target organ' for psychosomatic processes (Taylor 1987; see Graham 1967). In this view, psychodynamic explanations of alexithymia do not stand in competition or opposition to neurobiological ones, but rather as their complement. Psychodynamic explanations cluster around what is called a 'deficit model'. This model, as we have seen, essentially relies on the idea that early developmental difficulties in the process of separation of the infant from its mother may lead to deficits in the capacity for symbolic elaboration or 'mentalization' of bodily experiences.

Starting from the proposition that 'alexithymia is a valid and quantifiable construct' and that research supports the 'theoretical formulation of an association between alexithymia and somatic illness' (Taylor *et al.* 1991: 158), we may now turn to the descriptions given of the alexithymic patient and of his or her relation to the self and to others. The most salient features of alexithymia are summarized by Taylor *et al.* into four points as: difficulty in identifying and describing feelings; difficulty in distinguishing between feelings and the bodily sensations of emotional arousal (or visceral emotions); constricted imaginative processes as evidenced by a paucity of fantasies and a cognitive style that is literal, utilitarian, and externally oriented (Taylor *et al.* 1991: 155; see also Lesser 1981; Nemiah *et al.* 1976; Taylor 1984). To these, Pedinielli (1992) adds the tendency to resort to action in order to avoid or resolve conflicts, and the high degree of social conformity and submission to cultural stereotypes that alexithymic patients often manifest. These aspects cover, albeit too synthetically, a rich set of clinical observations as well as some inferences that are derived from them (the proofs of an absence or constriction of imagination, for instance, are only indirect and it is difficult to know whether subjects actually lack imaginative activities or whether they lack the capacity to express them). In this context, the difference between the observations and the derived inferences will not concern us. The reason is that the inferences, however debatable they are, also enter the descriptions given of the alexithymic as characteristic features, not unlike the observations themselves. In order to examine these features in more detail, it is worth starting from the accounts provided by clinicians of the quality of their encounters with patients that were later labelled 'alexithymic'. We may return to the famous article of 1970 where Nemiah and Sifneos explicitly address the assumption against which these patients appeared as a striking anomaly to the psychiatrist: 'From his experience with psychoneurotic patients', they write,

> the psychiatrist has learned that merely giving the patient the opportunity to talk about his troubles will usually draw forth from him a wealth of affect-laden material that enables the doctor to empathize with the patient and provides him with an immediate, insightful understanding of the latter's emotional problems.
>
> (Nemiah and Sifneos 1970: 156)

When faced with patients presenting with somatic complaints, however,

> our own introspections revealed a sense of frustration when interviewing the patients, and a feeling that they were dull, lifeless, colorless and boring.
>
> (ibid.: 159)

'I can't say', or 'I can't put it into words' are reported as frequent responses to requests on the part of the therapist to describe what these patients felt, in situations to which 'one would normally expect [them] to respond emotionally' (ibid.: 157). Another conspicuous feature of clinical reports is the boredom provoked by alexithymic patients in their therapists. This boredom is also related in many reports to their 'endless description of physical symptoms, at times not related to an underlying medical illness', as well as 'elaborate description of trivial environmental detail' (Apfel and Sifneos 1979: 181). Sometimes this appearance of a lack of feelings is contradicted by the fact that alexithymic patients do use words that refer to affects, as in being 'nervous', 'sad' or 'angry', and by the fact that they report experiencing chronic dysphoria or may manifest outbursts of crying or rage. In such cases, 'intensive questioning' or being 'pressed by the interviewer to describe their inner experience' (Taylor *et al.* 1991: 155) reveals that these patients 'know very little about their own feelings and, in most instances, are unable to link them with memories, fantasies, or specific situations' (Nemiah 1978: 29). So-called alexithymic patients thus confront clinicians with the appearance of being a shell without a core, someone whose outer appearance descriptively exhausts the contents of inner experience. As Marty and de M'Uzan put it, 'the subject is present, but empty' (1963: 348). They appear only able to relate to the outer concreteness of things and to the present, as if they had neither an interiority nor a past. This mode of relating exclusively to the materiality of facts is reproduced in the relation with the therapist who also figures, for the patient, as a 'utensil' without an interiority:

> Judging from [the patient's] attitude, the therapist does not represent for him anything other than a function, someone to whom he *entrusts* his symptoms and from whom he expects nothing apart from the cure. There is no question of an affective engagement on either part.
> (Marty and de M'Uzan 1963: 346)

These patients thus appear to deliver themselves into the hands of clinicians just as they would leave an object for repair with a mechanic or other technician. Their insensitivity to the feelings of boredom and frustration they arouse in the therapist, and equally their indifference towards the interest the therapist manifests for their own personal characteristics, also forms an important part of the picture. Clinicians feel unrecognized and unacknowledged as subjects in the same way as the alexithymic patient appears not to acknowledge his or her own subjectivity. Just as the patient's personal feelings, and therefore their difference with respect to the objectivity of 'facts' appears absent, so the difference between patient and therapist is ignored except in so far as it relates to their objective institutional roles: 'The other is ultimately considered as identical to the subject, and as endowed with the same mode of *pensée opératoire* as himself' (Marty and de M'Uzan 1963: 349; see also Krystal 1979).

These clinical impressions, let me state it once more, illustrate that the conspicuousness of characteristics called 'alexithymic' emerges against the background of a cultural expectation that each of us possesses a rich and unique 'inner life': an inner life made of feelings, fantasies and imagination, whose prototypical example is provided by the dream, that most private and subjective of all experiences. This cultural expectation finds its formal statement in classic psychoanalytic discourse, and meets with disappointment when confronted, in a psychotherapeutic setting, with so-called alexithymic individuals. These are individuals who are usually referred to a psychiatrist by departments of general medicine for unexplained medical symptoms or for a 'classic' psychosomatic disease; individuals who do not complain of any psychic disturbance and appear, both to themselves and to the referring physician, as perfectly 'normal' from a psychological point of view (Apfel and Sifneos 1979). What is the novelty introduced with alexithymia in respect to the psychodynamic concept of defensive denial? This novelty lies in the suggestion that if these patients do not reveal their inner life and hidden fantasies in the therapeutic setting it is not because their defence mechanisms are particularly efficient in keeping them hidden. Rather, it is because they do not have anything to hide. With the emergence of alexithymia as a conceptual tool, it is possible for investigators to resort to 'intensive questioning' to confirm the underlying lack of an inner life that alexithymia designates, even despite the fact that the patients sometimes do appear to experience strong emotions. In the clinical encounter alexithymia refers to a modality of relating to the self (devoid of any reference to an 'interiority', lacking introspection, a disinvestment of the subjective) that is reflected in a modality of relating to the other (as an inability to acknowledge the other's difference on the point of experiencing feelings). Thus the alexithymic patient, as a construct, seems to contradict the cultural assumption about the universal character of a rich 'inner life' in two different senses. In one sense, he or she fails to display any evidence of having an inner life. In a second sense, he or she does not appear to share in the assumption itself with regard to other individuals.

The proposition that alexithymic patients *do not have anything to hide* is an apt rendering of another noteworthy aspect that is reported about these individuals, namely their high degree of social conformity and adaptation to the requirements of external reality. Alexithymic patients largely appear adequate to their tasks and sometimes particularly efficient, producing a strong 'impression of normality' in the observer who abstracts from the psychotherapeutic setting (Pedinielli 1992: 24). Marty and de M'Uzan illustrate what they mean by *conformisme* with reference to the case of a woman they had in treatment who said one day, as she arrived for her session: 'My father is dead, what does one do in a situation like this?' (Marty and de M'Uzan 1963: 350). In the middle of the distressing event of the loss of her father, and with a psychotherapeutic setting readily available, this woman sought help by appealing to something external to the therapeutic relationship. She asked for a behavioural formula derived from impersonal patterns dictated by custom or by socialization. Joyce McDougall refers to this type of person as 'normopaths', that is,

> individuals who, while deeply disturbed, seemed to seek shelter behind a wall of 'pseudo-normality' that was relatively devoid of awareness of emotional experience . . . . I was unable to see further into this curious condition, except to conjecture that it was probably rather widespread among the population at large, and might well characterize what many would refer to as 'normal people'.
>
> (McDougall 1989: 93)

The observation that this 'curious condition' may well characterize a large portion of what many would refer to as 'normal people' is reminiscent of Marty's (1980) suggestion that the group of what he calls 'badly mentalized' neurotics comprises the majority of individuals in our civilization. What seems particularly significant is that the 'normality' addressed here refers to something more than the mere absence of psychopathological symptoms. It refers to 'normality' as the positive qualities manifested by individuals who are generally considered to be well-adapted to the social environment. The notions of *pseudonormality* and *normopathology* thus call into question the psychopathological inconspicuousness of so-called 'normal' individuals, and of 'normality' itself. In this perspective, it seems strangely possible to be pathologically normal.

The notion of 'pathological normality' (or of a normality that may be pathogenic) that characterizes alexithymia appears as a contradiction in terms unless we specify the distinction between the medical and the sociological definitions of normality that are simultaneously implied within it. The problem of distinguishing between social and organic perspectives in the definition of the normal has been discussed at some length in chapter three with reference to the work of Georges Canguilhem. It is worth recalling Canguilhem's argument for not assimilating psychic health to social adaptation. He writes,

> we are taking care not to define the normal and the pathological in terms of their simple relation to the phenomenon of adaptation . . . . The psychosocial definition of the normal in terms of adaptedness implies a concept of society which surreptitiously and wrongly assimilates it to an environment, that is, to a system of determinisms when it is a system of constraints . . . . To define abnormality in terms of social maladaptation is more or less to accept the idea that the individual must subscribe to the fact of such a society, hence must accommodate himself to it as a reality which is at the same time a good.
>
> (Canguilhem 1989: 282–3)

McDougall's concept of pseudonormality addresses the relation between social adaptedness and health in terms that seem to highlight the possibility of a contrast between psycho-medical and sociocultural definitions of normality. In her use, the *pseudo*normality of alexithymic individuals is a psychological and a medical concept (framed by the opposition of the normal to the pathological) that stands in contrast precisely to the normality of such individuals from a sociological point of view (opposing normality to deviance). The notion of pseudonormality appears *prima facie* to carry within it a noteworthy critical import. It problematizes conformity to social norms as a self-evident social good, to the extent that this conformity may constitute a risk factor in producing disease – which is also, albeit not only, a social problem. The title of McDougall's book *Plea for a Measure of Abnormality* (1978) is an apt illustration of these critical implications. As we shall see further below, the construct of alexithymia addresses the pathological quality of certain forms of adaptedness precisely in the terms pointed to by Canguilhem, articulating the difference between apprehending social norms as determinisms as opposed to constraints. The construct of alexithymia subordinates the value of social adaptedness to a specification of this value from the viewpoint of organic norms, by stating the superordinate value of 'inner life' as a variable that defines the possible qualities of social adaptedness as healthy or pathological.

But why is the notion of 'pseudonormality' critical of social norms only *prima facie*? The contradiction between the social and the medical perspectives suggested by this concept appears less radical when we consider it in a broader context. Let us retrace the steps that lead to the psycho-medical notion of pseudonormality, and to its implications with respect to sociocultural normality. In the construct of alexithymia, the violation of the expectation that each of us possesses a rich inner life is addressed as a medical problem relative to organic norms. As such, the superficial normality of the alexithymic is revealed as a pseudo-normality from a medical point of view. However, the psycho-medical concept falls short of considering the lack of a personal distance from 'role', or from normative prescriptions, as itself a form of sociocultural abnormality. In other words, it is assumed that the sociocultural definition of normality excludes the possession and display of 'inner life' qualities from its requirements. Following Foucault and other cultural theorists such as Erving Goffman (1961a, 1961b), we can argue that the current social definition of 'normality' does indeed include the measure of 'abnormality' that is represented by the non-perfect coincidence between the self and its roles. The commonsense assumption is precisely the contrary, that there is a genuine 'self' over and above, or behind, the mask of the role. If this is so, we must wonder whether alexithymic individuals are, after all, 'normal' even from a sociocultural point of view. We must ask whether the notion of 'pseudonormality' does not apply to them in the sociocultural sense beside the medical one. And this leads to a renewed overlap and confusion between these two perspectives, the medical and the sociocultural.

As in the medical perspective specified by Canguilhem, also from a sociocultural viewpoint the subject must be 'more than normal' in order to be said to be well adapted to the social environment. After all, it is this being 'more than normal' that is implied by the liberal-democratic values of autonomy and self-determination, by the exercise of choice and critique that are presumed to underlie the social outcomes we define as 'norms', and 'normality' as being in compliance with them. Alternatively, being 'more than normal' may stand for the symmetrical equivalent of these very assumptions, or the belief that we all possess an irrational kernel of freedom that is a bizarre reservoir of creativity, motivation and desire; an untameable kernel that emerges in the interstices of formal interaction to reveal that there is someone acting his or her social part, someone who is not identical with that part. In any case, either of these options implies a notion of the 'normality' of individuals that includes something more than the mere compliance with rules or with 'what should be done'. If this point can be sustained, the medical statement concerning the pseudonormality of alexithymic patients may be regarded as a formalized expression of sociocultural requirements relating to the qualities the self must possess in order to be socioculturally 'normal'. Viewed under this perspective, there is nothing critical at all about the concept of pseudonormality, on the contrary: the concept is symptomatic of the sociocultural *status quo* and appears merely to reinforce it. Yet, things are not quite as simple as this. In order to see how they are more complex, we must dwell a little longer on the figure of the alexithymic.

The hidden truth and the 'inner life'

How does the quality of social adaptedness of alexithymic individuals come to be regarded as pathological? How does it relate to the descriptions of their styles of communication, of their poverty of imagination, and of their lack of an 'inner life'? The conceptual hinge between all these aspects is the function of symbolization. In the last chapter, we saw how the discourse of psychosomatics links a deficit in this function to the proneness towards somatic or psychotic responses, as opposed to neurotic ones. We saw that the structure of the mental apparatus is believed to mediate the quality of the subject's encounter with reality, and that this mediation is said to give rise to different ways of falling ill. Hysteria and the psychoneuroses (the classical instances of Freudian psychopathology) stand in a positive correlation with the function of symbolization, and with the personal history of the subject which this function metabolizes. The hysterical pseudosomatic symptom can be effectively explained and resolved in terms of its being a symbol. In this sense, hysteria is perhaps rightly addressed as an 'imaginary disease' or, better still, as a 'disease of the imagination'. Somatization and psychosis, on the other hand, are negatively correlated with the function of symbolization. They allegedly stem from the fact that this buffer is not available between the subject and reality. At this stage in the discussion we are no longer concerned with examining questions of aetiology or topography, or with the specific technical passages that link a deficit in symbolization to the possibility of somatic pathology. We can take these links at face value, to examine what they imply in terms of the subjective relations to the self and to others. We will highlight the features that link the terms of truth, self, and illness at the surface of discourse, in a purely descriptive sense.

Before mediating the transition between health and pathology, the function of symbolization mediates a relation with reality, a way of being in the world wherein medical and 'existential' concerns appear to interlock and partly overlap. What is at stake in the healthy development of this function, in a medical as well as in an existential sense, is the very possibility of being in the world as a subject. Being in the world as a subject indicates the possibility of experiencing a quality of identity with oneself in difference that is equivalent to not being determined – or being so to a lesser degree – by changes in the outer and intersubjective world. The function of symbolization substantiates this possibility by allowing for a translation of present experience into forms that are recognizable in terms of a past experience, despite the fact that the experience of the past is not identical with the experience of the present. The function of symbolization allows for a margin of negotiation with the events of reality, and for the possibility of devising a 'compromise' wherein both terms of the relationship – the subject and the social, the past and the present – are actively engaged. It is this capacity of being in the world as a *subject* that the alexithymic patient is described as lacking. They lack such a capacity in their relation to themselves and to others, to the extent that their self-recognition has its source in external, 'objective' items of experience rather than internally, in the 'inner life'. The quality of adaptedness of alexithymic individuals therefore proceeds from the misapprehension or a distortion of the boundaries between self and other, a substitution of the external, 'objective', socially shared vectors of identity for identity itself. The 'excessive' dependence of such individuals on other people, or on the stability of their life-situations, stems thus from the fact that through the inability to develop and sustain the distinction between self and other, subject and object, their psychobiological balance or self-regulation is susceptible to changes in the other as veritable challenges to the integrity of the self.

Thus, the coincidence between the features displayed by these patients and the 'normal' qualities of identity or conduct does not testify to a deliberate engagement and intercourse with social prescriptions. It testifies instead to an inability to be otherwise, and therefore to a form of pathology. For the alexithymic patient, social norms of conduct and sentiment are the main sources for the boundaries of the self, boundaries which depend on the subject's (positive or negative) correspondence with them: the price of forgetting the rule is the threat of disintegration or madness. When the function of symbolization is defective, the alternative to this inclusion and absorption of the self by the other is its psychotic converse, the inclusion of all exteriority into an absolute, psychotic interiority. The psychotic, as we have seen, is characterized as presenting a similar rigidity with respect to imagination, whose contents are deprived of all (symbolic) ambiguity and are apprehended literally. If the alexithymic apprehends society as an 'environment', as a system of determinisms rather than a system of constraints, it is because one pole of the dialectic which allows for negotiation with society itself, the pole of subjectivity, is absent. There is no margin for negotiation because the two poles of the relationship are indistinguished. This indistinction, and the lack of a margin for negotiation, means that no response-ability is possible: what responds is the autonomic nervous system left to its own devices, unable to discriminate between an actual need or value and a symbolic one, between the organic self and the psychological self. Finally, this impossibility to be otherwise is projected onto the object (or the other) itself, upon which the constancy of the self depends. The projection becomes manifest in the failure to acknowledge the other as such, as possessing needs or interests that differ from the ones assumed or taken for granted by the subject.

Alexithymic patients are therefore described as lacking a quality of 'distance' with respect to reality, the quality of distance that is implicit in the form of the symbol on account of its ambiguity. This lack affects the forms of their experience of reality and of their engagement with it. Marty and de M'Uzan describe this feature as follows:

> Undoubtedly their thought is adequate to its task, even practically effective, but this adaptation represents the sheer limit of its possibilities for expansion and communication . . . . [I]ts lack of distance with respect to *things* is in fact a lack of freedom. Everything happens as if it were imposed on the subject.
>
> (Marty and de M'Uzan 1963: 348)

And similarly,

> Clinging thus to actuality as to a safeguard, without benefiting from the possibilities for receding and temporizing made available by phantasmic activity, the subject who is only able to think in terms of *pensée opératoire* undergoes reality more than he lives it deeply, he does not participate in it except in an empirical sense.
>
> (ibid.: 350)

The dimension of hiddenness or interiority that alexithymic patients seem to lack is thus the region that provides the condition of possibility for a receding (*recul*). The receding is a return that recreates the self as such precisely by 'returning' to it. The receding, in other words, splits experience into a duality of being and appearing, and enables the subject to re-signify the self in relation to the real, and the real in relation to the self, without allowing the two to become perfectly coextensive or identical.

Through this image we may begin to see the sense in which the 'inner life' is a necessary feature for the constitution of the self as a *true* subject, and somatic illness the expression of a relation between the self and its truth. The 'inner life' is not the truth 'contained' by the subject, but it is the term of reference that allows for the setting in place of a dialectic between subject and object, self and other. The 'inner life' is the history of the subject not as mere chronology, but as an imaginative construction that is unique in how its elements symbolically relate to one another. As such, it provides a constant principle of doubt and the possibility for a constant re-signification of experience: the present in terms of the past, the past in terms of the present. Winnicott explicitly used the expressions 'true self' and 'false self' to denote possible outcomes of the mother–infant relationship in the process of separation (Winnicott 1965). Dejours adopts this terminology to suggest that different mental structures imply different modalities of the 'relationship of the subject to his or her own truth' (Dejours 1986: 161–2). The figure of the *caractéropathe*, like that of the alexithymic, is a false self. Both figures cheat themselves into adaptation. Their compliance with the demands of reality, when these exceed the limits of what is psychologically tolerable, does not stem from a psychic negotiation through which a compromise is derived. It stems, as we have seen, from a preemptive annihilation of what spontaneously reacts, within the subject, to the encounter with the real. Somatization is the result of a shortcut, and it is the price paid to avoid confronting the possibility of psychic disintegration, the discovery of an empty self. Disease remains, for these patients, the only available form for the constitution of self as a *true* subject: they have disease in the place of a true identity, of the inner life, of the imaginary (Ammon 1974; Sami-Ali 1987). The subjective quality of experience is restored through disease to these individuals, who remain biological subjects despite themselves, as it were.

The healing powers of truth, or a re-evaluation of disease

A re-evaluation of the value of disease is implicit in the terms which link disease and truth within psychosomatic discourse. As a surrogate form of truth, disease may represent the extreme instance of an attempt at psychic self-healing (an 'attempt to survive' in McDougall's words), through a retrieval of the distance and difference between self and other. In this case, the retrieval occurs in the order of the actual, or of the real itself. The physical dimension of dis-ease, in other words, accomplishes for the individual what his or her psychic functioning cannot accomplish through having no psychic, hidden region within which to retreat. Disease itself becomes that region: it may afford, for instance, the possibility of a moratorium, of a postponement of decisions or activity, and in this it resembles the *recul*, or standing back, that the neurotic performs through unconscious activity. The experience of pain, similarly, affords the possibility of physically experiencing the boundaries of the self, when these are violated by alterations in the world of objects upon which the subject symbiotically depends, under normal circumstances, for that experience. Seen from this perspective, physical symptoms and somatic disease constitute a stabilizing factor with respect to the psychological balance of the individual, and not the mere and senseless consequence of a deficit. The symptom, as Dieter Beck (1981) writes, is almost the 'most intact' part of the patient, a precious asset without which the possibility of severe psychic suffering may be not avoidable. This point recalls the theme of an alternative or alternation between psychic and somatic suffering that is also reported clinically: a schizophrenic crisis or an endogenous depression may subside, if only temporarily, with the insurgence of a bronchial asthma or an ulcerative colitis (Spielberg *et al.* 1970). In psychiatry, the use of electroshock therapy, convulsive treatment, induced sleep, fever, and insulin coma can be read as somatic dis-ease that is artificially provoked under controlled conditions in order to obtain psychic healing (Bleuler, in Beck 1981).

Disease as an attempt at self-healing may succeed or, more often, it may fail. Failure here means that the persistence or recurrence of physical suffering is the only possible way of preserving psychic homeostasis. Success, on the other hand, means that the experience of disease is able to institute a confrontation between the self and its truth – that is equivalent to a resignification of the past in terms of the present, and vice versa – and to restore through it a margin of psychic agency and autonomy. From all that has been previously discussed, it should be superfluous to add that an authentic experience of psychic agency and autonomy is presumed to feed back into the physiological processes which underlie disease. Processes of 'miraculous' healing that occur as the result of a confrontation of the self with its truth are repeatedly described in autobiographical accounts of the experience of terminal diseases, as I will illustrate below. Conversely, the confrontation with the truths of agency and autonomy – the retrieving of a true self – is presented as a therapeutic option especially when the stakes are between life and death, as in the case of cancer. The 'wild' Georg Groddeck, whose work aimed less at finding scientific explanations than at being itself a form of medication, clearly expressed this point of view in the lectures delivered to the patients of his sanatorium. According to Groddeck, when human beings attain sincereness with respect to themselves they are no longer ill: either they die, or they get well again, whether literally or in the sense that they will be happy and no longer suffer from their illness (Groddeck 1978b: lecture 57). The re-evaluation of disease thus also implies a redefinition of health, not even as more than the mere absence of disease, but as something other than the absence of disease (see Abraham and Peregrini 1991).

Groddeck's own therapeutic practice, as we can now fully appreciate, was based on instituting such a confrontation between the subject and truth. How? By facilitating a reactivation of the imaginary through the constant spur towards engaging in symbolic interpretations: the wilder the better, in this case. The discursive pillars of this practice, examples of which are scattered throughout Groddeck's work, were precisely the re-evaluation of disease, claiming disease to be a good, and its resignification in terms of intentionality. They were veritable therapeutic tools, whose humorous content worked in synergy towards the same therapeutic end. Groddeck believed that the medical profession was irretrievably damaged by the Great War because physicians were called on to perform police tasks, and thereby to associate the notion that disease is intentional with the notion of simulation (Groddeck 1978b: lecture 59). Groddeck insisted that the function of a doctor is radically different from that of a policeman, and must be so. Whether or not someone lied, he proclaimed, had nothing to do with his task. There was no reproach in his asking: 'What do you want to obtain with your illness?', since this question could be asked and should be asked of every illness (Groddeck 1978a:

lecture 32). Similarly, the 'purpose of illness' as a form of truth is not equivalent, for Groddeck, to the static scientific 'truth' of an aetiology. The work of establishing the purpose of illness served to institute a meaning for illness. This meaning, if believed, could become the internal term of reference that is necessary for the constitution of the self as a *true* subject: a true subject in ways other than through disease. A re-signification, to recall Chiozza's expression, is also a change of state.

The therapeutic value ascribed in psychosomatics to the confrontation between the subject and its truth can be well illustrated through accounts provided by patients of their 'spontaneous remissions' from terminal diseases such as cancer. Spontaneous remissions are exceptional events, but what is of interest here is that they are now being studied in the context of what has been termed a 'salutogenic' approach, which aims at identifying factors capable of restoring or maintaining health (Antonovsky 1987). It is worth quoting at length from one of these pioneer studies, to show how the elements of adaptedness versus adaptability, and the relationship with oneself and one's choices, enter a discourse that is likely to be applicable, for the sake of prevention, to the majority of individuals in our society. The 'experiment' consisted in open interviews with a number of individuals from diverse social backgrounds and intellectual training, who had cancer and who lived better and longer than expected, or who had recovered completely despite hopeless medical prognoses. The interviews were geared towards investigating the subjective experience the individuals had of their illness, whether and how they thought they had changed in the course of it, and what they thought their own role was in the process. Superficially, each story seemed radically different from all others: in terms of the therapies employed, in terms of the extent to which lifestyles had changed, in terms of the time-span that changes took to occur. Upon closer investigation, however,

> The analogies between the experiences of these people became more apparent . . . . Looking back on their experiences, in particular the change in 'inner attitude' was remarkable. 'Inner attitude' refers to what these people would approximately describe as 'experience of one's relationship with life, oneself, the environment, etc.'. Usually these people talked about themselves before having cancer as being nice, friendly, cooperative, 'doing what I was supposed to do', living up to experiences, etc. . . . Invariably, a period came when these people realized the gravity of their illness . . . . [They] said that in this period they started to become more aware . . . of their, hitherto unconscious, mental concepts about life and themselves. These concepts described, e.g., a life in which one lives according to others' wishes, in which illness, health and death are a matter of chance, in which no real choices exist and in which meaning (as an experience) does not exist . . . . Then, after a period lasting days to one year, they

> *experienced* having choice . . . . Part of this altered outlook was a realization that also in the past they somehow had made a choice to follow the patterns and, in a way, had chosen themselves not to have choice . . . . The experience of free will and of naturally acting upon one's own intuition and insight seems to be a prerequisite for being a 'participant'.
>
> (Rijke 1985: 135–7, 138)

A second pilot study was performed by the same author after the initial results of the study reported here. Its purpose was to investigate the effect of providing people with advanced stages of cancer through counselling with a developmental context similar to the one described by 'survivors'. This second study yielded the conviction that:

> necessary to the discovery and development of the will is what may be called 'willingness'. The willingness to 'look into oneself', 'to let go of control', 'to suffer pain', 'to take risks in relation to the life-partner, working-situation, etc.', 'to make choices', 'to make mistakes' . . . . These issues, which may be a reflection of more general conceptions in society and culture, constitute an important part of the counselling.
>
> (ibid.: 140)

Although the term 'alexithymia' is not mentioned even once in the course of these studies, we may easily recognize in the patients Rijke describes, before undergoing their process of self-transformation, the characteristics I reviewed. Exceptional cancer patients describe themselves prior to their disease as hyperadapted individuals: individuals who experienced having no choice except in favour of 'normality'. Speaking from his salutogenic perspective, Rijke maintains that the pre-cancerous condition of these patients may be regarded, if not as an illness, as a 'lack of health' that can and should be acted upon for the sake of a better life, before and beyond the problem of disease. The exercise of will retrieved through the development of a true self attains the status of an organic norm.

Disease as an option: agency and response-ability

What is at stake in psychosomatics as a form of problematization? In the genealogy of this project we found the will to know, to define, and to spell out the possibilities of a newly perceived power: the power to generate and to exploit physical illness as an inconspicuous form of 'madness'. The strategic dimension of illness had its epitome in the figure of the hysteric, whose 'truth' Freud articulated together with psychoanalysis. With all the due modifications and differences with respect to the model of hysterical conversion, I propose that a theme of illness as a subjective strategy is still central to the propositions of psychosomatics. In what sense, then, can disease be said to reveal and hide the motives of a subject, if its condition of possibility is located in the structure of a subject who is not one? A subject, that is, who has only emptiness to oppose to the prescriptions of social reality? As a first move to answer this question, we must shift to a higher level of abstraction with respect to the proposition that disease expresses a compromise solution found by the subject to preserve and guarantee his or her social existence.

Disease, in the sense I have reviewed above, is not the direct expression of an immediate and contingent compromise, but the eventual outcome of a general mode of being, a more remote and more fundamental 'choice' with respect to the conflicts and dilemmas of existence. The quality of adaptedness attributed to alexithymics protects and shields these individuals from these conflicts and dilemmas, in the sense that social standards of conduct provide ready-made answers and values, leaving no space for self-doubt, self-questioning or guilt. This delegation of responsibility however is also, as we have seen, a partial delegation of response-ability: the margin of agency that disease appropriates and thereafter defines is the margin of agency the subject renounced by practising his or her liberty as if it were not one. The problem of physical illness thus bears on the constitution of the self as an ethical subject, in the sense that it concerns what we do with our freedom, the extent to which we acknowledge it and, with it, the extent to which we engage with attributions of responsibility, of guilt, of agency, on the part of the self already and before than on the part of others.

Before considering what these propositions yield in terms of therapeutic options, we must meet an objection that spontaneously arises after what has just been said. The objection is the following: How can we think of the features of alexithymia – the quality of social adaptedness it denotes, with all its consequences – as a form of subjective strategy, with respect to the real and to the social, since it appears to befall individuals as a result of interactive processes as remote in time as the mother–infant relationship? Is alexithymia as a deficit not 'inherited', much like any other genetic defect? There is a sense in which this is, of course, the case. There is however a strong argument for maintaining that the strategic dimension is necessarily implied in the construct of alexithymia. Generally speaking, the construct addresses an aspect of the individual that can supposedly be modified, but only through an active participation of the individual (the 'willingness' of which Rijke speaks). Once the features and the consequences of this way of 'being in the world' are made present in discourse to the individual, it is only his or her reticence towards engaging in a work upon the self and to undergo a process of relearning and self-transformation – which may yield important modifications in a life hitherto considered 'acceptable' except for disease itself – that accounts for the persistence of these characteristics. The problem of illness as a work of thought, in other words, does not have the same status before and after it is thematized as such. The task of addressing alexithymic characteristics and disease in terms of their strategic value (as 'having chosen not to choose') enters medical discourse as the ultimate theoretical option for their resolution. While the techniques proposed through behavioural medicine – relaxation techniques, meditation exercises, biofeedback and visualization – can be seen as unconscious ways of improving the capacity for self-regulation through a retrieval of the capacity for a true self (see Taylor 1987), their successful implementation presupposes the willingness or the ability to relinquish a prior balance. It is perhaps not surprising that these methods work sometimes spectacularly in relation to terminal diseases, where disease constitutes a hardly viable option for the individual as a solution to problems in living (Schützenberger 1991; Simonton *et al.* 1978). Each time the solutions proposed by behavioural medicine fail, largely through the failure on the part of patients actively to integrate them in their daily lives outside the therapeutic setting, the question returns to psychoanalysis and to the motivations underlying such failures: Who benefits from the homeostatic balance disease affords, and what is at stake in eliminating disease? At an immediate and contingent level, this is a question psychosomatics poses to the individual; at a more fundamental level, it is a question psychosomatics addresses to the medical establishment, and to society as a whole.

Both in its conditions of possibility and in the possibilities for its resolution, disease, in the discourse of psychosomatics, implies a confrontation of the subject with his or her own use of freedom, and with his or her own truth understood as the form in which this freedom is embodied. In his 1949 address to the Deutsche Gesellschaft für innere Medizin, Von Weizsäcker maintained that a psychosomatic perspective on the pathological allows us to see that illness has a purpose; that this purpose is to facilitate reflection on the meaning of existence; and that this reflection should lead to a re-evaluation of the values that previously informed that existence. Groddeck shared this conviction and formulated it in more commonsense terms: 'In the first place', he wrote:

> I claim the validity of this sentence for all illnesses, every form of illness and at any age – the meaning of illness is the warning 'do not continue living as you intend to do'; this warning increases, could become a compulsion or lead to arrest and ultimately even to death.
>
> (Groddeck 1977 [1925]: 199)

It is now possible to appreciate the full density of this assertion and also of its converse: namely, that the attitude of naturalistic medicine prevents us from making this important realization. The privilege assigned to biomedical epistemology in medical practice functions precisely to exclude the pertinence of questions relating to the purpose and motivations disease serves. In this sense, social norms of evaluation collude with the subject in producing disease, to the extent that they sanction it as a region that is exempt from the critique of values and ends. The consequences of this predicament affect both the possibilities for individual recovery and the relations between medicine and its clients:

> The patient experiences disease as the source of a right: as the legal foundation of insurance and indemnification. He even regards it as an uncertain and often contested right. Through this, we bury a most profound experience of every sick person, an experience that should be fundamental to his development and that is probably indispensable for his recovery: namely, the feeling of a condition that should not be there.
>
> (Von Weizsäcker 1986 [1930]: 42)

This proposition may be translated in terms borrowed from Canguilhem in the following way. Society as a system of constraints contains collective norms for evaluating the qualities of relations between its members and the environment (Canguilhem 1989: 282–3). In the case of modern Western societies, these norms are such as to render physical disease a minor risk, from the viewpoint of the general well-being of the individual, compared to the risks entailed by a different exercise of freedom. This point reverses the attribution of responsibility and strategy, from the individual who is sick through a faulty exercise of freedom to the social organization that prizes such an exercise above others.

For Von Weiszäcker, as for Groddeck, the attribution of a strategic quality to disease is subordinate to a re-evaluation of its value. This implies that the critique of motives and ends must apply to medicine, as an agency of the social, at the same time as it applies to the agency of the individual. The indiscriminate 'fight against disease' is not necessarily the best value in terms of the health of the patient, but it does reflect a value judgement proper to the 'entrepreneurial state' (Von Weizsäcker 1986 [1930]). It is within this social context that health is assimilated to the capacity for work and therapy is made equal to indemnification. This conflation has important consequences for the therapeutic prognosis in Von Weizsäcker's view, as I have already indicated. But he maintains that it also has counterproductive consequences for the economy of work itself. On the assumption that the medical task is equivalent and interchangeable with a task of indemnification, medicine is called upon to articulate judgements about whether and to what extent someone is impaired on the basis of 'objective' parameters. From a medical point of view, this is impossible: someone whose both legs are paralysed may be entirely vital and able to work, while a neurotic without any evidence of organic disease may be totally unfit to perform normal duties. Yet, the former will receive indemnity and aid, while the latter will be suspected of malingering. For Von Weizsäcker, the therapy of disease understood as a subjective strategy is inseparable from the therapy of a social conflict. The analysis of the patient should be accompanied by the analysis of the parts involved in the conflictual situation: of the social system as well as of medicine and doctors (Von Weizsäcker 1986 [1930]). These come across as the suggestions of an unconstrained imagination: they rightly testify to the 'revolutionary' and perhaps utopian character of psychosomatics as a form of problematization. But what are the therapeutic options in the *status quo*?

On account of the active role of the individual in substantiating illness and in possibly contrasting it, on account of the intrinsic link between health and the exercise of freedom, psychosomatics is not in a position to deliver 'prescriptions' in the same way as the medical knowledge that has gone before. Analysts themselves acknowledge that psychoanalysis as a form of treatment may not be indicated as a solution for physical disease in its immediacy. The confrontation it deliberately attempts to institute between the subject and its (lack of) truth may entail a concrete risk of further disintegration rather than the promise of restored health. The choice is left to the patient, between a series of therapeutic alternatives which correspond to as many modalities of relating to the question of truth. They differ, in other words, on the point of whether they aim at strengthening the individual in his or her current mode of functioning (as a false self), or whether they aim at facilitating a more fundamental autonomy through the retrieval of a true self. Dejours has outlined these alternatives in terms of three therapeutic 'positions'. The *psychotherapeutic* position offers patients the opportunity of learning how to organize their life in such a way as to avoid the situations which threaten to destabilize their psychosomatic economy. It is a vicarious exercise of judgement that bypasses the question of what makes the subject vulnerable to those situations in the first place (Dejours 1986: 210–11). Therapists may lend themselves as 'self-objects' to restore, through the therapeutic relationship, the threatened boundaries of the self and thereby stabilize or improve the patient's illness. As Taylor underlines, these types of empathic therapeutic intervention:

> actively gratify the patients' narcissistic needs rather than analyze the transference relationship and the patients' pathological internal object relations. Patients . . . therefore fail to acquire new psychic structure and self-regulating capacities and remain vulnerable to the vicissitudes of their symbiotic . . . relationships.
>
> (Taylor 1987: 260)

The risk for the patient in this type of option is to substitute for his or her illness the need for a permanent 'life-line' to the therapist, as both Taylor and Dejours remark. In its configuration, the psychotherapeutic position resembles the *psychiatric* and the *biomedical* positions, both of which act on the biological body as if it were independent from the structure of psychic functioning. By focusing on the immediacy of disease as the problem to be resolved, all these positions have in common the set task of protecting or restoring the patient to a prior balance.

The *psychoanalytic* position, on the other hand, exploits disease as an occasion for a more profound reorganization of experience, thanks to which the subject may hope to become his or her own source of protection, and to live without fearing the challenges posed by the encounters with reality. The price entailed by this position is that of relinquishing the focus on disease itself as the immediate problem to be resolved. Ideally, both analyst and patient should be 'free' from the desire to cure in order for the work of analysis to progress effectively. As Chiozza observes, the fact that the analyst works without keeping his or her objective in mind does not mean that therapy is aimless. However, especially in relation to severe conditions, analysts cannot rely on the fact that a psychoanalytic treatment will work in time to protect the patient from a serious threat to his or her life. This is the main problem posed by somatic illness to psychoanalysis, for which solutions in the form of revisions of technique and of cooperation with organic therapy are sought (Chiozza 1988).

The differences between each of these positions, in the context of this analysis, are less relevant than the similarities between them. They can all be regarded as different strategies that involve a choice on the part of the individual, a choice to be employed against disease and for the constitution and the transformation of the self as a subject. These two aspects appear inextricably linked, whether positively or negatively. The event of disease, in other words, calls upon the individual to opt for one type of technology as opposed to another. This choice quite explicitly does not only concern the more or less remote possibility of recovery, but the possibility of a different experience of self, of social reality, and of life itself. Dejours illustrates this general point with unusual clarity:

> Psychoanalysis is possible as soon as the neurotic manifests a desire . . . to find his way through a work that concerns the search of his own truth. The indication of psychoanalytic treatment for the other structures similarly rests on this fundamental question: is the subject asking the analyst to reinforce his internal split, or is he asking to contend with the truth, not only the truth of his neurotic guilt, but also the truth of his unconscious and of its violence? In the first case, it is best to address him to a psychotherapist, to a physician, or to a psychiatrist. In the second case, it is possible to contemplate the analytic adventure. But this choice is fundamental and only belongs to the patient. The analyst should be able to understand and respect the position of the patient that comes to him, even if this should lead him to abandon the idea of taking on the patient's treatment.
>
> (Dejours 1986: 224–5)

This point can only reinforce the suggestion that the event of disease, in a psychosomatic perspective, points to the truth of an intentionality, to a deliberate practice of one's liberty. Over and above the question of its aetiology, the event of disease involves a taking position with respect to disease itself. And this, at the same time, is a taking position with respect to one's relationship to oneself and to others. Although the choice is left to the patient, it remains to be seen whether these positions are equivalent with respect to the 'societal reaction' with which they meet. On the one hand, we may wonder what status is likely to be ascribed, in our society, to a deliberate choice against the development of autonomy and the search for a 'true self'. On the other hand, we may wonder whether a choice in favour of such a development would produce socially approved results. Beck among others underlines that the success of disease as a form of psychic self-healing entails progresses towards autonomy which, in their concrete forms, may easily be in contrast with social norms (Beck 1981). Von Weizsäcker draws similar conclusions from an application of his 'logic of mutual occultation':

> If organic disease is the surrogate of an unresolved conflict; if it can be defined as a flight from conflict into disease; if it is therefore a materialization of conflict; then, even with its spiritualization, the conflict remains unresolved. In other words, the successful outcome of the psychotherapy of an organic disease is at the same time the reproduction of a conflict. When this conflict leads to thoughts previously unheard of, and to even more unlikely actions, this produces a surrounding environment that may not find the change acceptable at all. Whether the change in question is a divorce, a political subversion or a religious one, in all these cases the person who *thus* recovers comes to contradict the customary order of things, and his therapist comes to be blamed by his friends and by the beneficiaries of the prior social situation. If what I am saying is for one half a kind of fantasy, for the other half it is nonetheless a description of what actually happens.
>
> (Von Weizsäcker 1986 [1949]: 461)

This is what is at stake, for the subject, in psychosomatics as a form of problematization.

Conclusions: the 'alexithymia construct' in context

Drawing from comparisons of his clinical experience in Egypt and France, Sami-Ali is the first author, to my knowledge, to have linked explicitly the prevalence of alexithymia to a diagnosis of the sociocultural specificity of the modern West. Alexithymia and what he calls the 'pathology of adaptation' are surface symptoms of a mode of life instituted by the absence or preclusion of the duality of being and appearing, for which Sami-Ali (1980) proposes the term 'banal'. As absence of thought within a simulacrum of thought, the banal is fostered by a type of social organization underpinned by a certain mode of production and by certain forms of technology. This type of organization favours a form of the 'real' that corresponds to the 'concrete' and to the 'literal', substituting for the abstract and dialectical form of identity 'concrete contents of the identical that embody the social norms of a sensibility' (ibid.: 10). In the order of the literal, meaning is fixed and being is exhausted by what something *is*; even the unconscious and the symbol can be reduced to transparent instances 'whose codified deciphering draws less on a subjective exploration than on a general consensus' (ibid.: 26). The banal is thus a way of speaking about the ineffable, a drawing of experience into an absolute visibility without residue, a flattening of the signified into the signifier. Perception is organized through stereotypes which render different objects, and different subjects, apparently interchangeable. Since it feeds on de-personalized meanings which belong to everyone and no one at the same time, the banal implies the neutrality of affect. The concept of the banal addresses, therefore, a form of identity 'that does not result from a dialectical reversal but from the impossibility of maintaining the two opposite terms in their difference' (ibid.: 28).

Classical Freudian theory does not permit an analysis of the banal as such. In that context, whatever is banal has, like everything else, the quality of an appearance or of an illusory cover pointing to a subjectively significant hidden content. Freudian theory, Sami-Ali suggests, has not exploited the theoretical possibility that the banal may actually exist as such and not as a mere illusion. And indeed, by his own admission, Freud did not explore what happens when and if the mechanism of repression does not fail, and thus does not give rise to the 'returns of the repressed' through which we know and we experience the unconscious. For Sami-Ali (1987), the pathology of adaptation is a 'pathology of the banal', of banal life and of banal identity, stemming from the unavailability of the inherently hidden dimension of interiority.

These considerations offer the opportunity for a contextualization of the construct of alexithymia. They may be usefully connected to the discussion of the relation between medical and social definitions of normality and pseudonormality. As we have seen, the medical perspective addresses the lack of an 'inner life' as a problem relative to organic norms. This perspective is in contrast to a social definition of normality that is assumed to exclude the possession and display of 'inner life' qualities from its requirements. If, however, we accept that this is not the case; if we acknowledge that there is a sociocultural requirement to behave as a self with an interiority, over and above the formal qualities of 'role', then, Sami-Ali's account acquires a new intelligibility. Like the unconscious and the symbol, then the 'true self' and true identity may be rendered banal by a social organization where these concepts have themselves acquired a functional value and have thereby become reified, so to speak. The pathology of adaptation stems from the peculiar opportunities for self-deception offered by the requirement to act 'true to oneself' and by the socially shared perceptual schemes which sanction acting 'true' as such. It is through their socially sanctioned experience of sincerity that subjects acquire and consolidate a 'false self'. In the wake of Freudianism, this process is facilitated by the cultural assumption about the universal character of the unconscious and of its 'inner life'. Subjects need not experience it: it will suffice for them to *know* that they possess one in order to act in ways they believe to be 'true' to themselves.

These propositions link in an interesting way with some of the recent work that stems from Elias' thesis of the civilizing process. I am referring to Cas Wouters' (1986) work on 'informalization' and to Abram De Swaan's (1981) work on 'management through negotiation' as opposed to 'management through command'. These works illustrate the thesis that, in its latest developments, the civilizing process has seen the 'true self' rising as a figure functional to the workings of human figurations. The process later named as 'informalization' was indicated by Elias himself in the lectures he delivered at the University of Amsterdam in 1970–1, and referred to the then frequent 'social experiments' towards 'controlled decontrolling of emotional controls'. Like virtually any other process considered from an Eliasian perspective, informalization is provoked and made possible by changes in the structure of interdependencies between people, and particularly by what Elias termed the process of 'functional democratization'. Functional democratization allegedly removed 'the necessity of distinguishing oneself from other individuals and from lower groups by way of instruments of possession and prestige instead of individual achievement' (Wouters 1986: 3). This precondition made informalization possible as a psychological development. A certain number of self-constraints, those inherited as part of the aristocratic legacy of civilization (e.g. etiquette), become no longer necessary or even desirable for the modern individual. Informalization as a psychological process is defined as 'becoming aware of deeper feelings and learning to surmount hidden fears', a process of which Freud represents the first leading spokesman (ibid.: 2). Central to Wouters' account is the argument that informalization does not represent a reverse movement with respect to the general direction of the civilizing process; in other words, it does not imply a decrease of self-constraints but rather a finer modulation of them, a change in their type and quality, resulting possibly in an overall increase in the general requirement for self-control in individuals. For De Swaan, as a result of increasing interdependency and relative equalization of power differentials, a typically modern type of self-constraint concerns the expression of:

> all those manners of feeling and conduct with which one puts oneself above others . . . . This is not to say that people in fact no longer attempt to rise above others, but that they try to control the expression of these strivings in themselves, and especially in others, and that

> they attempt to convey the impression that they never sought aggrandizement – it just befell them.
>
> (De Swaan 1981: 371–2)

De Swaan's description provides a perfect example of an added type of self-constraint which is working, however, in the direction of informalization. A change is therefore indeed present, but it involves new and different forms of self-control geared towards the ability to negotiate consent between relatively equal partners who can no longer appeal to 'blood', 'property', or sheer 'power' as justifications for authoritative commands. De Swaan underlines that in the transition from management through command to management through negotiation a central role must be ascribed to the rising profession of psychotherapy and to the process of 'proto-professionalization' through which psychotherapeutic concepts reached related helping professions, then clients, then the general public of potential clients (ibid.: 375).

The argument for the transition towards management through negotiation is also an argument for the functional value acquired, in the current social configuration, by the notion of having a 'true self' and by the activities through which it is searched for and displayed. What must be stressed is that management through negotiation does not necessarily imply a greater fairness or dignity of arrangements, for 'such negotiations always occur within a wider social context in which one party generally holds better alternative options than another' (De Swaan 1981: 376). What it does imply, by shifting the focus of tensions on micro or face-to-face relations, is a legitimation of the social order in which mutual consent is being achieved. 'Management through negotiation paralyzes rebellion', De Swaan writes, and I might add that it does so in the very name of liberty and autonomy. This predicament is taken by De Swaan to explain the occurrence of modern psychopathology in general, and the phenomenon of agoraphobia in his specific example:

> Some people . . . forego these options and steer clear of such threatening involvements, or they avoid the negotiations and the ensuing engagements. They do not rebel but they reject, not with so many words, but tacitly, implicitly, with a strategy that denies itself, until it is expressed in a vocabulary of psychic problems, as depersonalization, as a pleasure-less promiscuity . . . , or as phobia . . . . The transition to management through negotiation is onerous and hazardous. Where no command can be heard within or without, people may adopt fears and compulsions to help them refrain from what they are now allowed to do by others but what they find too difficult, too dangerous, and too lonesome.
>
> (ibid.: 377)

Through the notion of alexithymia, psychosomatics goes further than De

Swaan in suggesting that the very engagement in the process of negotiation, rather than the forgoing of its (limited) options, may underlie the pathology of somatic disease. The alexithymic mistakes the exercise of available options for a veritable form of liberty, and is no longer capable of distinguishing the social requirements of informality from the expression of his or her own desire.

What conclusions may be drawn from these suggestions? On the one hand, the construct of alexithymia may serve to institute a perpetual principle of dissatisfaction with what we believe to be true about ourselves, against any too-ready identification with received or commonsense wisdom. It may also serve to highlight that what we believe to be true about ourselves entails concrete effects on a personal as well as a societal level. On the other hand, we cannot fail to notice that this principle of dissatisfaction is derived from the reference to a superordinate notion of a 'true self', whose attainment is valued above all else in the name of health. In this sense, the construct of alexithymia must be regarded itself as an expression of the very movements whose effects it diagnoses as pathological. The essential point to be remarked on alexithymia, is therefore perhaps the double-edged character of the phenomenon when considered from an ethico-political point of view. De Swaan would seem to agree with this proposition, when he argues against Christopher Lasch that:

> Granted all that is wrong with the mental health movement, the contemporary therapy cults, the helping professions, and the social security bureaucracies, most Europeans and Americans may still be suffering more from a lack of what these institutions have to offer than from an overdose . . . . [W]hat the maligned professions and service bureaucracies are at present engaged in is mediation between individuals and families, on the one hand, and the state apparatus and capitalist enterprise on the other. They are essentially of a double nature, both helping *and* controlling institutions. Ignoring either aspect invalidates the analysis.
>
> (De Swaan 1981: 382)

However, it remains an all-important consideration to be made that the 'true self' as it is envisaged in the alexithymia construct is neither a necessary universal given awaiting to be revealed, nor its attainment a necessary option for the relative well-being of the individual. These impressions must be regarded as an effect of the assessment of alexithymia from within a social organization where health is defined as material autonomy and is held as such to be an irrenounceable value. In and of itself, the alexithymia construct substantiates the option of choosing against the search for a true self – a search that must be understood as a deliberate construction – at the price of accepting disease as a meaningful aspect of one's life. As we have seen, disease itself comes to be regarded as an expression of the self's truth, albeit one that the subject may wish to modify. In the perspective of psychosomatics, as

Groddeck put it, it is better to produce an interesting disease than a mediocre painting (Groddeck 1978b: lecture 61). The 'true self', if and when it is envisaged as the key to a 'health' understood as the absence of disease, has the same status as a concept of freedom envisaged as yielding only the 'right' actions. The construct of alexithymia contains the elements for a critique of the normative effects of the use of concepts such as freedom and health, and therefore for a critique of the unintended effects its own implementation may produce through these concepts. Even so, this concrete, historically overladen social context of appropriation is the unavoidable condition that will shape the predicament of psychosomatics.

9

CONCLUSIONS

A political double-edge[1]

In this book I have surveyed the general forms of psychosomatics as a space of problematization in the domain of thought. I have not paid detailed attention to more local forms of this problematic as they emerge from specific regional or national contexts (for an overview see Warnes and Blustein (1987)). The differences in nuance and emphasis and therefore in practical implications are likely to be significant, especially in the light of the important connection between different forms of medicine and different forms of state regulation. A comparative historical analysis in terms of local political economies of health would highlight how the different ways of conceiving the relationship between individuals and the state may inflect the problematic of psychosomatics in one direction or another, and vice versa. Such an analysis remains deferred to another context. In conclusion to this work, however, I wish to point to the ambivalence of what psychosomatics yields theoretically in terms of a political consciousness of health, to suggest that this ambivalence plays a role in defining the marginal status of psychosomatic discourse. For this purpose, even a superficial contrast between different national contexts is quite useful as an illustration. Karl Figlio's (1987) research on aspects of interwar social medicine in the UK, for instance, has shown a link between the formulation of 'psychosomatic' diagnoses and what he terms a 'reconceptualization of the social', whose culminating expression was the publication of James Halliday's *Psychosocial Medicine* in 1948 (Figlio 1987: 80). Figlio seems to suggest that the consideration of patients from a psychoanalytic perspective that retrieves the dimension of subjectivity is inherently conducive to a critique of the social, such as we find it in Halliday's book. Psychosomatics, from this perspective, appears to provide the foundation in knowledge of an individual 'right to health' against the losses incurred through interaction with a pathogenic social environment. And yet we cannot fail to notice that the immediate context of Halliday's book is that of Great Britain immediately after the Second World War; it is a context characterized, if not positively shaped, by the Beveridge plan and by the new relationship between the state and its citizens that the plan symbolically inaugurated. It is difficult here to establish any clear order of priority between the forms taken by psychosomatic knowledge and the forms of political engagement.

To see that nothing points inherently or unilaterally to an individual 'right to health' in psychosomatic discourse we may contrast Halliday's book with another text of psychosomatic medicine produced in the USA in 1943. Flanders Dunbar's *Psychosomatic Diagnosis* reports on the results of twelve years of research and clinical investigation carried out in the psychiatric and medical divisions of Columbia University at the Presbyterian Hospital Medical Center in New York. Dunbar quotes approvingly from Halliday's own earlier publications, but she outlines a problematic that differs strikingly in its implications from a reconceptualization of the social. Instead of the concept of a sick society, Dunbar's work yielded a set of personality profiles correlated respectively to fractures, hypertensive cardiovascular disease, coronary occlusion and anginal syndrome, rheumatic disease, cardiac arrhythmias, recurrent decompensation and, finally, diabetes. Halliday coined the expression 'psychosomatic affection' in order to unify localized diseases into a single category, which he believed would act as a lens through which the underlying social sickness, which is the true object of his work, could be recognized as such (Halliday 1948: 58–9, 225). Over half of Halliday's book is devoted to specifying the characteristics of this social sickness with a 'clinical' reference to the case of Great Britain and of specific regions throughout the UK. Throughout Dunbar's long work, on the other hand, textbook headings are reproduced to reinforce rather than to deny their specificity. Her 'specificity of personality' theory focused on individual predisposing factors, rather than collective ones. Even if Dunbar herself might have regarded underlying social constraints as significant in producing individual styles of response, the blueprint of her work easily lends itself to entirely different modes of interpretation, and specifically to an ideology of 'victim blaming' as opposed to that of a 'right to health' to be secured by the state. Dunbar's and Halliday's books taken together usefully point to the wide spectrum of political solutions that psychosomatics can be addressed to.

An authoritative counterweight to Figlio's optimism in relation to psychosomatics can be found in a number of articles written by Karl Jaspers between 1950 and 1955 on the subject of medicine in the age of technology (Jaspers 1986a [1950], 1986b [1953], 1986c [1955]). These articles can be read as a direct response to the position advocated by Von Weizsäcker around the same years. Jaspers was in fact called to arbitrate between Von Weizsäcker and psychiatrist Kurt Schneider on the question of whether an institute for psychotherapy should be established within the medical faculty of the University of Heidelberg, and he voted against this proposal. Like Von Weizsäcker, Jaspers supposed that the goal of an anthropological psychosomatics could be summarized as the 'introduction of the subject' within medicine. But, unlike Von Weizsäcker, he maintained that this slogan promoted a dangerous representation of human perfectibility identified with health, a representation based on the wilful or unwilful denial of the antithesis between liberty and knowability. Objectification, Jaspers argued, is a precondition of any finalized intervention based on knowledge. It is certainly true that human beings in their *Gestalt* are not amenable to objectification; but for exactly this reason it is wrong to seek to include this variable as an object for a new science. Precisely where it fulfils the programme of an anthropological medicine, psychosomatics treats human freedom as a 'fact', as something which exists and may be known through research, and on which we may count as 'factor'. Psychosomatics appears to forget that wherever research and therefore objectification extend, there can be no liberty.

Jaspers admits that there are certain conditions that present an insoluble problem, namely those in which patients themselves favour disease through their own actions or where, in a sense, patients are themselves the disease. This is the point where the medical perspective founded on scientific objectification is no longer viable. However, and here Jaspers argues in a diametrically opposite way to Von Weiszäcker, the relevant point from a medical point of view is not that these conditions have a comprehensible meaning or content, but rather that these relations of meaning have their correlate in somatic mechanisms or phenomena. If we could act on these mechanisms, their psychological consequences would also disappear. Through comprehension, on the other hand, we cannot establish with these mechanisms a relationship capable of ensuing in effective, finalized intervention. To the extent that medical knowledge aspires to the capacity for intervention towards definite goals, these relations of meaning should remain outside the province of medicine itself. An anthropological medicine would render the concept of 'health' akin to that of 'salvation', and this would mean that anyone could deem themselves sick in one way or another, and they could not be contradicted. Jaspers sees the emergence of psychosomatics as the effect of an epoch devoid of faith, yet where individuals have not lost the need for spiritual care. He stresses that we should not underplay the difference between self-revelation before a therapist and self-revelation before a spiritual confessor; we should not confuse the reflection on the self promoted for the attainment of health and the spiritual exercises addressed to God or being. In the contemporary promise of salvation, the means-ends relationship regarding health is inverted: health itself is the supreme value, rather than the means to attain a supreme value. Yet, surely, human beings should need health in order to attain their goals in life, rather than live in order to attain health. Jaspers feared that this inversion would eventually paralyse all possibilities for action (Jaspers 1986b [1953]).

Jaspers rightly observed that a psychosomatic conception of disease implies a displacement of the medical focus of intervention, away from the body-as-object and onto the embodied subject. For him, the consequences of this displacement could only be fearsome, in the form of an objectification of human liberty. The risk of moral principles being proclaimed as something similar to natural laws in the name of the value of health is indeed present in the application of a psychosomatic perspective. In fact, it is an inherent danger to the extent that psychosomatics aspires to the status of a form of knowledge capable of 'finalized intervention', short of a public redefinition of the goal of intervention itself. As I argued in chapter eight, the displacement operated by psychosomatics logically involves a re-evaluation of disease, and therefore a redefinition and a relativization of what is recognizable as 'health'. This predicament may contribute to explain the 'marginal' character of psychosomatic hypotheses in the everyday practice of mainstream medicine. As I argued in chapter two, a biomedical epistemology offers the technical and pragmatic solution to the problem of sanctioning and delimiting the right of entry into the sick-role. This function may well be challenged, but cannot easily be supplanted in a society where the sick status is in turn a tool for the differential allocation of both rights and duties (Gerhardt 1987; Parsons 1950, 1951, 1964). Paradoxically, the more that new territory of personal experience is made relevant to questions of health and disease through psychosomatics, the more indispensable a biomedical epistemology appears for the purpose of setting limits both on the duties and on the authority of the medical establishment in relation to the individual bearer of a 'right to health'. In practical terms, this invisible complementarity between biomedicine and psychosomatics is maintained through a rigid schedule of clinical inferences and consultations. At first, illness is treated as if it were merely somatic; only when biomedical approaches fail will psychosomatic considerations rise to the status of formal statements within medical and psychiatric institutions.

For the purpose of assessing the impact of psychosomatics on the contemporary experience of individuals, however, its formal relevance within medical institutions gives us only half of the story. If in the clinical context a psychosomatic rationality is confined to the management of what biomedicine itself cannot explain, at the level of information divulged by the media the presence of psychosomatics is increasingly being affirmed. As Arney and Bergen suggest, an interpretation of the modern medical encounter should start:

> not in the doctor's office but in the modern bookstore . . . . Indeed the modern bookstore suggests that patients, ex-patients and would-be patients are forming themselves into a social movement that is not unlike a rebellion. It seems that the self is asserting itself against medical indifference to the experiences and emotions that make up life, and its seems that the self is calling into question the power of the physician.
>
> (1984: 2)

The increasing popularization of some key terms of psychosomatic discourse has had the effect of producing a consciousness, and a conspicuousness of behaviour, either for health or against it. The media, one might say, have done for the collectivity of our time what medicine itself could not do for each individual: the rendering visible, conscious, and therefore amenable to some kind of rational decision, of the motivational components of illness. There are two important implications of this process, both originating in the fact that medicine and the media are structures (or technologies) with different competences and tools. The first implication is of an epistemological order. The fact that the media can only address an anonymous subject implies that they can only ever speak of susceptibility and of risk factors in generalized terms. Variables that might well have opposite valences in a psychosomatic perspective when applied to different individuals are transferred into 'causes' or at best into factors that 'can cause'. These reified factors, therefore, acquire a generalized negative value irrespective of the unique and personal constellation of which they form part in concrete life. In the media treatment of this vast new health-relevant domain, behaviours and attitudes have the same logical status as viruses or germs in the theory of infectious diseases. The nature of this transposition of psychosomatic concepts is that of a banalization, in the sense given to this term by Sami-Ali and reviewed in the course of the last chapter. The second implication arises from the fact that the media, unlike medicine, have no curative power. They can inform for the purposes of prevention, but they cannot assume responsibility for intervention. Individuals may still feel compelled to 'abdicate judgment' before the authority of knowledge, but this is no longer so that a physician might act or make decisions on their behalf. In other words, the individual – but also his or her employer or insurance company – is in a position to 'diagnose' the unhealthy aspects of his or her life much earlier than the stage at which medicine will sanction the 'reality' of a medical problem.

The preventive strategies applicable to the individual *by* the individual have become innumerable, ranging from the imperative to 'think positively' in the face of stress, to the self-monitoring and modification of physiological responses (Carroll 1984; Klausner 1965). There is, in fact, no limit to the scope of application of this will towards health, since the very failure to exert one's preventive capacity can be the object of a rational decision in the form of seeking psychotherapy. Yet, to the extent that any such failure is not treated itself as an illness – to the extent that it is not inserted in the structure of a doctor–patient relationship – it no longer involves a purely guiltless responsibility, but something more. A moral responsibility has become associated with prevention which represents an extension of the duties Parsons described as those incumbent upon the sick-role. As Crawford has rightly suggested, it is as if the sick-role became operative before the onset of illness itself, where the 'duty to get well' becomes retranscribed as a 'duty to say well' (Crawford 1977, 1980). In this somewhat modified reciprocity disease always implies a personal fault, yet one for which the patient must still (for how long?) be excused. The phenomenon of 'healthism' appears to suggest that some of the outcomes Jaspers feared and condemned are coming into being despite the fact that a psychosomatic rationality is kept from providing the mainstream line of approach within medical institutions. To make a stronger suggestion, it seems that the failure to have developed a medico-institutional structure of psychosomatic management may be co-responsible for the moral tones acquired by individualistic health movements developed extra-institutionally. As an alternative to this situation, however, we must ask: Would we want the 'personal failures' to which disease is traced to be inserted within the structure of the doctor–patient relationship as this structure currently stands? This would ensure the predicament of guiltlessness for them, in so far as they are reported as a problem. Clearly, it would also sanction them as unequivocally 'pathological' and therefore undesirable: what would then become of individual liberty?

Recent critiques of the phenomenon of healthism construe its moralism as a question of ideology and false consciousness, implying that political and economic motives of social control directly underlie the displacement of responsibility for health onto the individual. To construe the problem in this way, in my view, is to misapprehend the roots and rootedness of the issue. The phenomenon of healthism may be regarded, at least partly, as one effect of a profound modification in the possibilities of medical thinking which has not yet found a viable accommodation at an institutional level – and which therefore combines with a prior normative order to produce peculiar outcomes, both in a practical and in a theoretical sense. The biomedical definition of health as the absence of disease continues to provide an 'objective', institutionally sanctioned measure of value against which individual lifestyles and attitudes might be assessed in terms of their alleged health-preserving or health-denying function. In Western culture the medical effort continues primarily to be justified as an effort to eliminate disease as a meaningless and unnecessary aspect of human life. The 'finalization' of intervention in this sense substantiates the authority of the physician at least as much as his or her knowledge does. Each of these three aspects of medical rationality – health as an objectively definable condition, the elimination of disease as an unquestioned value, and the need to produce a capacity for finalized intervention – are problematized in the discourse of psychosomatics. Yet these fundamental and perhaps less visible aspects of what is involved in calling illness 'psychosomatic' are hardly ever acknowledged in public discourse about psychosomatic health.

The purpose of this book has not been to provide the elements for an immediate endorsement or rejection of the phenomenon of psychosomatics, still less to offer suggestions of how these developments could or should modify current norms of institutional functioning. The purpose has been to identify how the problem of 'illness as a work of thought', as it is posed for and by modern subjects, modifies the coordinates in terms of which we think of health, disease, and ourselves. The discourse of psychosomatics shifts the question of health from an ontology of disease to a genealogy of disease. The task of defining what disease is becomes subordinate and logically secondary to the task of asking what value disease represents in the context of an intersubjective environment where individuals interact, constantly trading the options available to them against each other. This operation yields and rests on a certain conception of the human subject. In this conception, the subject's psychophysiological functioning is not immune, and cannot be abstracted, from the predicament of epistemic dualism and of its normative concomitants. It is for this reason that the diagnosis of disease in terms of its strategic value can only hope to be effective – in a therapeutic sense – if it is applied to the agencies that provide care as well as to each individual patient. The discourse of psychosomatics ultimately yields a prescription towards reflection in the form of asking: What do we want under the name of 'health'? The risks of moralism, of individualistic politics, or of a totalizing dominance on the part of medical institutions, are inherent in any partial application of psychosomatic propositions, or any one-sided re-evaluation of the value of disease.

NOTES

1 THE SYMPTOMS OF TRUTH: A HISTORICAL SEARCH

1 Elias' analysis may be used to provide a macro-sociological and historical perspective complementary to Erving Goffman's concept of 'role distance' (Goffman 1961a).

2 The material presented in the Howison Lectures of 1980 (here cited) mostly overlaps with that of two lectures given at Dartmouth on 17 and 24 November of the same year. A transcript of these edited by Mark Blasius was published in 1993 under the title: 'About the beginning of the hermeneutics of the self'.

3 I borrow this expression from Stefan Rossbach (personal communication).

4 An example of what is meant by this 'multiplication' is provided by Foucault's description of the disappearance of an autonomous body of literature concerning the 'art of living' during the Christian era, and especially from the Renaissance onwards. In Antiquity, the literature on the art of living addressed the question of 'how to be', how to afford a certain type of experience (how not to fear death, for example, or how to face exile). During the Middle Ages and up to the moralists of the seventeenth century, the problem of the 'art of living' is increasingly addressed in manuals as a problem of 'how to do', and particularly of 'how to appear' within the collectivity. The 'art of dying', for instance', becomes an art concerning the appropriate clothes, gestures, words and countenance to be maintained before an event of death. This development signals the emergence of a difference (and possibly of a contradiction) between a truth of the self for the self, and a truth of the self for the other (see Foucault 1981b).

5 See Foucault's discussion of Cassian (1993: 218–19), for whom there is a specific virtue of verification in the act of verbalization itself. One can attest to the value of thoughts based on the extent to which they resist verbalization or not (evil thoughts cannot be referred to without difficulty).

6 This point can be fruitfully linked to Elias' account of a developing distinction betwen 'fantasy' and 'reality'. The consolidation of what we might call, with Goffman, 'backstage' and 'frontstage' truths may arguably imply that such truths about the self also acquire difference valences in terms of their 'fantasy' and 'reality' status. In this sense, we may ask whether 'immediate impulses' at later stages in the civilizing process possess in this sense a status likely to represent an actual threat or difference, should they be revealed. This line of reasoning may potentially be extended to explore the functional value of 'revealing one's fantasies' in contemporary processes of 'informalization' (Wouters 1986) and 'management through negotiation' (De Swaan 1981).

7 For a definition of 'return of the repressed' and for the sources of this concept in Freud, see Laplanche and Pontalis' (1988: 398–9).

2 HIDE AND SEEK: MEDICINE AND 'SOMATIZATION'

1 Portions of this and the next chapter appear in Greco (1998).
2 This expression, initially coined by Freud in reverse (as the 'mysterious leap from the body to the mind'), was made widely known by Felix Deutsch (1959) to refer to the process of conversion, and more generically to the notion of 'psychogenesis'.
3 Micale himself argues that the notion that hysteria as a disorder has virtually disappeared is a 'historical illusion'. He shows how 'elements of earlier hysteria diagnoses were reshuffled and fitted into a new set of diagnostic pigeonholes in twentieth-century medicine'. Accordingly, he offers no view on whether hysterical disorders are any more or less prevalent than they were, since 'insuperable methodological and epistemological obstacles exist to answering [this] with any degree of accuracy and meaning' (1993: 523).
4 If Parsons was right in regarding (bio)medical practice as a form of 'unconscious psychotherapy' (1951) – and recent psychosomatic research would confirm that it can thus be regarded (e.g. Dejours 1986) – the effectiveness of medical treatment for somatizing patients cannot be simply dismissed.

3 THE VITAL AND THE SOCIAL

1 Katon *et al.* (1982a, 1982b) discuss how various social networks and agencies affect the patients' 'choice' to focus on somatic symptoms in the case of depression, starting with the premise that depression involves both somatic and affective components.
2 D.W. Winnicott has explored similar themes in greater depth (see e.g. 1958, 1965, 1988). Although his work is directly relevant to this discussion, it is always in many ways more specific (e.g. in his addressing 'mothers') than I want this argument to be here. This argument also clearly resembles Elias' account of any individual 'civilizing process', but with an all-important difference: Elias treats society, for this purpose, as necessarily a 'system of determinisms' rather than a 'system of constraints'. The important objections to this view have already been discussed in chapter one and in relation to Canguilhem.

4 DOES PSYCHOSOMATICS EXIST? AN INTRODUCTION

1 The event in question was the fourteenth conference organized by the Italian Society for Psychosomatic Medicine, held in Florence in May 1993.
2 Foucault therefore focuses on the clinic as a space of epistemological reorganization, and therefore as the object of an *epistemological* – not a historiographical – problem (Osborne 1992). This marks off Foucault's 'history' from other accounts of the emergence of nineteenth-century medicine, where emphasis is placed on other elements or issues. For references on other perspectives, see e.g. Bynum (1980).

5 THE DISPERSION OF PSYCHOSOMATICS

1 Von Weizsäcker was actively engaged in these debates. However, the foundation of a 'psychosomatic clinic' in Heidelberg is connected to the name of his disciple

Alexander Mitscherlich, whose views diverged from Von Weiszäcker's in fundamental respects (Henkelmann 1990).

2 I refer here to Foucault's description of the human sciences in *The Order of Things* (1970). The human sciences are governed by the paradoxical figure of 'Man', a figure that is both the object and the condition of knowledge. For this reason, they are inevitably in the predicament of facing 'in two directions, towards the domains of life, labour and language whose determinations are represented in his being and towards philosophy where the status of the knowledge of those determinations is itself determined and fixed' (Cousins and Hussain 1984: 50). The task of questioning biomedical knowledge as a foundation of representations corresponds therefore only to one direction in the movement of perennial oscillation between the 'empirical' and the 'transcendental'. In relation to medical sociology, this oscillation is evident in the distinction between a 'sociology *in* medicine' and a 'sociology *of* medicine' (Straus 1957).

3 The German original of this text is unavailable in published form. My translation is from a version published in Italian (to my knowledge, the only existing published version).

4 For the notion of understanding to the point of belief see also Ricoeur (1970: 121), who discusses Freud's concept of 'double registration' as 'the provisional way of noting the difference in status of the same idea, at the surface of the unconscious and in the depth of the repressed'. For Freud, this concept explains why the communication to a patient of the meaning of his or her trouble does not automatically result in relief or cure.

7 INTERPRETING THE SIGNS OF EMBODIMENT

1 On the function of the dream as a psychic organizer and as a biological regulator see Dejours (1986: chapter 3) and also Taylor (1987: chapters 7–8). From the perspectives of these two authors, both based on extensive comparisons of neurophysiological and psychoanalytic research, the dream has a fundamental role in the psychosomatic economy. Thus, it is not a mere witness to the existence of a psychic life. Both authors insist on the need to distinguish between oneiric activity and REM phases of sleep, and therefore the psychological process of dreaming from its neurophysiological correlates. The psychological capacity to dream, as Taylor suggests, requires the capacity to reconstruct reality symbolically. It is not surprising, therefore, that the onset of oneiric activity is said to coincide with the phase of 'transitional objects' in the process of separation of the infant from its mother (see Metcalf (1977); Metcalf and Spitz (1978)).

2 The term 'foreclosure' (or repudiation) was introduced by Jacques Lacan and derived by him particularly from Freud's case history of the Wolf Man, where the words *verwerfen* and *Verwerfung* appear several times. It is a 'furtherance of a constant injunction of Freud's – the injunction, namely, to define a defence mechanism specific to psychosis' (Laplanche and Pontalis 1988: 167). The mechanism of foreclosure consists in an expulsion of a fundamental 'signifier' from the subject's symbolic universe; foreclosed signifiers differ from repressed ones in that they are not integrated into the subject's unconscious and they return 'from the outside', as opposed to 'from the inside'.

9 CONCLUSIONS: A POLITICAL DOUBLE-EDGE

1 Parts of this chapter have appeared in Greco (1993).

BIBLIOGRAPHY

Abraham, G. and Peregrini, C. (1991) *Ammalarsi fa bene: la malattia a difesa della salute*, Milan: Feltrinelli.

Abraham, K. (1927) *Selected Papers on Psychoanalysis*, London: Hogarth Press.

Alexander, F. (1925) 'Einige unkritische Gedanken zu Ferenczis Genitaltheorie', *Internationale Zeitschrift für Psychoanalyse* 11: 444–56.

—— (1943) 'Fundamental concepts of psychosomatic research', *Psychosomatic Medicine* 5: 205–10.

—— (1950) *Psychosomatic Medicine*, New York: W.W. Norton.

Alexander, F. *et al.* (1968) *Psychosomatic Specificity*, Chicago, IL: University of Chicago Press.

American Psychiatric Association (1987) *Diagnostic and Statistical Manual of Mental Disorders* (DSM-IV), Washington, DC: American Psychiatric Association, revised 3rd edn.

—— (1994) *Diagnostic and Statistical Manual of Mental Disorders* (DSM-IV), Washington, DC: American Psychiatric Association, 4th edn.

Ammon, G. (1974) *Psychoanalyse und Psychosomatik*, Munich: Piper & Co.

Antonovsky, A. (1987) 'The salutogenic perspective: toward a new view of health and illness', *Advances* 4.

Apfel, R.J. and Sifneos, P.E. (1979) 'Alexithymia: concept and measurement', *Psychotherapy and Psychosomatics* 32: 180–90.

Armstrong, D. (1983) *The Political Anatomy of the Body*, Cambridge: Cambridge University Press.

—— (1987) 'Theoretical tensions in biopsychosocial medicine', *Social Science and Medicine* 25: 1213–18.

Arney, W.R. and Bergen, B.J. (1984) *Medicine and the Management of Living*, Chicago, IL: University of Chicago Press.

Asher, R. (1972) *Richard Asher Talking Sense*, London: University Park Press.

Bachelard, G. (1951) *L'activité rationaliste de la physique contemporaine*, Paris: Presses Universitaires de France.

Barsky, A.J. (1988a) 'The paradox of health', *New England Journal of Medicine* 318: 414–18.

—— (1988b) *Worried Sick: Our Troubled Quest for Wellness*, Boston, MA: Little, Brown.

Barsky, A.J. *et al.* (1986) 'Medical and psychiatric determinants of outpatient medical utilization', *Medical Care* 24: 548–60.

Bass, C. and Benjamin, S. (1993) 'The management of chronic somatisation', *British Journal of Psychiatry* 162: 472–80.

Bass, C., Benjamin, S. and Murphy, M. (1990) 'The chronic somatizer and the government white paper', *Journal of the Royal Society of Medicine* 83: 203–5.

Beck, D. (1981) *Krankheit als Selbstheilung*, Frankfurt: Insel Verlag.

Bernard, C. (1878) *Leçons sur les phénomènes de la vie communs aux animaux et aux vegetaux*, Paris: Baillière.

Bion W.R. (1962) *Learning From Experience*, London: Heinemann Medical.

Blackwell, B. (1992) 'Sick-role susceptibility: a commentary on the contemporary database (1989–91) and classification system', *Psychotherapy and Psychosomatics* 58: 79–90.

Bonaparte, M. *et al.* (eds) (1954) *The Origins of Psychoanalysis: Letters to Wilhelm Fliess. Drafts and Notes 1887–1902*, London: Imago.

Boorse, C. (1975) 'On the distinction between disease and illness', *Philosophy and Public Affairs* 5.

Brede, K. (1972) *Sozioanalyse psychosomatischer Störungen*, Frankfurt: Athenäum.

Brown, T. M. (1985) 'Descartes, dualism, and psychosomatic medicine', in W.F. Bynum *et al.* (eds) *The Anatomy of Madness: Essays in the History of Psychiatry*, London: Tavistock.

Bury, M.R. (1986) 'Social constructionism and the development of medical sociology', *Sociology of Health and Illness* 8: 137–69.

Bynum, W. F. (1980) 'Health, disease and medical care', in G.S. Rousseau and R. Porter (eds) *The Ferment of Knowledge: Studies in the Historiography of Eighteenth-Century Science*, Cambridge: Cambridge University Press.

Canguilhem, G. (1975) 'Gaston Bachelard et les philosophes', in *Études d'histoire et de philosophie des sciences*, Paris: Vrin.

—— (1989) *The Normal and the Pathological*, New York: Zone Books.

Cannon, W.B. (1932) *The Wisdom of the Body*, New York: W.W. Norton.

Carroll, D. (1984) *Biofeedback in Practice*, London: Longman.

Chiozza, L. A. (1981) *Corpo, affetto e linguaggio: Psicoanalisi e malattia somatica*, Turin: Loescher.

—— (1988) *Perché ci ammaliamo? La storia che si nasconde nel corpo*, Rome: Borla.

Chodoff, P. (1954) 'A re-examination of conversion hysteria', *Psychiatry* 17: 75.

Chodorow, N. (1978) *The Reproduction of Mothering and the Sociology of Gender*, Berkeley, CA: University of California Press.

—— (1989) *Feminism and Psychoanalytic Theory*, New Haven, CT and London: Yale University Press.

Codignola, E. (1977) *Il vero e il falso. Saggio sulla struttura logica dell'interpretazione psicoanalitica*, Turin: Boringhieri.

Cohen, R. (1983) 'Stress, emotions, and illness', in L. Temoshok *et al.* (eds) *Emotions in Health and Illness*, New York: Grune & Stratton.

Conrad, P. and Schneider, W. (1980a) 'Looking at levels of medicalization: a comment on Strong's critique of the thesis of medical imperialism', *Social Science and Medicine* 14A: 75–9.

—— (1980b) *Deviance and Medicalization: From Badness to Sickness*, St Louis, MO: Mosby.

Corsi Piacentini, T. *et al.* (1983a) 'Mente e corpo in Freud. Alcune considerazioni', *Psicoterapia e Scienze Umane* 1: 3–21.
—— (1983b) 'Mente e corpo in Freud: "come è" e "come se"', *Psicoterapia e Scienze Umane* 2: 41–67.
Cousins, M. and Hussain, A. (1984) *Michel Foucault*, London: Macmillan.
Crawford, R. (1977) 'You are dangerous to your health: the ideology and politics of victim-blaming', *International Journal of Health Services* 7: 663–80.
—— (1980) 'Healthism and the medicalization of everyday life', *International Journal of Health Services* 10: 365–88.
Creed, F. and Guthrie, E. (1993) 'Techniques for interviewing the somatising patient', *Journal of Psychiatry* 162: 467–71.
Cunnien, A.J. (1988) 'Psychiatric and medical syndromes associated with deception', in R. Rogers (ed.) *Clinical Assessment of Malingering and Deception*, New York and London: Guilford Press.
Dean, M. (1994) *Critical and Effective Histories*, London: Routledge.
De Swaan, A. (1981) 'The politics of agoraphobia: on changes in emotional and relational management', *Theory and Society* 10: 359–85.
Dejours, C. (1980) 'La psychosomatique avec et sans Groddeck', *L'arc* 78: 51–8.
—— (1986) *Le corps entre biologie et psychanalyse*, Paris: Payot.
—— (1989) *Recherches psychoanalytiques sur le corps: répression et subversion en psychosomatique*, Paris: Payot.
Deutsch, F. (1922) 'Psychoanalyse und Organkrankheiten', *Internationale Zeitschrift für Psychoanalyse* 8: 290–306.
—— (1959 [1924]) 'On the formation of the conversion symptom', in *On the Mysterious Leap from the Mind to the Body: a Workshop Study on the Theory of Conversion*, New York: International Universities Press.
—— (1959) 'Symbolization as a formative stage of the conversion process', in *On the Mysterious Leap from the Mind to the Body: a Workshop Study on the Theory of Conversion*, New York: International Universities Press.
Dreyfus, H.L. and Rabinow, P. (1982) *Michel Foucault: Beyond Structuralism and Hermeneutics*, Brighton: Harvester.
Dunbar, H.F. (1935) *Emotions and Bodily Changes: A Survey of Literature on Psychosomatic Interrelationships 1910–1933*, New York: Columbia University Press.
—— (1943) *Psychosomatic Diagnosis* London: Hoeber.
—— (1947) *Mind and Body: Psychosomatic Medicine*, New York: Random House.
—— (1959) *Psychiatry in the Medical Specialities* , New York: McGraw-Hill.
Elias, N. (1969) 'Sociology and psychiatry', in S.H. Foulkes and G. Stewart Prince (eds) *Psychiatry in a Changing Society*, London: Tavistock.
—— (1978a) *What is Sociology?*, London: Hutchinson.
—— (1978b) *The Civilizing Process*, Oxford: Basil Blackwell.
—— (1982a) *State Formation and Civilization*, Oxford: Basil Blackwell.
—— (1982b) 'Civilization and psychosomatics', unpublished transcript, Elias Foundation, Amsterdam.
—— (1984) 'On the sociogenesis of sociology', *Sociologisch Tijdschrift* 11: 14–52.
—— (1987) 'On human beings and their emotions: a process sociological essay', *Theory, Culture and Society* 4: 339–61.
—— (1991) *The Society of Individuals*, Cambridge: Basil Blackwell.

—— (1992) *Time: An Essay*, Oxford: Basil Blackwell.
—— (1994) *Reflections on a Life*, Cambridge: Polity Press.
Ellenberger, H.F. (1970) *The Discovery of the Unconscious*, London: Fontana Press.
Engel, G. L. (1967) 'The concept of psychosomatic disorder', *Journal of Psychosomatic Research* 11: 31–9.
—— (1968) 'A life setting conducive to illness: the giving up–given up complex', *Annals of Internal Medicine* 69: 293–300.
—— (1977) 'The need for a new medical model: a challenge for biomedicine', *Science* 196: 129–36.
Engel, G.L. and Schmale, A.H. (1967) 'Psychoanalytic theory of somatic disorder: conversion, specificity and the disease onset situation', *Journal of the American Psychoanalytic Association* 15: 344–65.
Entralgo, P. Lain (1955) *Mind and Body – Psychosomatic Pathology: A Short History of the Evolution of Medical Thought*, London: Harvill.
Eve, M. (1983) 'L'opera storica di Norbert Elias', *Rivista di storia contemporanea* 3: 396–408.
Ewald, F. (1986) *l'État providence*, Paris: Grasset.
Fabrega, H.F. (1976) 'Disease viewed as a symbolic category', in H.T. Engelhardt and S.F. Spicker (eds) *Mental Health: Philosophical Perspectives*, Dordrecht and Boston: Reidel.
—— (1980) 'The position of psychiatric illness in biomedical theory: a cultural analysis', *Journal of Medicine and Philosophy* 5: 145–68.
—— (1990) 'The concept of somatization as a cultural and historical product of Western medicine', *Psychosomatic Medicine* 52: 653–72.
Fava, G.A. (1992) 'The concept of psychosomatic disorder', *Psychotherapy and Psychosomatics* 58: 1–12.
Fava, G.A. and Wise, T.N. (eds) (1987) 'Methodological issues in psychosomatic research', *Research Paradigms in Psychosomatic Medicine*, Basel: Karger.
Fédida, P. (1969) 'Le psychanalyste sauvage', *Les Temps Modernes* 25.
Feldman, M.D. and Escalona, R. (1991) 'The longing for nurturance: a case of factitious cancer', *Psychosomatics* 32: 226–8.
Fenichel, O. (1945) 'Nature and classification of the so-called psychosomatic phenomena', *Psychoanalytic Quarterly* 14: 287–312.
Ferenczi, S. (1955) *Final Contributions to the Problems and Methods of Psychoanalysis*, New York: Basic Books.
Figlio, K. (1977) 'The historiography of scientific medicine: an invitation to the human sciences', *Comparative Studies in Society and History* 19: 262–86.
—— (1982) 'How does illness mediate social relations? Workmen's compensation and medico-legal practices, 1890–1940', in P. Wright and A. Treacher (eds) *The Problem of Medical Knowledge*, Edinburgh: University of Edinburgh Press.
—— (1985) 'What is an accident?', in P. Weindling (ed.) *The Social History of Occupational Health*, London: Croom Helm.
—— (1987) 'The lost subject of medical sociology', in G. Scambler (ed.) *Sociological Theory and Medical Sociology*, London: Tavistock.
Ford, C.V. (1983) *The Somatizing Disorders: Illness as a Way of Life*, New York: Elsevier Biomedical.
Foucault, M. (1970) *The Order of Things*, London: Routledge.

—— (1972a) *Histoire de la folie à l'âge classique*, Paris: Gallimard.
—— (1972b) *The Archaeology of Knowledge*, London: Routledge.
—— (1973) *The Birth of the Clinic*, London: Routledge.
—— (1976) 'La crisis de la medicina o la crisis de la antimedicina', *Educación Médica y Salud* 10: 152–70.
—— (1977a) 'Nietzsche, genealogy, history', in D.F. Bouchard (ed.) *Michel Foucault: Language, Counter-Memory, Practice*, New York: Cornell University Press.
—— (1977b) *Discipline and Punish*, London: Penguin.
—— (1978) *The History of Sexuality: An Introduction*, London: Penguin.
—— (1980a) 'The confession of the flesh', in C. Gordon (ed.) *Power/Knowledge*, Brighton: Harvester.
—— (1980b) 'Truth and subjectivity', Howison Lecture, 20 October 1980, Archives Foucault, Bibliothèque du Saulchoir, Paris.
—— (1980c) 'Truth and subjectivity', Howison Lecture , 21 October 1980, Archives Foucault, Bibliothèque du Saulchoir, Paris.
—— (1980d) 'The politics of health in the eighteenth century', in C. Gordon (ed.) *Power/Knowledge*, Brighton: Harvester.
—— (1981a) 'Subjectivité et vérité', unpublished lecture, 6 January 1981, Archives Foucault, Bibliothèque du Saulchoir, Paris.
—— (1981b) 'Subjectivité et vérité', unpublished lecture, 13 January 1981, Archives Foucault, Bibliothèque du Saulchoir, Paris.
—— (1981c) 'Omnes et singulatim: towards a critique of political reason', in S.M. McMurrin (ed.) *The Tanner Lectures on Human Values* 2, Cambridge: Cambridge University Press.
—— (1982) 'The subject and power', afterword to H.L. Dreyfus and P. Rabinow, *Michel Foucault: Beyond Structuralism and Hermeneutics*, Brighton: Harvester.
—— (1984a) 'Polemics, politics, and problemizations', in P. Rabinow (ed.) *The Foucault Reader*, New York: Pantheon Books.
—— (1984b) 'What is Enlightenment?', in P. Rabinow (ed.) *The Foucault Reader*, New York: Pantheon Books.
—— (1984c) 'Preface to *The History of Sexuality*, Volume II', in P. Rabinow (ed.) *The Foucault Reader*, New York: Pantheon Books.
—— (1987) *Mental Illness and Psychology*, Berkeley, CA: University of California Press.
—— (1988a) 'The concern for truth', in L.D. Kritzman (ed.) *Michel Foucault: Politics, Philosophy, Culture*, New York: Routledge.
—— (1988b) 'On problematization', *History of the Present* 4 (Spring): 16–17.
—— (1988c) 'The ethic of care of the self as a practice of freedom', in J. Bernauer and D. Rasmussen (eds) *The Final Foucault*, Cambridge, MA: MIT Press.
—— (1988d) 'Technologies of the self', in L.H. Martin *et al.* (eds) *Technologies of the Self*, London: Tavistock.
—— (1988e) 'The political technology of individuals', in L. Martin *et al.* (eds) *Technologies of the Self*, London: Tavistock.
—— (1990) *The Use of Pleasure: History of Sexuality: Volume II*, New York: Vintage Books.
—— (1993) 'About the beginning of the hermeneutics of the self', *Political Theory* 21: 198–227.
—— (1997) *The Essential Works 1: Ethics*, London: Penguin.

Freidson, E. (1970) *Profession of Medicine*, New York: Dodd Mead.

Freud, S. (1893) 'Some points for a comparative study of organic and hysterical paralyses', in J. Strachey (ed.) *The Standard Edition of the Complete Psychological Works of Sigmund Freud*, London: Hogarth Press, Vol. 1.

—— (1895) 'On the grounds for detaching a particular syndrome from neurasthenia under the description "anxiety neurosis"', in *The Standard Edition of the Complete Psychological Works of Sigmund Freud*, Vol. 3.

—— (1896) 'Heredity and the aetiology of the neuroses', in *The Standard Edition of the Complete Psychological Works of Sigmund Freud*, Vol. 3.

—— (1898) 'Sexuality in the aetiology of neuroses', in *The Standard Edition of the Complete Psychological Works of Sigmund Freud*, Vol. 3.

—— (1914) 'On narcissism: an introduction', in *The Standard Edition of the Complete Psychological Works of Sigmund Freud*, Vol. 14.

—— (1915) 'Instincts and their vicissitudes', in *The Standard Edition of the Complete Psychological Works of Sigmund Freud*, Vol. 14.

—— (1915–17) 'Introductory lectures on psychoanalysis', in *The Standard Edition of the Complete Psychological Works of Sigmund Freud*, Vol. 16.

—— (1926) 'The question of lay analysis', in *The Standard Edition of the Complete Psychological Works of Sigmund Freud*, Vol. 20.

—— (1930) 'Civilization and its discontents', in *The Standard Edition of the Complete Psychological Works of Sigmund Freud*, Vol. 21.

—— (1933) 'New introductory lectures on psychoanalysis', in *The Standard Edition of the Complete Psychological Works of Sigmund Freud*, Vol. 22.

—— (1950) 'Two encyclopaedia articles', in *Collected Papers*, London: Hogarth Press.

Freund, P.E.S. (1988) 'Bringing society into the body: understanding socialized human nature', *Theory and Society* 17: 839–64.

—— (1990) 'The expressive body: a common ground for the sociology of emotions and health and illness', *Sociology of Health and Illness* 12: 452–77.

Furlan, P.M. and Mancini, A. (1980) 'La consultazione psicosomatica: problemi di metodo e implicazioni operative', *Psicoterapia e Scienze Umane* 4: 45–59.

Gaddini, E. (1982) 'Fantasie difensive precoci e processo psicoanalitico', *Rivista di Psicoanalisi* 1: 1–14.

Gaddini, R. (1980) 'Patologia psicosomatica come difetto maturativo', *Rivista di Psicoanalisi* 3: 381–8.

Garma, A. (1953) 'The internalized mother as harmful food in peptic ulcer patients', *International Journal of Psychoanalysis* 34: 102–10.

—— (1958) *Peptic Ulcer and Psychoanalysis*, Baltimore, MD: Williams & Wilkins.

Gerhardt, U. (1987) 'Parsons, role theory, and health interaction', in G. Scambler (ed.) *Sociological Theory and Medical Sociology*, London: Tavistock.

—— (1989) *Ideas About Illness: An Intellectual and Political History of Medical Sociology*, London: Macmillan.

Goffman, E. (1961a) *Encounters*, Indianapolis, IN: Bobbs Merrill.

—— (1961b) *Asylums*, New York: Anchor.

Gorman, W.F. (1982) 'Defining malingering', *Journal of Forensic Sciences* 27: 401–7.

Goudsmit, E.M. and Gadd, R. (1991) 'All in the mind? The psychologisation of illness', *The Psychologist* 4.

Gove, W.R. (1970) 'Societal reaction as an explanation of mental illness: an evaluation', *American Sociological Review* 35: 873–84.

—— (1974) 'Individual resources and mental hospitalization: A comparison and evaluation of the societal reaction and psychiatric perspectives', *American Sociological Review* 39: 86–100.

Grace, W.H. and Graham, D.T. (1952) 'Relationships of specific attitudes and emotions to certain bodily diseases', *Psychosomatic Medicine* 14: 243–51.

Graham, D.T. (1967) 'Health, disease, and the mind–body problem: linguistic parallelism', *Psychosomatic Medicine* 29: 52–71.

Greco, M. (1993) 'Psychosomatic subjects and the "duty to be well": personal agency within medical rationality', *Economy and Society* 22: 357–72.

—— (1998) 'Between social and organic norms: reading Canguilhem and somatization', forthcoming in *Economy and Society*.

Grinker, R.R. (1973) *Psychosomatic Concepts*, New York: Jason Aronson.

Grinker, R.R. and Robbins, F.P. (1953) *Psychosomatic Case Book*, New York: Blakiston.

Groddeck, G. (1977a [1917]) 'Psychic conditioning and the psychoanalytic treatment of organic disorders', in *The Meaning of Illness*, London: Karnac Books.

—— (1977b [1925]) *The Meaning of Illness*, London: Karnac Books.

—— (1977c [1927]) 'The human being, not the patient, requires help', in *The Meaning of Illness*, London: Karnac Books.

—— (1978a) *Conférences psychanalytiques à l'usage des malades*, Vol. 1, Paris: Éditions 10/18.

—— (1978b) *Conférences psychanalytiques à l'usage des malades*, Vol. 2, Paris: Éditions 10/18.

Grosz, E. (1994) *Volatile Bodies: Toward a Corporeal Feminism*, Bloomington and Indianapolis, IN: Indiana University Press.

Grotstein, J.S. (1980) 'A proposed revision of the psychoanalytic concept of primitive mental states: I. Introduction to a newer psychoanalytic metapsychology', *Contemporary Psychoanalysis* 16: 479–546.

Gutting, G. (1989) *Michel Foucault's Archaeology of Scientific Reason*, Cambridge: Cambridge University Press.

Hacking, I. (1986) 'Making up people', in T.C. Heller *et al.* (eds) *Reconstructing Individualism: Autonomy, Individuality, and the Self in Western Thought*, Stanford, CA: Stanford University Press.

Halliday, J.L. (1948) *Psychosocial Medicine: A Study of the Sick Society*, New York: W.W. Norton.

Harrington, R. (1996) 'The "railway spine" diagnosis and Victorian responses to PTSD', *Journal of Psychosomatic Research* 40: 11–14.

Henkelmann, T. (1990) 'Viktor Von Weizsäcker: l'uomo e la sua opera', in Von Weizsäcker, *Filosofia della medicina*, Milan: Guerini e Associati.

Helman, C.G. (1985), 'Psyche, soma, and society: the social construction of psychosomatic disorders', *Culture, Medicine and Psychiatry* 9: 1–26.

Hinkle, L.E. (1961) 'Ecologic observations of the relation of physical illness, mental illness, and the social environment', *Psychosomatic Medicine* 23: 289–96.

Hofer, M.A. (1978) 'Hidden regulatory processes in early social relationships', in P.G. Bateson and P.H. Klopfer (eds) *Perspectives in Ethology*, Vol. 3, New York: Plenum.

—— (1983) 'The mother–infant interaction as a regulator of infant physiology and behavior', in L. Rosenblum and H. Moltz (eds) *Symbiosis in Parent–Offspring Interactions*, New York: Plenum.

—— (1984) 'Relationships as regulators: a psychobiologic perspective on bereavement', *Psychosomatic Medicine* 46: 183–97.

Holmes, T.H. and Rahe, R.H. (1967) 'The social readjustment rating scale', *Journal of Psychosomatic Research* 11: 213–18.

Holroyd, K.A. and Lazarus, R.S. (1982) 'Stress, coping, and somatic adaptation', in L. Goldberg and S. Breznitz (eds) *Handbook of Stress: Theoretical and Clinical Aspects*, New York: Free Press.

Hoppe, K.D. (1977) 'Split brains and psychoanalysis', *Psychoanalytic Quarterly* 46: 220–44.

Hoppe, K.D. and Bogen, J.E. (1977) 'Alexithymia in twelve commissurotomized patients', *Psychotherapy and Psychosomatics* 28: 148–55.

Horney, K. (1952) 'The paucity of inner experiences', *American Journal of Psychoanalysis* 12: 3–9.

Jaspers, K. (1986a [1950]) 'Zur Kritik der Psychanalyse', in *Der Arzt im technischen Zeitalter*, Munich: Piper Verlag.

—— (1986b [1953]) *Der Arzt im technischen Zeitalter*, Munich: Piper Verlag.

—— (1986c [1955]) 'Wesen und Kritik der Psychotherapie', in *Der Arzt im technischen Zeitalter*, Munich: Piper Verlag.

Jelliffe, S.E. (1919) 'The symbol as an energy container: a preliminary statement', *Journal of Nervous and Mental Diseases* 50: 540–50.

—— (1926) 'Psychoanalysis and organic disorder: myopia as a paradigm', *International Journal of Psychoanalysis* 7: 445–56.

—— (1933) 'The death instinct in somatic and psychopathology', *Psychoanalytic Review* 20: 121–32.

—— (1935–6) 'The bodily organs and psychopathology', *American Journal of Psychiatry* 92: 1051–76.

Jenkins, C.D. (1985) 'New horizons for psychosomatic medicine', *Psychosomatic Medicine* 47: 3–25.

Jennings, D. (1986) 'The confusion between disease and illness in clinical medicine', *Canadian Medical Association Journal* 135: 865–70.

Jewson, N.D. (1976) 'The disappearance of the sick-man from medical cosmology, 1770–1870', *Sociology* 10: 225–44.

Jonas, J.M. and Pope, H.G. (1985) 'The dissimulating disorders: a single diagnostic entity?', *Comprehensive Psychiatry* 26: 58–62.

Kaplan, H.S. and Kaplan, H.I. (1967) 'Current concepts of psychosomatic medicine', in A.M. Freedman and H.I. Kaplan (eds) *Comprehensive Textbook of Psychiatry*, Baltimore, MD: Williams & Wilkins.

Katon, W. *et al.* (1982a) 'Depression and somatization: a review', Part I, *American Journal of Medicine* 72: 127–35.

—— (1982b) 'Depression and somatization: a review', Part II, *American Journal of Medicine* 72: 241–7.

—— (1990) 'Distressed high utilizers of medical care: DSM-III-R diagnoses and treatment needs', *General Hospital Psychiatry* 12: 355–62.

Kelman, N. (1952) 'Clinical aspects of externalized living', *American Journal of Psychoanalysis* 12: 15–23.

Kimball, C.P. (1983) 'The biopsychosocial approach: liaison medicine and its models', *Psychotherapy and Psychosomatics* 40: 48–65.

King, L. (1994) 'There is no such thing as a mother', *Winnicott Studies: the Journal of the Squiggle Foundation* 9: 18–23.

Kirmayer, L.J. (1984) 'Culture, affect and somatization', *Transcultural Psychiatric Research Review* 21: 159–88.

—— (1986) 'Somatization and the social construction of illness experience', in S. McHugh and T.M. Vallis (eds) *Illness Behavior: A Multidisciplinary Model*, New York: Plenum.

Kirmayer, L.J. *et al.* (1994) 'Somatoform disorders: Personality and the social matrix of somatic distress', *Journal of Abnormal Psychology* 103: 125–36.

Klausner, S.Z. (1965) *The Quest for Self-Control*, New York: Free Press.

Kramer, P.D. (1994) *Listening to Prozac*, London: Fourth Estate.

Krasner, D. (1985) *Smith Ely Jelliffe and the Development of American Psychosomatic Medicine*, Ph.D. dissertation, Ann Arbor, MI: University Microfilms International.

Krohn, A. (1978) *Hysteria: The Elusive Neurosis*, New York: International Universities Press.

Krystal, H.A. (1979) 'Alexithymia and psychotheraphy', *American Journal of Psychotheraphy* 33: 17–31.

—— (1982–3) 'Alexithymia and the effectiveness of psychoanalytic treatment', *International Journal of Psychotherapy* 9: 353–78.

Krystal, H.A. and Raskin, H. (1970) *Drug Dependence: Aspects of Ego Function*, Detroit, MI: Wayne State University Press.

Kusch, M. (1991) *Foucault's Strata and Fields*, Dordrecht: Kluwer Academic Publishers.

Lacey, J.I. *et al.* (1953) 'Autonomic response specificity', *Psychosomatic Medicine* 15: 8–21.

Laplanche, J. and Pontalis, J.B. (1988) *The Language of Psychoanalysis*, London: Karnac Books.

Lask, B. (1996) ' "Psychosomatic medicine" *not* "psychosomatic disorders" ', *Journal of Psychosomatic Research* 40: 457–60.

Lemert, E.M. (1967) *Human Deviance, Social Problems and Social Control*, Englewood Cliffs, NJ: Prentice Hall.

Lerner, M. (1985) 'A report on complementary cancer therapies', *Advances* 2.

Lesser, I.R. (1981) 'A review of the alexithymia concept', *Psychosomatic Medicine* 43: 531–43.

Levin, D.M. and Solomon, G.F. (1990) 'The discursive formation of the body in the history of medicine', *Journal of Medicine and Philosophy* 15: 515–37.

Lewis, A.J. (1934) 'The psychopathology of insight', *British Journal of Medical Psychology* 14.

Lipowski, Z.J. (1984) 'Psychosomatic medicine – Past and present' Parts I–III, *Canadian Journal of Psychiatry* 31: 2–21.

—— (1988) 'Somatization: the concept and its clinical application', *American Journal of Psychiatry* 145: 1358–68.

Luban-Plozza, B. and Pöldinger, W. (1977) *Der psychosomatisch Kranke in der praxis*, Heidelberg: Springer Verlag.

Lumley, M. *et al*. (1996) 'How are alexithymia and physical illness linked? A review and critique of pathways', *Journal of Psychosomatic Research* 41: 505–18.

MacLean, P.D. (1949) 'Psychosomatic disease and the "visceral brain"', *Psychosomatic Medicine* 11: 338–53.

McDougall, J. (1978) *Plea for a Measure of Abnormality*, New York: International Universities Press.

—— (1989) *Theatres of the Body*, London: Free Association Books.

McGregor, J.A. and Duncan, L.S. (1988) 'Suing as an expression of somatization', *American Journal of Obstetrics and Gynecology* 158: 616–17.

Mahler, M.S. (1968) *On Human Symbiosis and the Vicissitudes of Individuation*, New York: International Universities Press.

Mahler, M.S. *et al*. (1975) *The Psychological Birth of the Human Infant: Symbiosis and Individuation*, London: Hutchinson.

Margetts, E.L. (1950) 'The early history of the word "psychosomatic"', *Canadian Medical Association Journal* 63: 402.

Marty, P. (1968) 'La dépression essentielle', *Revue Française de Psychanalyse* 32.

—— (1980) *L'ordre psychosomatique: les mouvements individuels de vie et de mort*, Paris: Payot.

—— (1991) *Mentalisation et psychosomatique*, Paris: Delagrange.

Marty, P. and De M'Uzan, M. (1963) 'La pensée opératoire', *Revue Française de Psychanalyse* 27: 345–56.

Mason, J.W. (1975a) 'A historical view of the stress field', Part I, *Journal of Human Stress* 1: 6–12.

—— (1975b) 'A historical view of the stress field', Part II, *Journal of Human Stress* 1: 22–36.

Mayou, R. (1983) 'Psychological factors and the course of illness', in D. Wetherall *et al*. (eds) *Oxford Textbook of Medicine*, Oxford: Oxford University Press.

—— (1993) 'Somatization', *Psychotherapy and Psychosomatics* 59: 69–83.

Mechanic, D. (1978) 'Effects of psychological distress on perception of physical health and use of medical and psychiatric facilities', *Journal of Human Stress* 4: 26–32.

Mechanic, D. and Volkart, E.H. (1960) 'Illness behavior and medical diagnoses', *Journal of Health and Human Behavior* 1: 86–94.

Meng, H. (1934) 'Das Problem der Organpsychose', *Internationale Zeitschrift für Psychoanalyse* 20: 439–58.

Mennell, S. (1989) 'Short-term interests and long-term processes: the case of civilization and decivilization', in J. Goudsblom *et al*. (eds), *Human History and Social Process*, Exeter: University of Exeter Press.

Metcalf, D.R. (1977) 'Sleep and dreaming: protodream and predream', in B.B. Wolman (ed.) *International Encyclopaedia of Neurology, Psychiatry, Psychoanalysis and Psychology*, New York: Van Nostrand Reinhold.

Metcalf, D.R. and Spitz, R.A. (1978) 'The transitional object: critical developmental period and organizer of the psyche', in S. Grolnik *et al*. (eds) *Between Reality and Fantasy: Transitional Objects and Phenomena*, New York: Aronson.

Micale, M.S. (1993) 'On the "disappearance" of hysteria: a study in the clinical deconstruction of a diagnosis', *Isis* 84: 496–526.

Morelli, R. (1982) 'Dove va la medicina psicosomatica', in R. Morelli (ed.) *Dove va la medicina psicosomatica*, Milan: Riza Libri.

Nemiah, J.C. (1978) 'Alexithymia and psychosomatic illness', *Journal of Continuing Education and Psychiatry* 39: 25–37.

Nemiah, J.C. and Sifneos, P.E. (1970) 'Psychosomatic illness: a problem in communication', *Psychotherapy and Psychosomatics* 18: 154–60.

Nemiah, J.C. and Sifneos, P.E. *et al.* (1976) 'Alexithymia: a view of the psychosomatic process', in O.W. Hill (ed.) *Modern Trends in Psychosomatic Medicine*, Vol. 3, London: Butterworths.

Noël, M.-P. and Rimé, B. (1988) 'Pensée opératoire, alexithymie et investigation psychosomatique: revue critique', *Cahiers de Psychologie Cognitive* 8: 573–99.

Osborne, T. (1992) 'Medicine and epistemology: Michel Foucault and the liberality of clinical reason', *History of the Human Sciences* 5: 63–93.

Osterweis, M. *et al.* (eds) (1987) *Pain and Disability*, Washington, DC: National Academy Press.

Parker, R. (1994) 'Maternal ambivalence', *Winnicott Studies: the Journal of the Squiggle Foundation* 9: 3–17.

Parsons, T. (1950) *The Social System*, New York: Free Press.

—— (1951) 'Illness and the role of the physician', *American Journal of Orthopsychiatry* 21: 452–60.

—— (1964) *Social Structure and Personality*, New York: Free Press.

Pedinielli, J.-L. (1992) *Psychosomatique et alexithymie*, Paris: Presses Universitaires de France.

Peters, D.L. (1971) 'Epilog', in D.N. Walcher *et al.* (eds) *The Development of Self-Regulatory Mechanisms*, New York: Academic Press.

Pilowski, I. (1969) 'Abnormal illness behavior', *British Journal of Medical Psychology*, 42: 347–51.

—— (1975) 'Dimensions of abnormal illness behavior', *Australia and New Zealand Journal of Psychiatry* 9: 141–7.

Pontalis, J.B. (1977) 'Entre Groddeck et Freud', *La Nouvelle Revue Française* (October).

Powell, R.C. (1977) 'Helen Flanders Dunbar (1902–59) and a holistic approach to psychosomatic problems: the rise and fall of a medical philosophy', *Psychiatric Quarterly* 49: 133–52.

Rabinowitz, S. *et al.* (1990) 'Malingering in the clinical setting: practical suggestions for intervention', *Psychological Reports* 67: 1315–18.

Rabkin, J.G. and Struening, E.L. (1976) 'Life events, stress, and illness', *Science* 194: 1013–20.

Rees, L. (1983) 'The development of psychosomatic medicine during the past 25 years', *Journal of Psychosomatic Research* 27: 157–64.

Ricoeur, P. (1970) *Freud and Philosophy: an Essay on Interpretation*, New Haven, CT: Yale University Press.

—— (1974) *The Conflict of Interpretations*, Evanston, IL: Northwestern University Press.

Rijke, R.P.C. (1985) 'Cancer and the development of will', *Theoretical Medicine* 6: 133–42.

Rogers, R. (ed.) (1988) *Clinical Assessment of Malingering and Deception*, New York: Guilford Press

Rogers, R. and Cavanaugh, J.L. (1983) '"Nothing but the truth . . . ": a re-examination of malingering', *Journal of Law and Psychiatry* 11: 443–60.

Ruesch, J. (1948) 'The infantile personality', *Psychosomatic Medicine* 10: 134–44.

Salmon, P. and May, C.R. (1995) 'Patients' influence on doctors' behavior: a case study of patient strategies in somatization', *International Journal of Psychiatry in Medicine* 25: 319–29.

Sami-Ali (1987) *Penser le somatique: Imaginaire et pathologie*, Paris: Bordas.

—— (1980) *Le banal*, Paris: Gallimard.

Sass, R. and Crook, G. (1981) 'Accident proneness: science or non-science?', *International Journal of Health Services* 11: 175–90.

Schimel, J.L. *et al.* (1973) 'Changing styles in psychiatric syndromes: a symposium', *American Journal of Psychiatry* 130.

Schmale, A.H. (1958) 'Relationship of separation and depression to disease', *Psychosomatic Medicine* 20: 259–77.

Schützenberger, A.A. (1991) *Vouloir guérir: l'aide au malade attaint d'un cancer*, Paris and Toulouse: Erès & La Méridienne.

Schwartz, G.E. (1979) 'The brain as a health care system', in G.C. Stone *et al.* (eds) *Health Psychology: a Handbook*, San Francisco, CA: Jossey-Bass.

—— (1981) 'A systems analysis of psychobiology and behavior therapy: implications for behavioral medicine', *Psychotherapy and Psychosomatics* 36: 159–84.

—— (1983) 'Disregulation theory and disease: applications to the repression/cerebral disconnection/cardiovascular disorder hypothesis', *International Review of Applied Psychology* 32: 95–118.

Sedgwick, P. (1972) 'Mental illness *is* illness', *Salmagundi* 20: 196–224.

Selye, H. (1946) 'The General Adaptation Syndrome and the disease of adaptation', *Journal of Clinical Endocrinology* 6: 117–230.

—— (1950) 'Adaptive reactions to stress', in H.G. Wolff *et al.* (eds) *Life Stress and Bodily Disease*, Baltimore, MD: William and Wilkins.

Shaw, J. and Creed, F. (1991) 'The cost of somatization', *Journal of Psychosomatic Research* 36: 307–12.

Shorter, E. (1984) 'Les désordres psychosomatiques sont-ils "hystériques"? Notes pour une recherche historique', *Cahiers Internationaux de Sociologie* 76: 201–4.

—— (1992) *From Paralysis to Fatigue: A History of Psychosomatic Illness in the Modern Era*, New York: Free Press.

Sifneos, P.E. (1972–3) 'Is dynamic psychotherapy contraindicated for a large number of patients with psychosomatic disease?', *Psychotherapy and Psychosomatics* 21: 133–6.

—— (1973) 'The prevalence of "alexithymic" characteristics in psychosomatic patients', *Psychotherapy and Psychosomatics* 22: 255–62.

—— (1975) 'Problems of psychotherapy of patients with alexithymic characteristics and physical disease', *Psychotherapy and Psychosomatics* 26: 65–70.

—— (1996) 'Alexithymia: past and present', *American Journal of Psychiatry* 153: 137–42.

Simonton, C. *et al.* (1978) *Getting Well Again*, Los Angeles, CA: Tarcher.

Speckens, A.E.M. *et al.* (1995) 'The acceptability of psychological treatment in patients with medically unexplained physical symptoms', *Journal of Psychosomatic Research* 39: 855–63.

Sperling, M. (1960) 'Symposium of disturbances of the digestive tract: II. Unconscious phantasy and object relationships in ulcerative colitis', *International Journal of Psychoanalysis* 41: 450–5.

—— (1973) 'Conversion hysteria and conversion symptoms', *Journal of the American Psychoanalytic Association* 21: 745–71.

Spielberg, U. *et al.* (1970) 'Syndromwechsel (syndrome shift) und Verstimmung', *Nervenartzt* 41.

Stefansson, J.G. *et al.* (1976) 'Hysterical neurosis, conversion type: clinical and epidemiological considerations', *Acta Psychiatrica Scandinavica* 53: 119–38.

Straus, R. (1957) 'The nature and status of medical sociology', *American Sociological Review* 22: 200–4.

Strong, P.M. (1979) 'Sociological imperialism and the profession of medicine', *Social Science and Medicine* 13A: 199–215.

Swartz, M. *et al.* (1986) 'Somatization disorder in a community population', *American Journal of Psychiatry* 143: 1403–8.

Szasz, T.S. (1956) 'Malingering: "diagnosis" or social condemnation?', *AMA Archives of Neurology and Psychiatry* 76: 432–3.

Taylor, G.J. (1984) 'Alexithymia: concept, measurement, and implications for treatment', *American Journal of Psychiatry* 141: 725–32.

—— (1987) *Psychosomatic Medicine and Contemporary Psychoanalysis*, Madison, WI: International Universities Press.

Taylor, G.J. *et al.* (1991) 'The alexithymia construct: a potential paradigm for psychosomatic medicine', *Psychosomatics* 32: 153–64.

Todarello, O. (1988) 'Modelli psicosomatici ed impotenza erettile', in A. Salvini (ed.) *Impotenza erettile*, Bologna: Monduzzi.

Todarello, O. and Porcelli, I. (1992) *Psicosomatica come paradosso*, Turin: Boringhieri.

Trimble, M. (1995) 'Medicine and the law: conflict or debate', *Journal of Psychosomatic Research* 39: 671–4.

Turco, R.N. (1991) 'Factitious disorders and the industrial accident system: winning and losing through deception', *International Journal of Offender Therapy and Comparative Criminology* 35: 35–44.

Tytell, P. (1980) 'Un précurseur des fictions théoriques', *L'arc* 78: 92–103.

Von Bertalanffy, L. (1964) 'The mind-body problem: a new view', *Psychosomatic Medicine* 26: 29–45.

Von Korff *et al.* (1988) 'An epidemiologic comparison of pain complaints', *Pain* 32: 173–83.

Von Uexküll, T. and Pauli, H.G. (1986) 'The mind-body problem in medicine', *Advances* 3: 158–74.

Von Weizsäcker, V. (1940) *Der Gestaltkreis: Theorie der Einheit von Wahrnehmen und Bewegen*, Leipzig: Thieme.

—— (1986 [1930]): 'Soziale Krankheit und soziale Gesundung', in *Gesammelte Schriften*, Vol. 8, Frankfurt: Suhrkamp Verlag.

—— (1986 [1949]) 'Psychosomatische Medizin', in *Gesammelte Schriften*, Vol. 6, Frankfurt: Suhrkamp Verlag.

—— (1990 [1946]) 'Anonyma Scriptura', in *Filosofia della Medicina*, Milan: Guerini e Associati.

Waitzkin, H. (1979) 'Medicine, superstructure and micropolitics', *Social Science and Medicine* 13: 601–9.

Warnes, H. and Blustein, J. (1987) 'International trends of therapy and research in psychosomatic medicine', *Psychotherapy and Psychosomatics* 47: 143–52.

Weiner, H. (1977) *Psychobiology and Human Disease*, New York: Elsevier.

—— (1982a) 'Contributions of psychoanalysis to psychosomatic medicine', *Journal of the American Academy for Psychoanalysis* 10: 27–46.

—— (1982b) 'The prospects for psychosomatic medicine: selected topics', *Psychosomatic Medicine* 44: 491–517.

Weiss, E. and English, O.S. (1949) *Psychosomatic Medicine*, Philadelphia, PA: W.B. Saunders.

WHO Expert Committee on Mental Health (1964) 'The psychosomatic concept', *WHO Chronicles* 18: 304.

Winnicott, D.W. (1958) 'Mind and its relation to the psyche-soma', in *Through Paediatrics to Psychoanalysis*, London: Karnac Books.

—— (1965) *The Maturational Processes and the Facilitating Environment*, New York: International Universities Press.

—— (1988) *Human Nature*, London: Free Association Books.

Wolff, H.G. (1950) 'Life stress and bodily disease: a formulation', in H.G. Wolff *et al.* (eds) *Life Stress and Bodily Disease*, Baltimore, MD: William & Wilkins.

Wouters, C. (1986) 'Formalization and informalization: changing tension balances in civilizing processes', *Theory, Culture and Society* 3: 1–18.

Wyss, D. (1957) *Von Weizsäcker: Zwischen Medizin und Philosophie*, Göttingen: Vandenhoeck und Ruprecht.

—— (1977) *Storia della psicologia del profondo: Sviluppo problemi crisi*, Rome: Città Nuova Editrice.

Zola, I.K. (1966) 'Culture and symptoms: an analysis of patients presenting complaints', *American Sociological Review* 31: 615–30.

—— (1973) 'Pathways to the doctor: from person to patient', *Social Science and Medicine* 7: 677–87.

Zonderman, A.B. *et al.* (1985) 'Does the illness behavior questionnaire measure abnormal illness behavior?' *Health Psychology* 4: 425–36.

INDEX